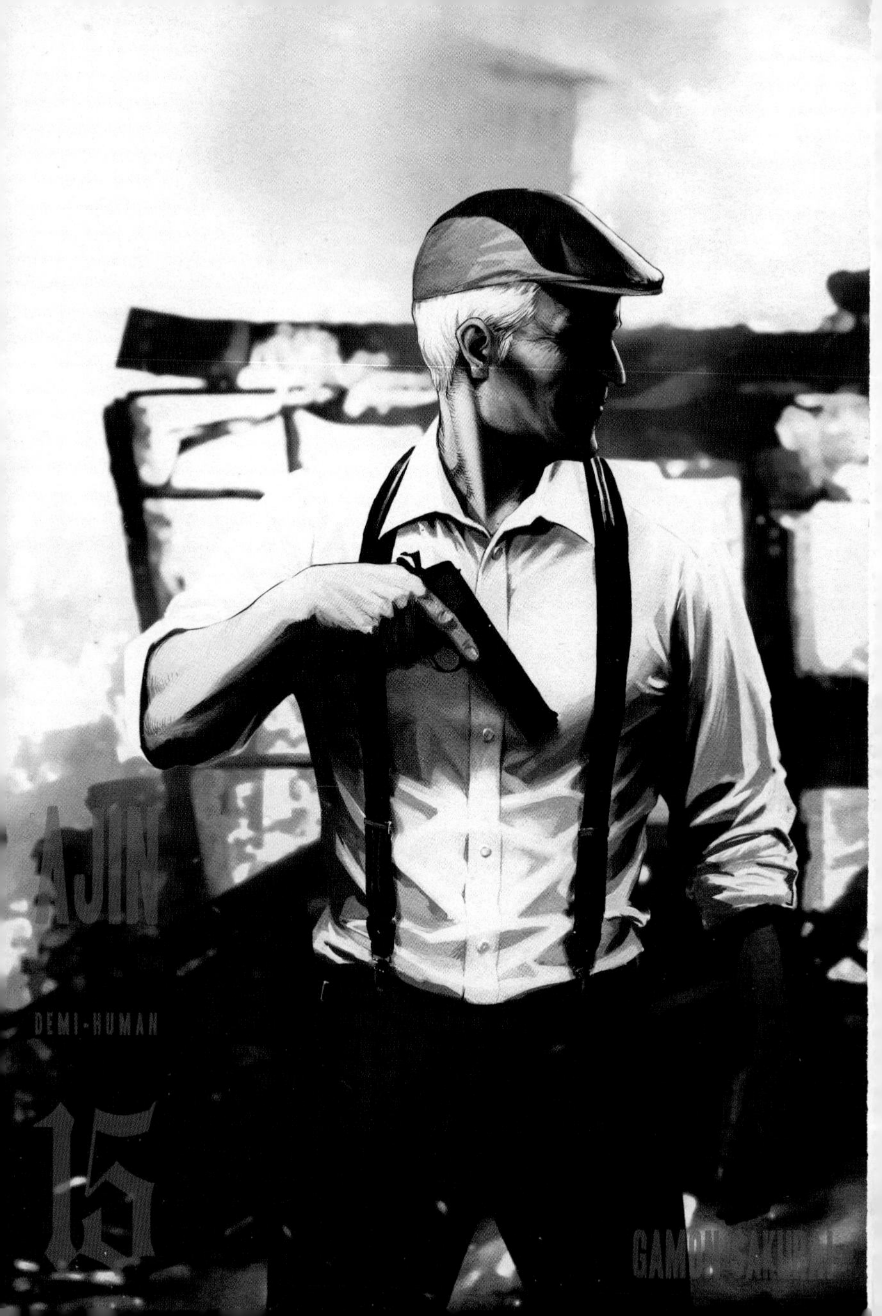
AJIN
DEMI-HUMAN
15

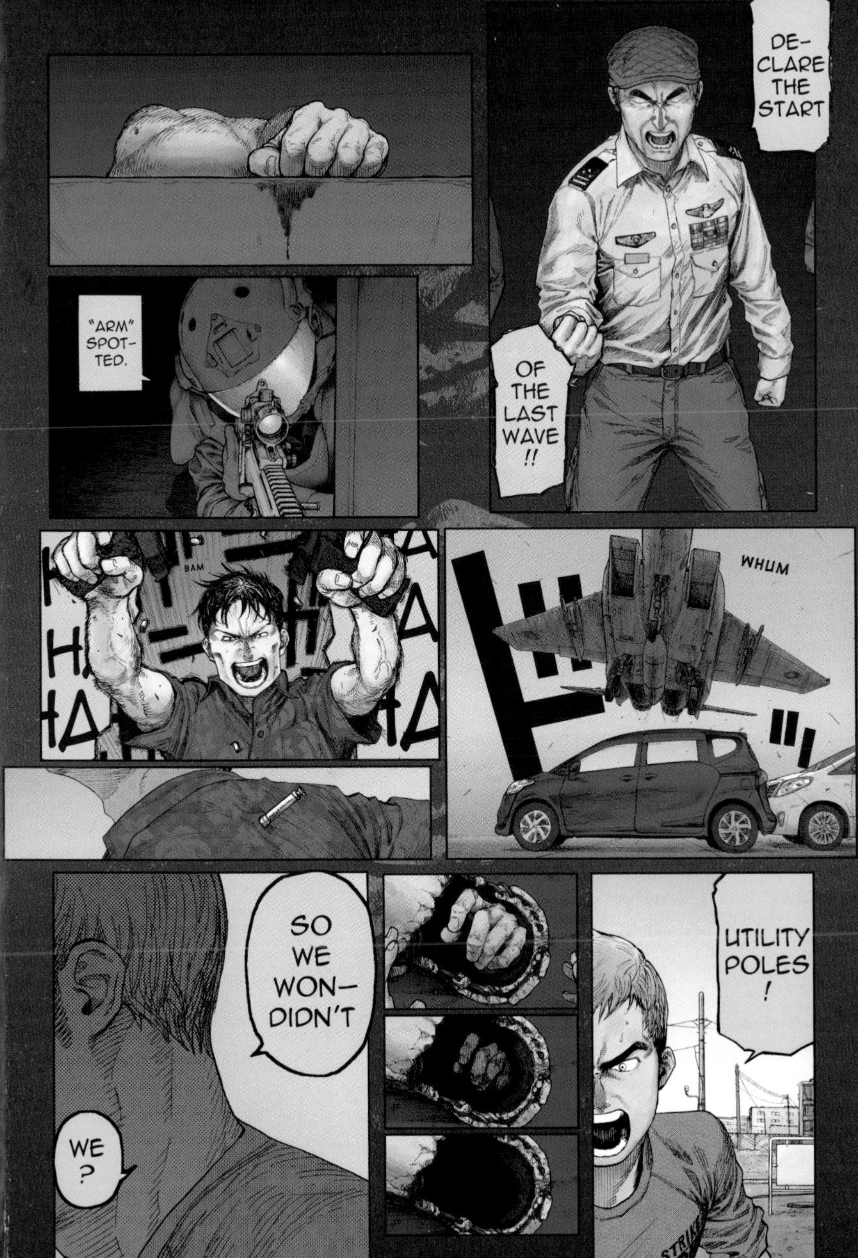
DE-CLARE THE START
OF THE LAST WAVE !!
"ARM" SPOT-TED.
WHUM
BAM
UTILITY POLES !
SO WE WON-DIDN'T
WE ?

DRAMATIS PERSONAE

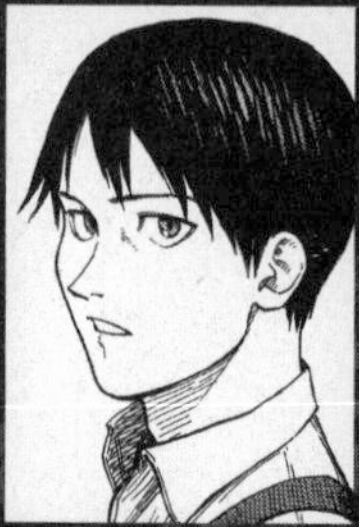
KEI NAGAI

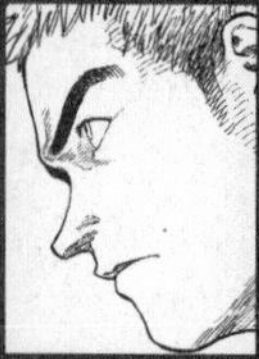
KO NAKANO

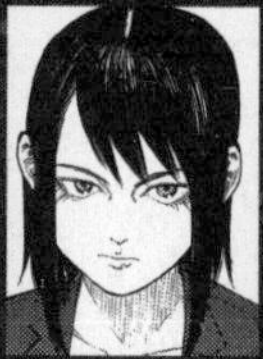
IZUMI SHIMOMURA

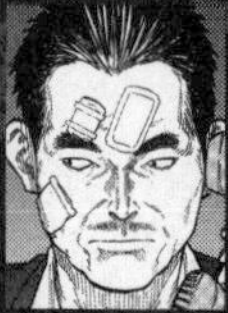
MANABE

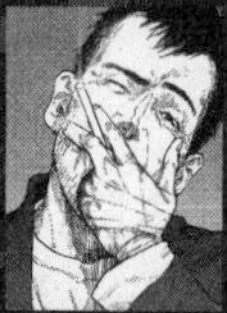
DR. IKUYA OGURA

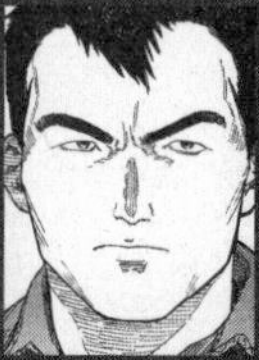
AKIYAMA

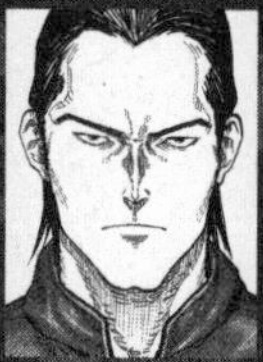
TANAKA

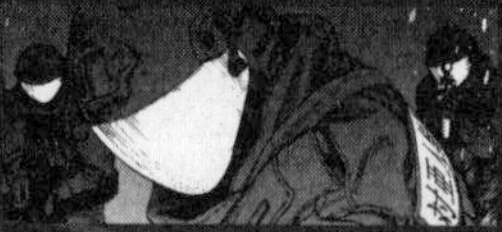
ANTI-DEMI SPECIAL FORCES

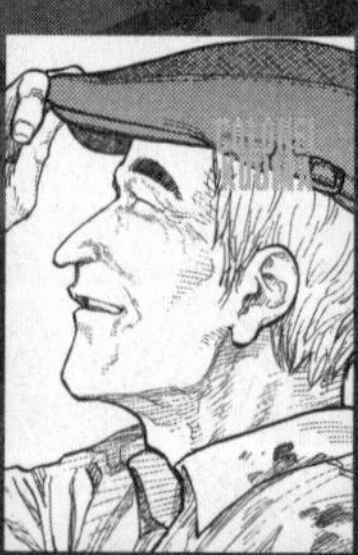
SATO

File:68

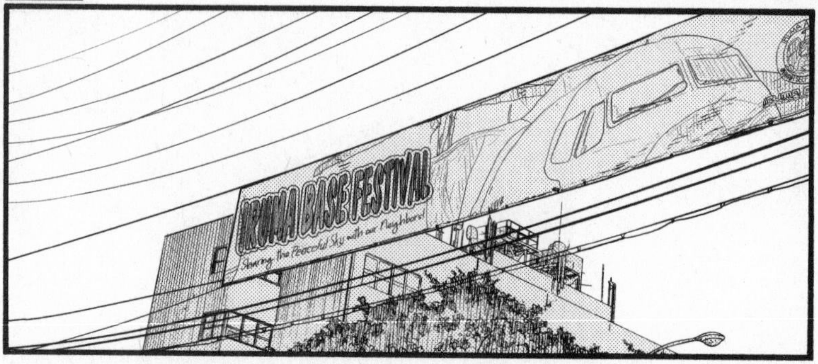
IRUMA BASE FESTIVAL
Sharing the Peaceful Sky with our Neighbors!

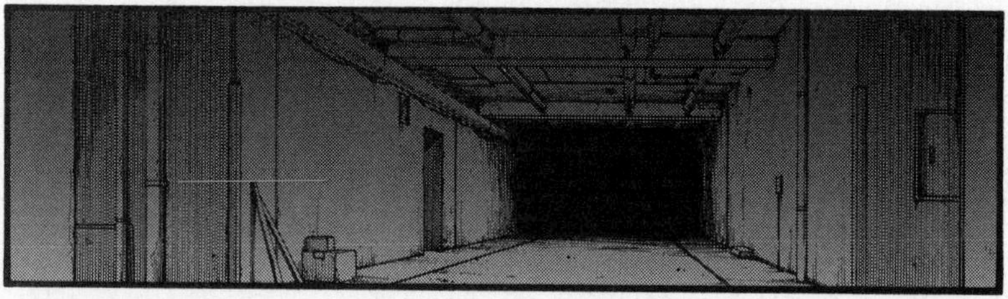

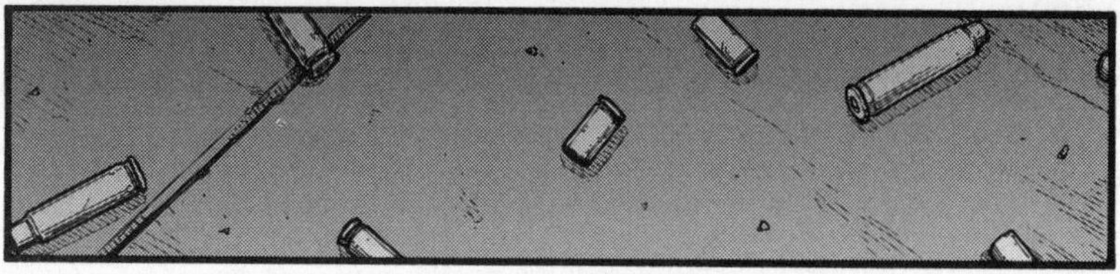

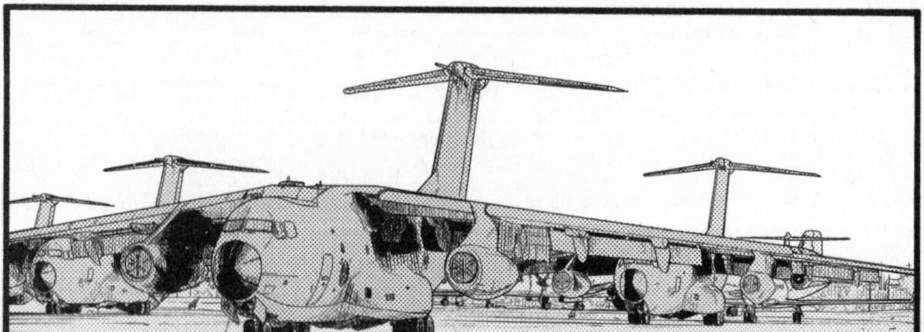

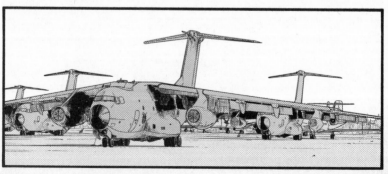

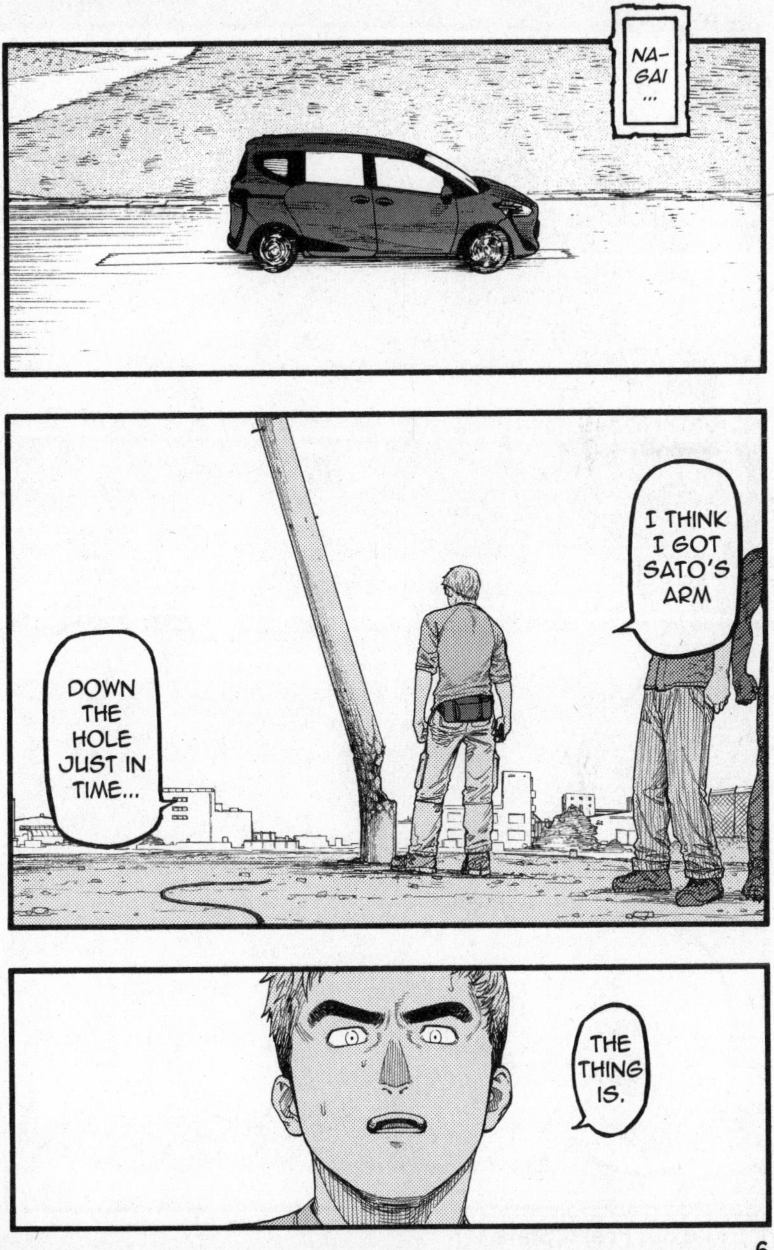
NA-GAI ...
I THINK I GOT SATO'S ARM
DOWN THE HOLE JUST IN TIME...
THE THING IS.

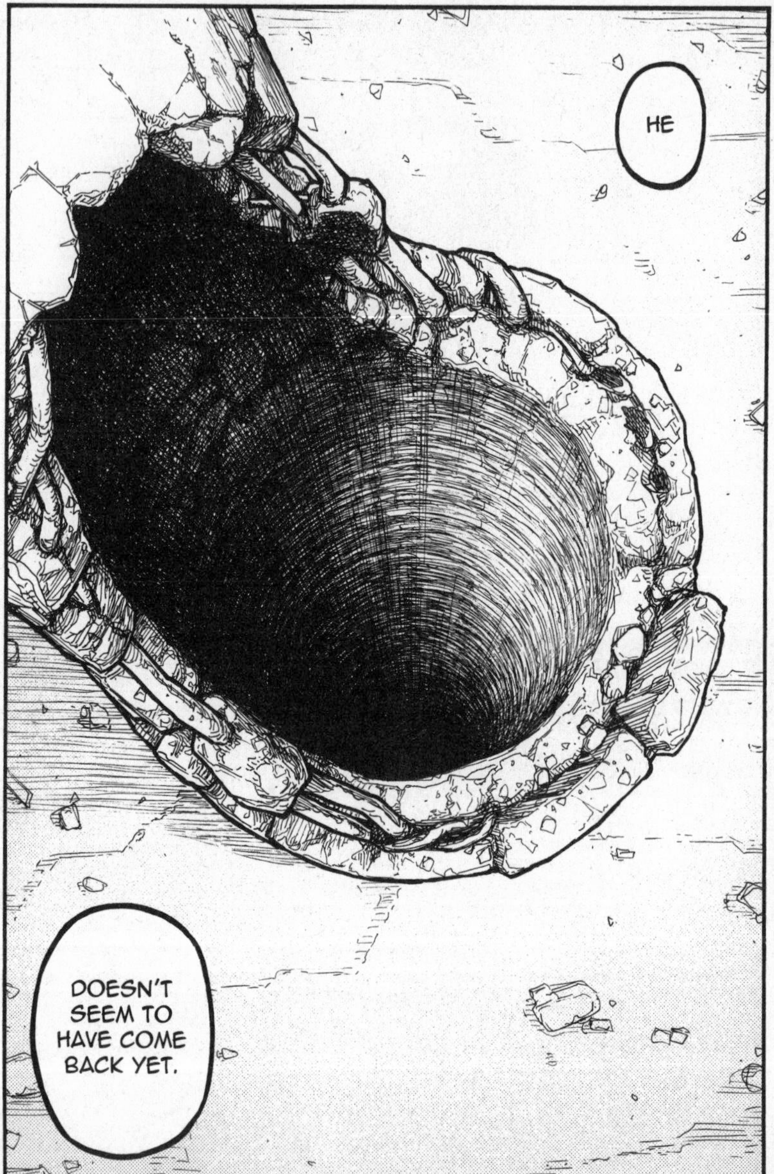
HE
DOESN'T SEEM TO HAVE COME BACK YET.

File 68: Fresh Slate

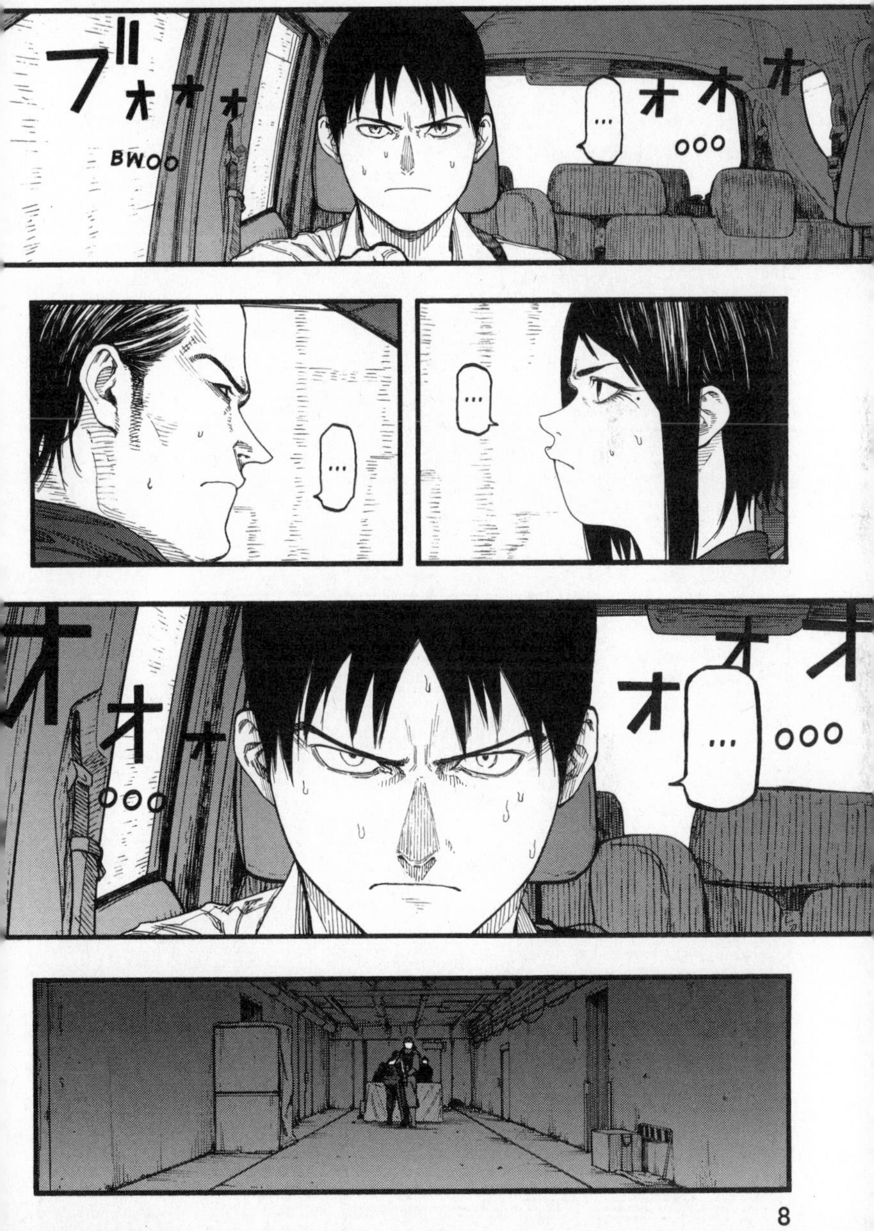

オオオ
OOO
...
ブォォォ
BWOO
...
...
オオオ
...
OOO
オオオ
OOO

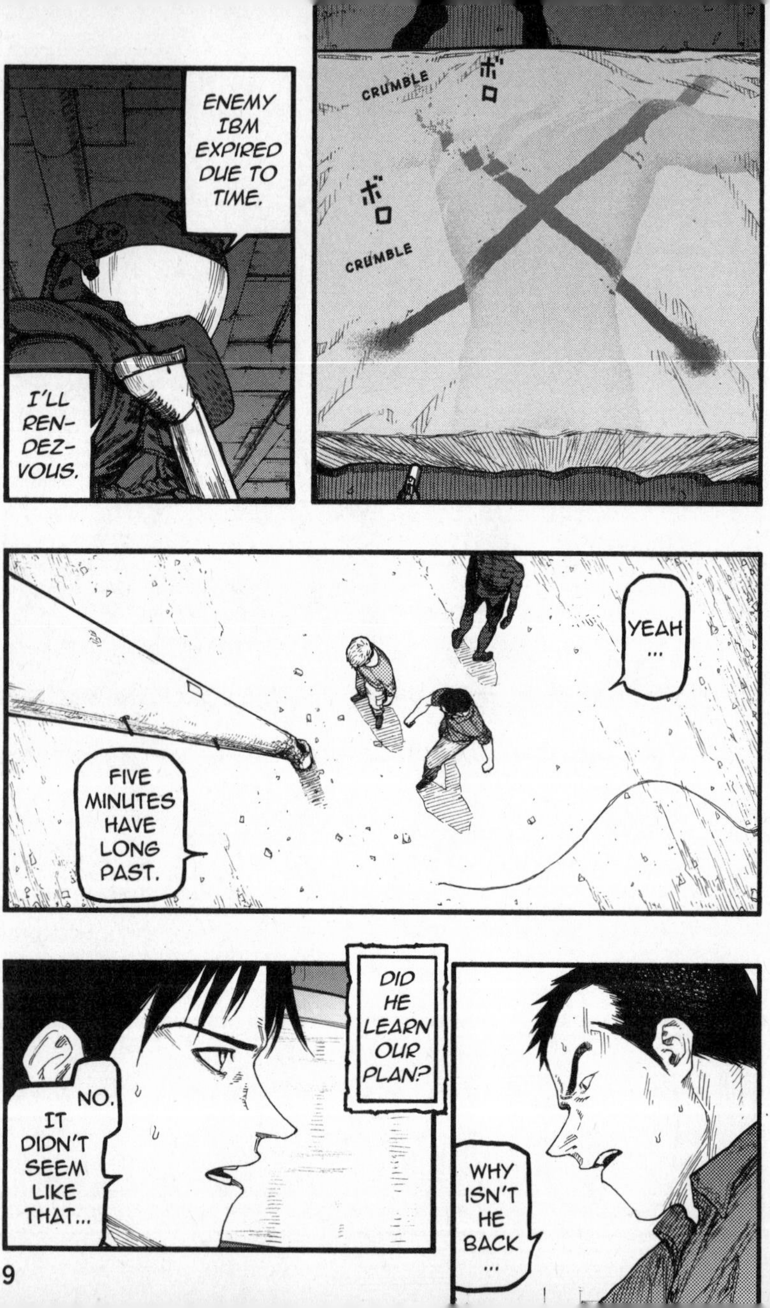
CRUMBLE
ボロ
ボロ
CRUMBLE
ENEMY IBM EXPIRED DUE TO TIME.
I'LL RENDEZVOUS.
YEAH...
FIVE MINUTES HAVE LONG PAST.
WHY ISN'T HE BACK...
DID HE LEARN OUR PLAN?
NO.
IT DIDN'T SEEM LIKE THAT...

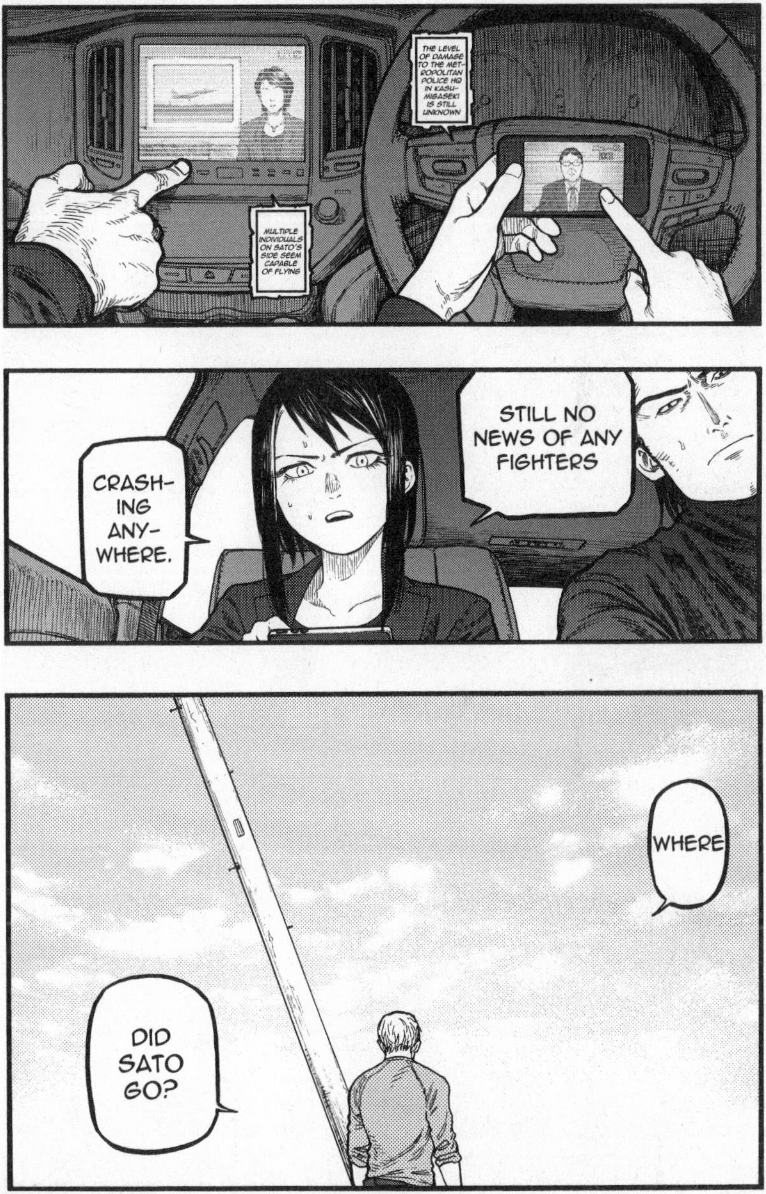
THE LEVEL OF DAMAGE TO THE MET-ROPOLITAN POLICE HQ IN KASU-MIGASEKI IS STILL UNKNOWN
MULTIPLE INDIVIDUALS ON SATO'S SIDE SEEM CAPABLE OF FLYING
STILL NO NEWS OF ANY FIGHTERS
CRASH-ING ANY-WHERE.
WHERE
DID SATO GO?

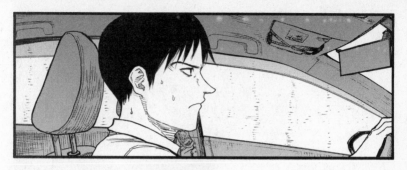

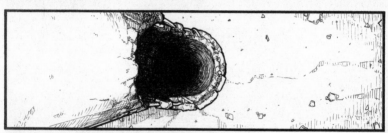

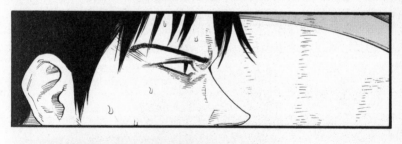

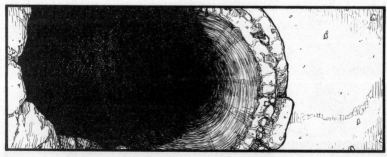

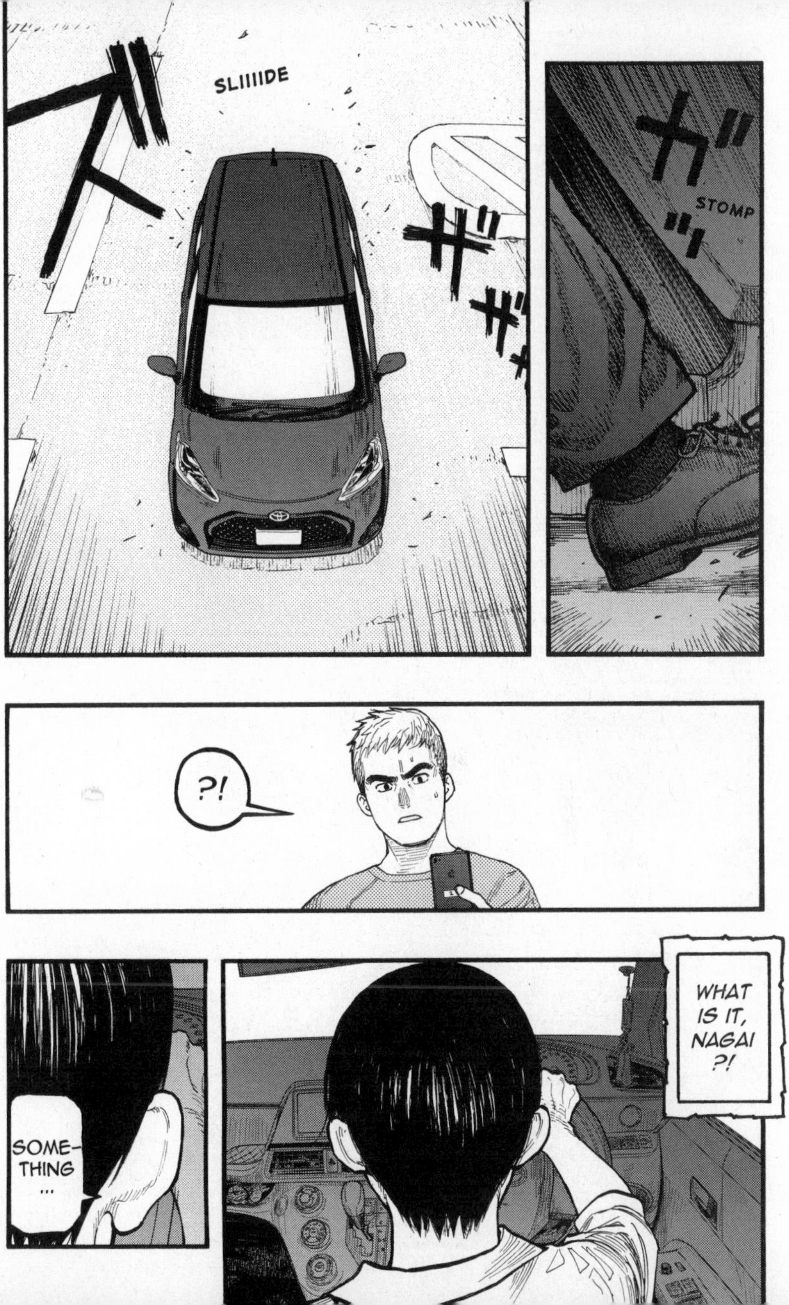
STOMP
SLIIIIDE
?!
WHAT IS IT, NAGAI ?!
SOME-THING ...

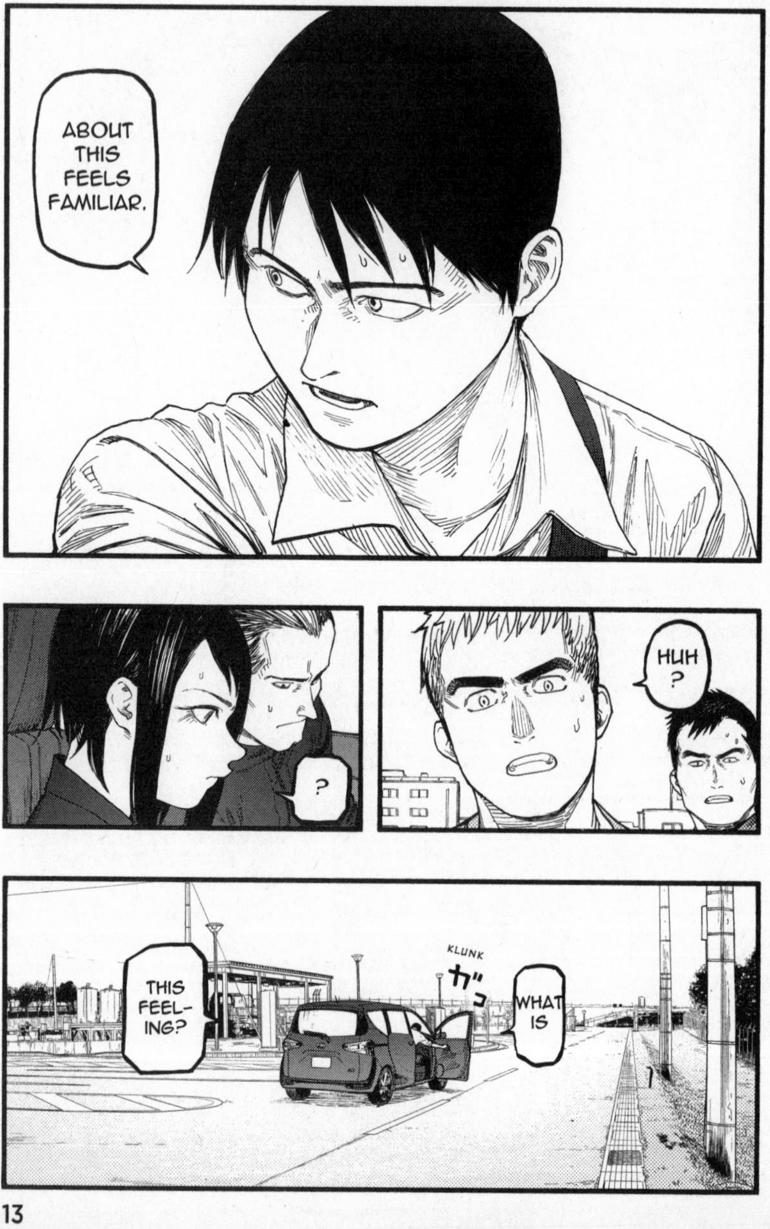
ABOUT THIS FEELS FAMILIAR.
HUH ?
?
WHAT IS
KLUNK
ガコ
THIS FEEL-ING?

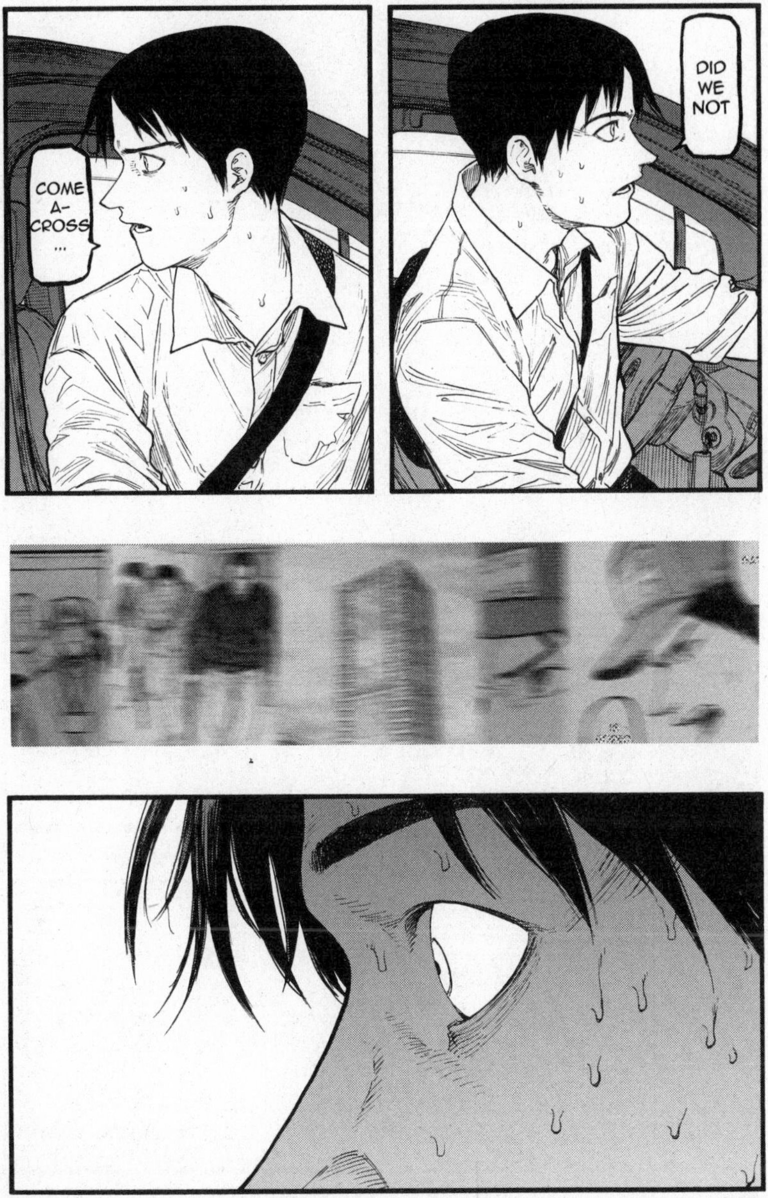
DID WE NOT
COME A-CROSS ...

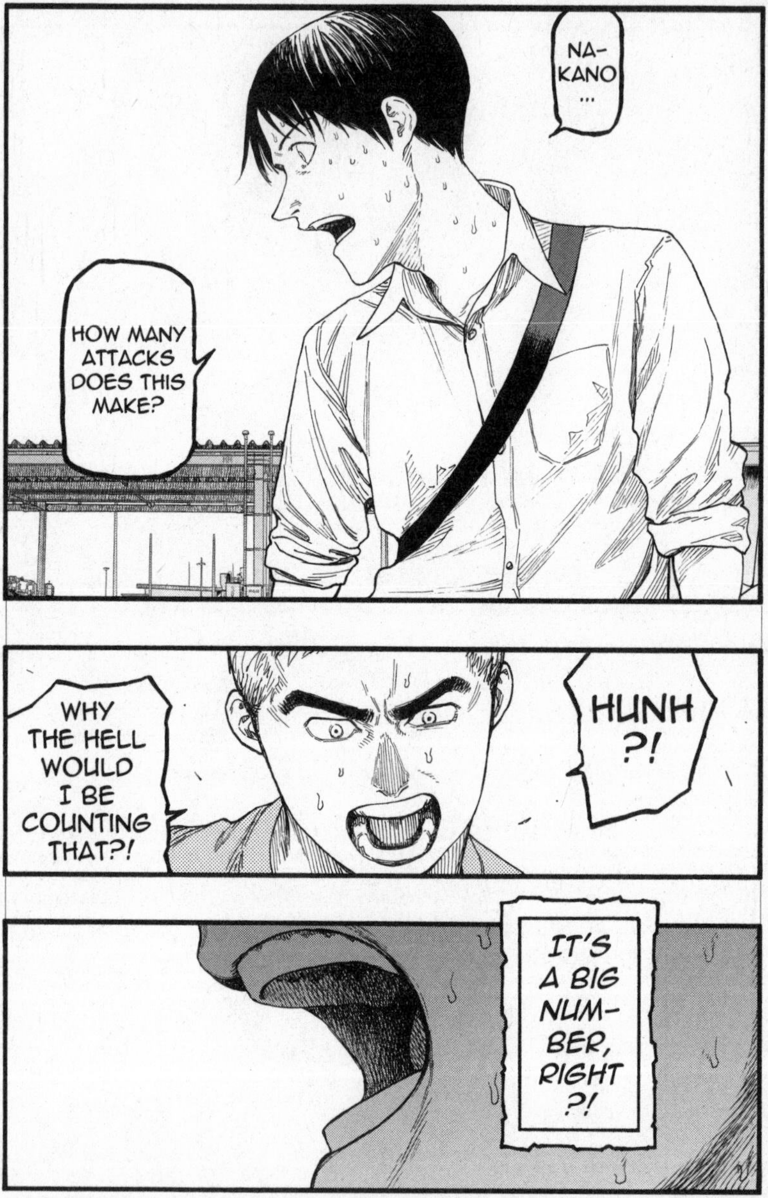
NA-KANO...
HOW MANY ATTACKS DOES THIS MAKE?
HUNH?!
WHY THE HELL WOULD I BE COUNTING THAT?!
IT'S A BIG NUMBER, RIGHT?!

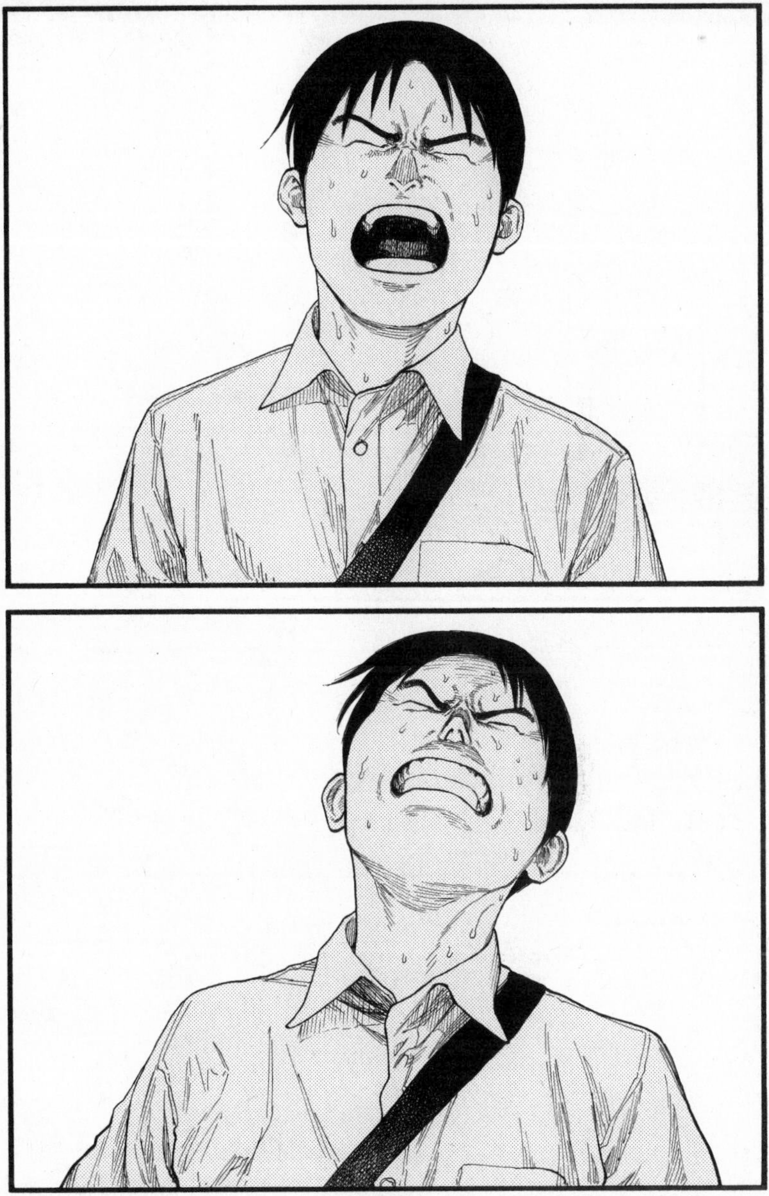

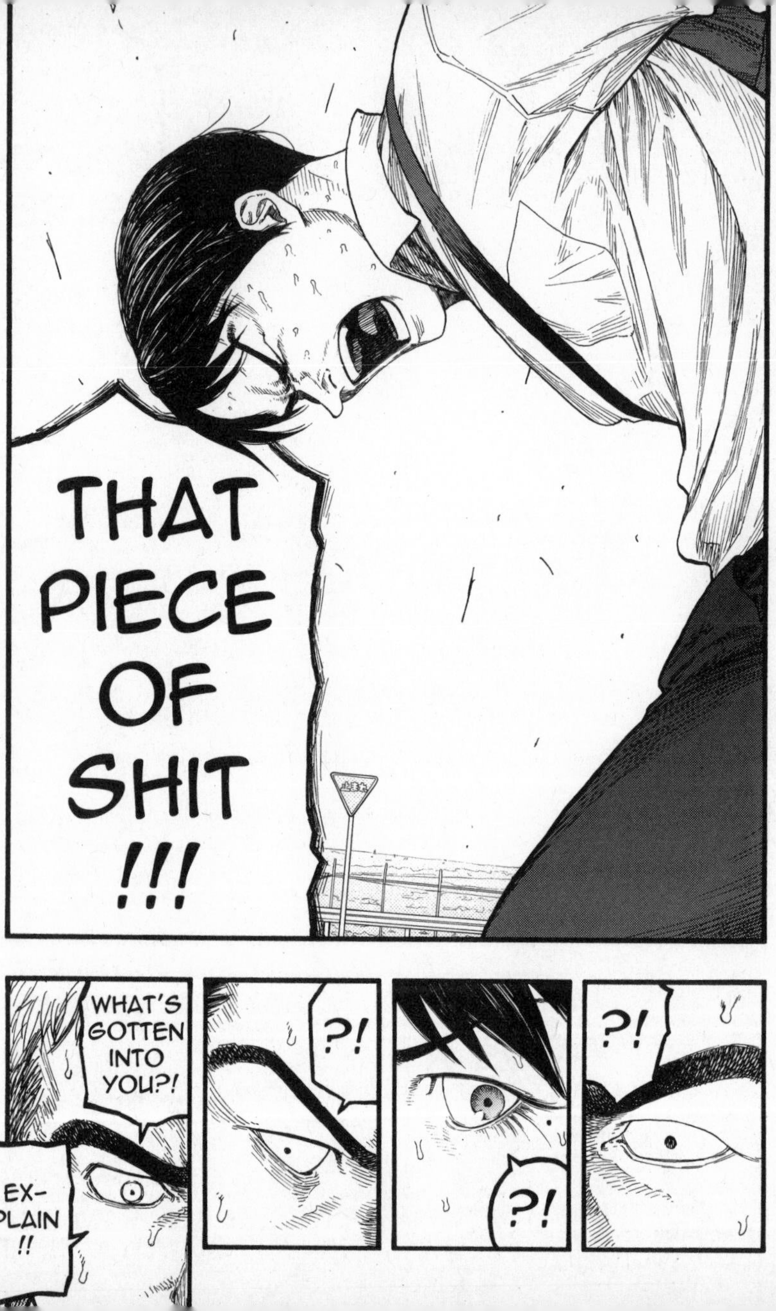
THAT PIECE OF SHIT !!!
?!
?!
?!
WHAT'S GOTTEN INTO YOU?!
EX-PLAIN !!

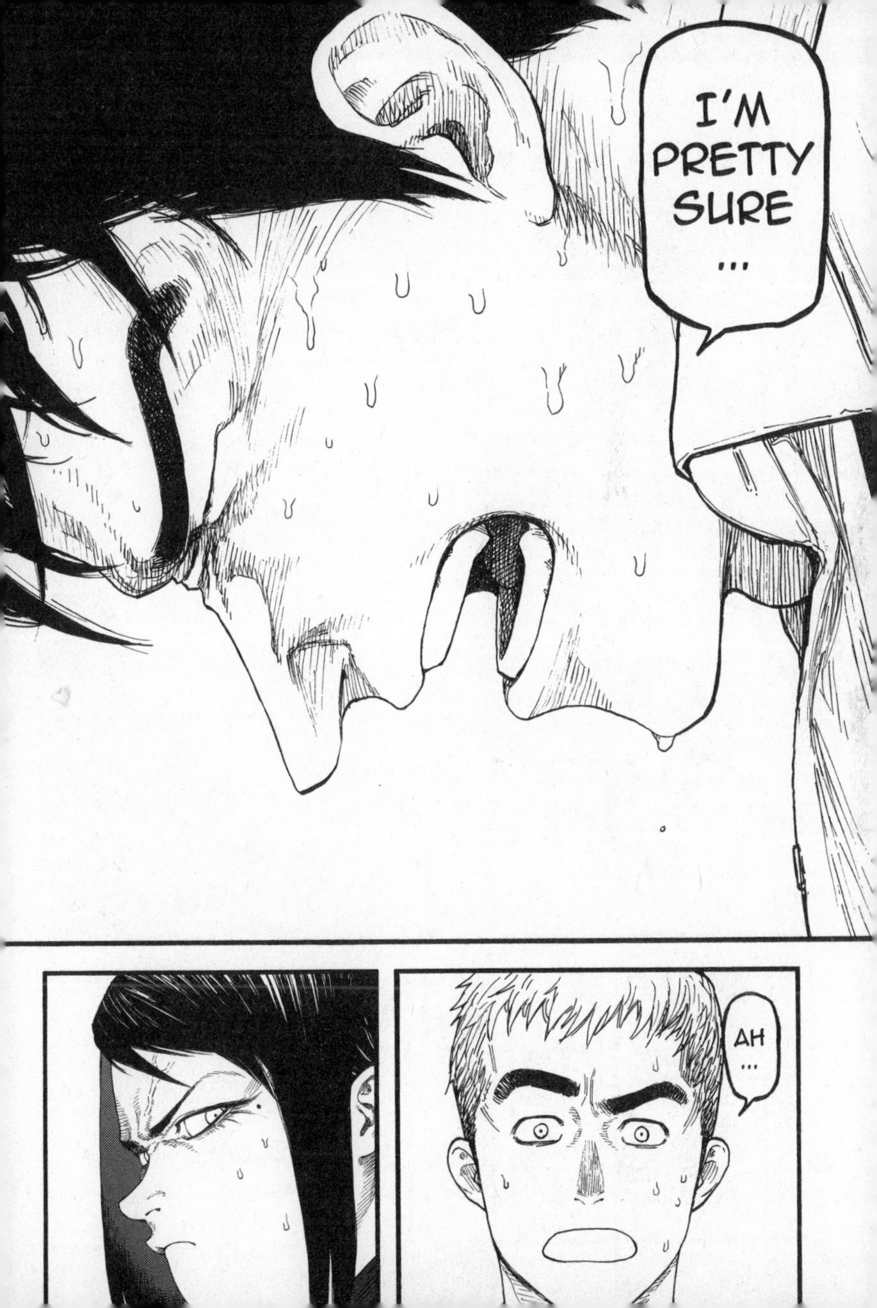
I'M PRETTY SURE ...
AH ...

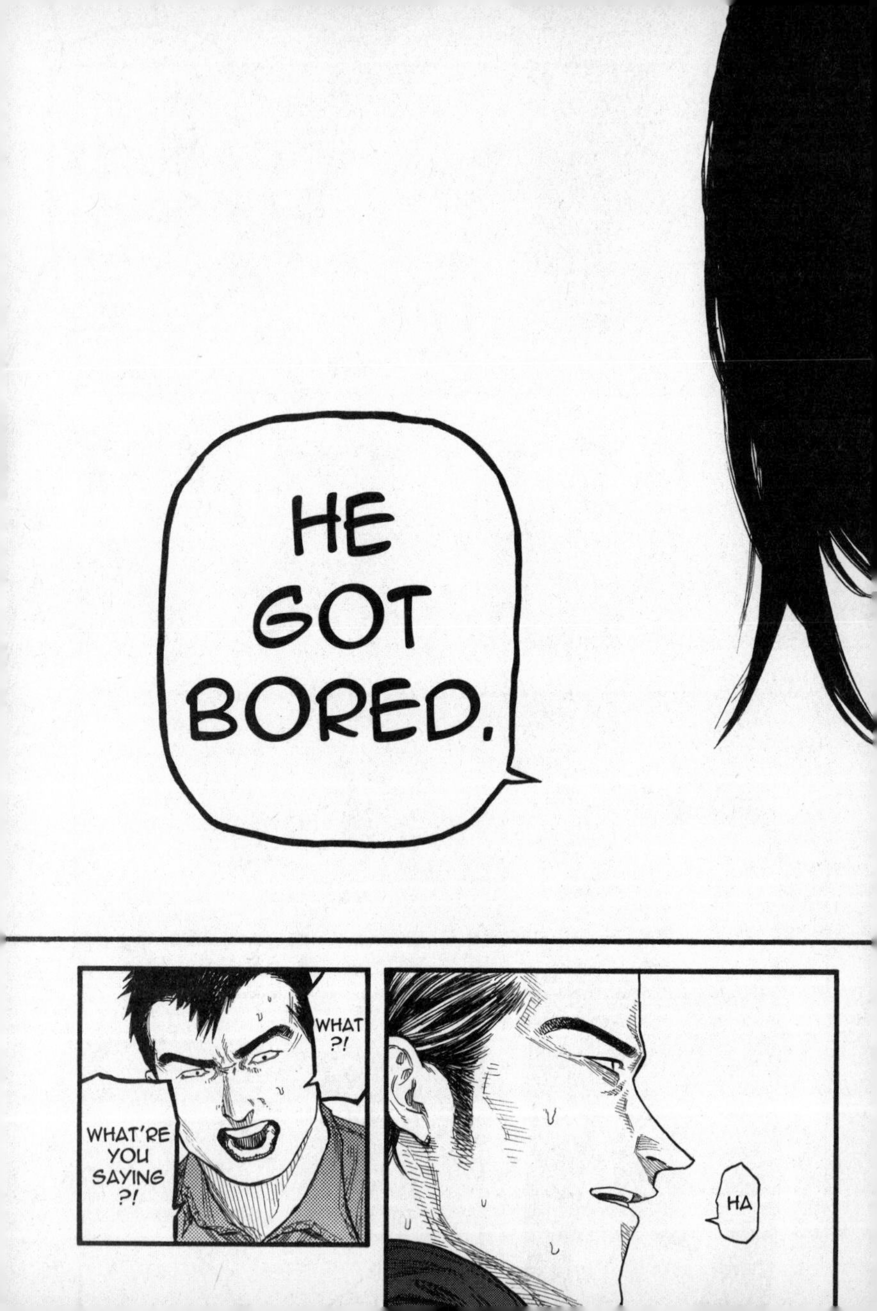
HE GOT BORED.
HA
WHAT ?!
WHAT'RE YOU SAYING ?!

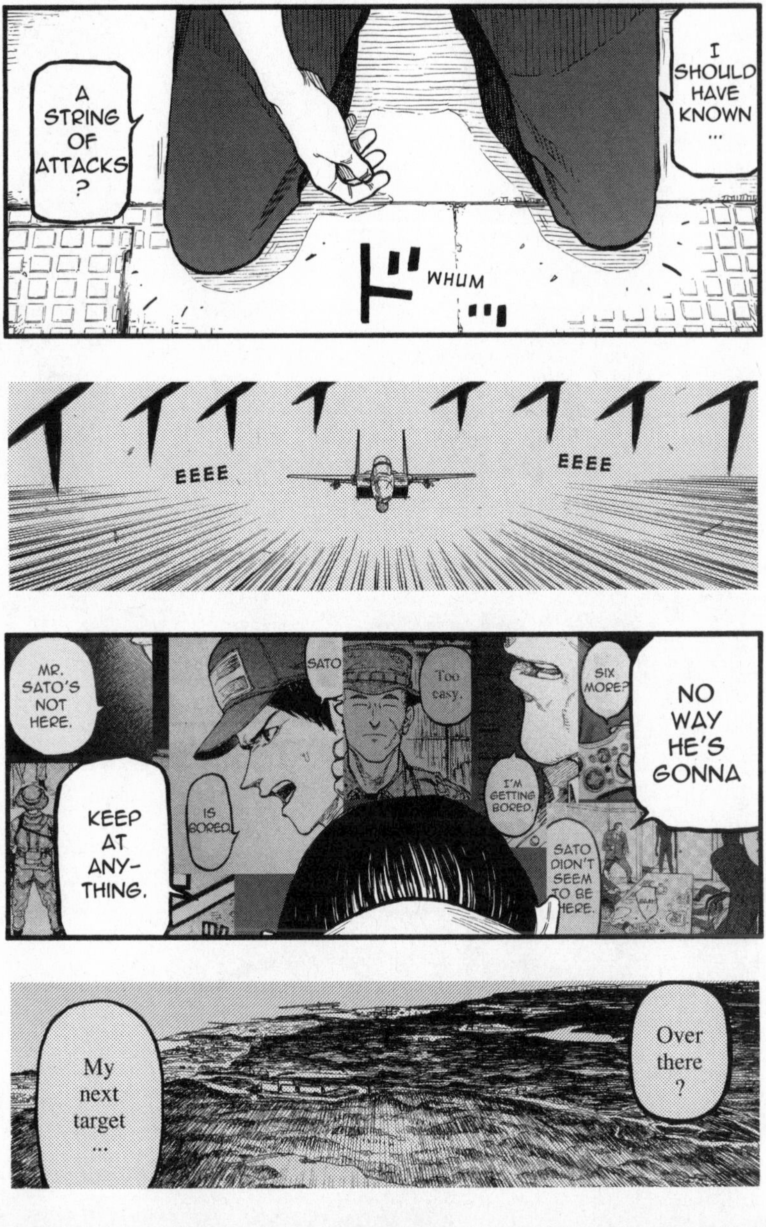
I SHOULD HAVE KNOWN ...
A STRING OF ATTACKS ?
ド
WHUM
EEEE
EEEE
NO WAY HE'S GONNA
SIX MORE?
I'M GETTING BORED.
SATO DIDN'T SEEM TO BE HERE.
Too easy.
SATO
IS BORED.
MR. SATO'S NOT HERE.
KEEP AT ANY-THING.
Over there ?
My next target ...

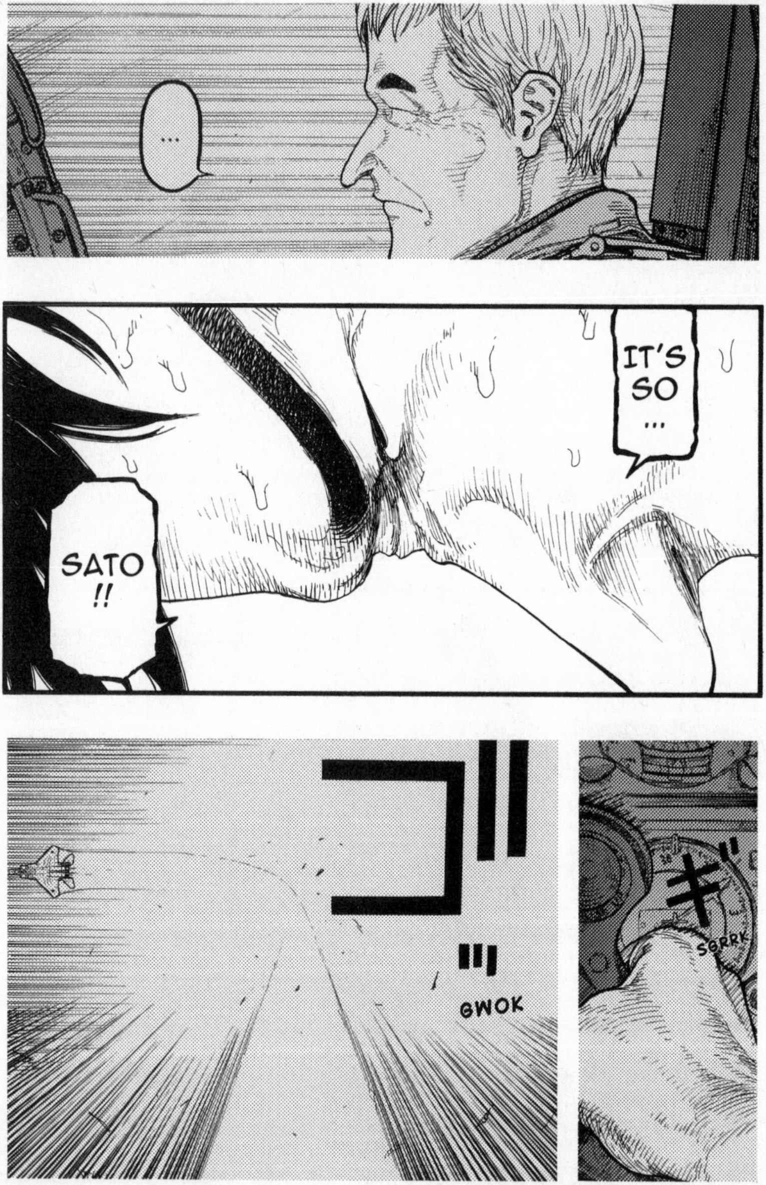
…
IT'S SO …
SATO !!
ギ
SGRRK
ゴッ
GWOK

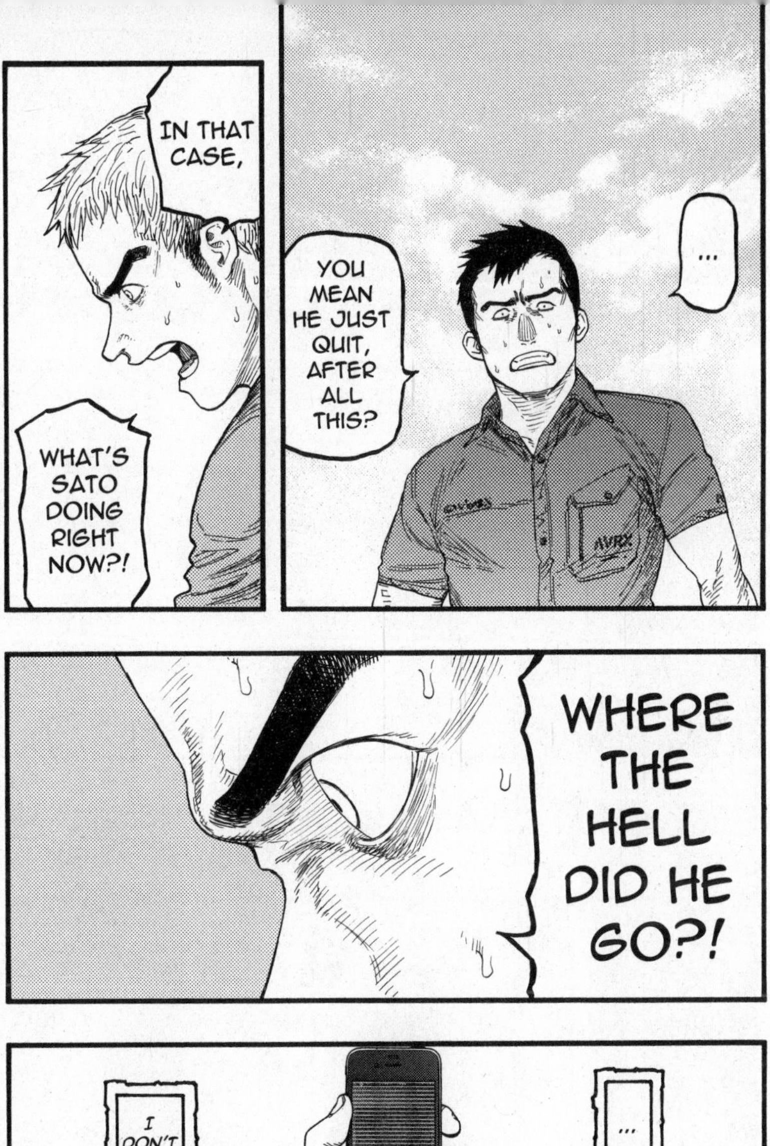
...
YOU MEAN HE JUST QUIT, AFTER ALL THIS?
IN THAT CASE,
WHAT'S SATO DOING RIGHT NOW?!
WHERE THE HELL DID HE GO?!
...
I DON'T KNOW ...

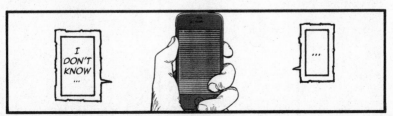

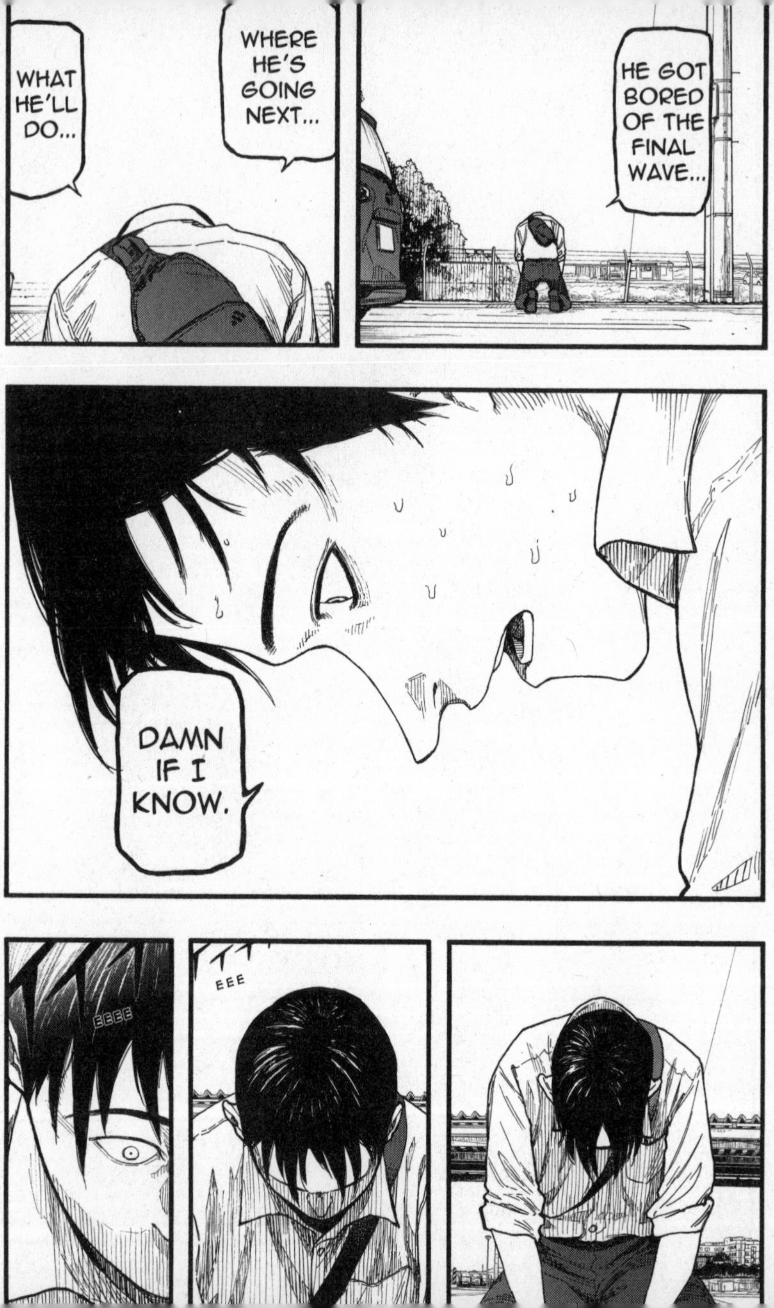
HE GOT BORED OF THE FINAL WAVE...
WHERE HE'S GOING NEXT...
WHAT HE'LL DO...
DAMN IF I KNOW.
EEE
EEEE

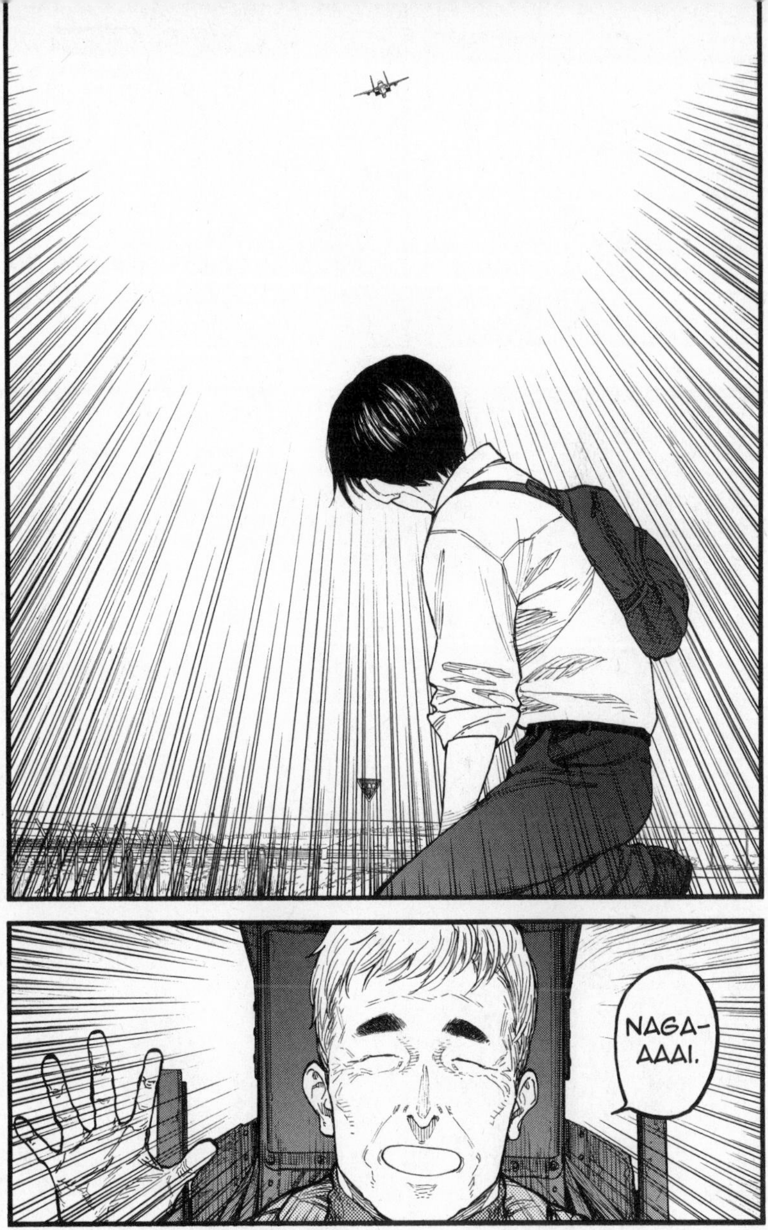
NAGA-AAAI.

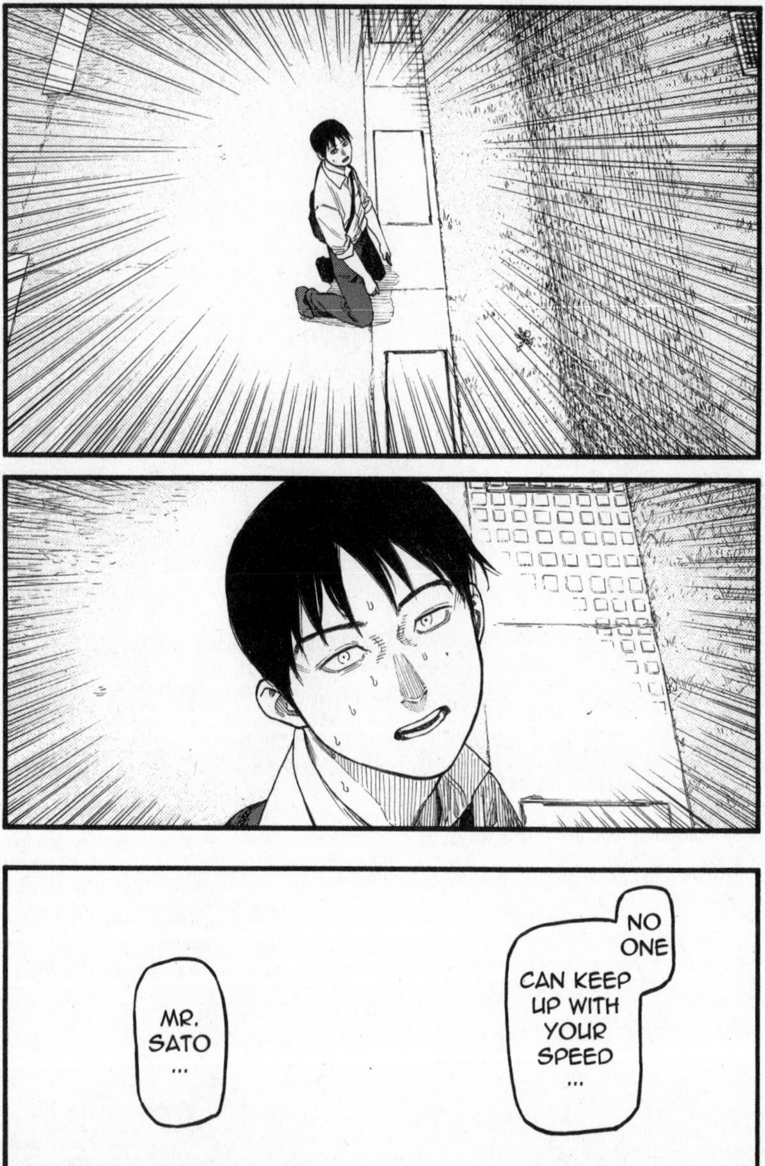

NO ONE CAN KEEP UP WITH YOUR SPEED ...
MR. SATO ...

File:68 End

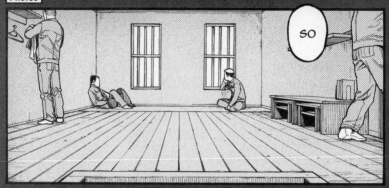

SO

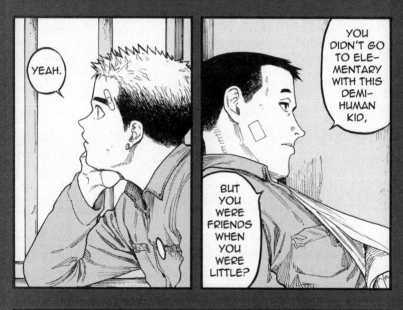

YEAH.

YOU DIDN'T GO TO ELEMENTARY WITH THIS DEMI-HUMAN KID,

BUT YOU WERE FRIENDS WHEN YOU WERE LITTLE?

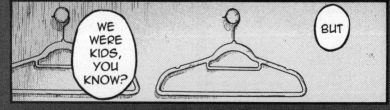

WE WERE KIDS, YOU KNOW?

BUT

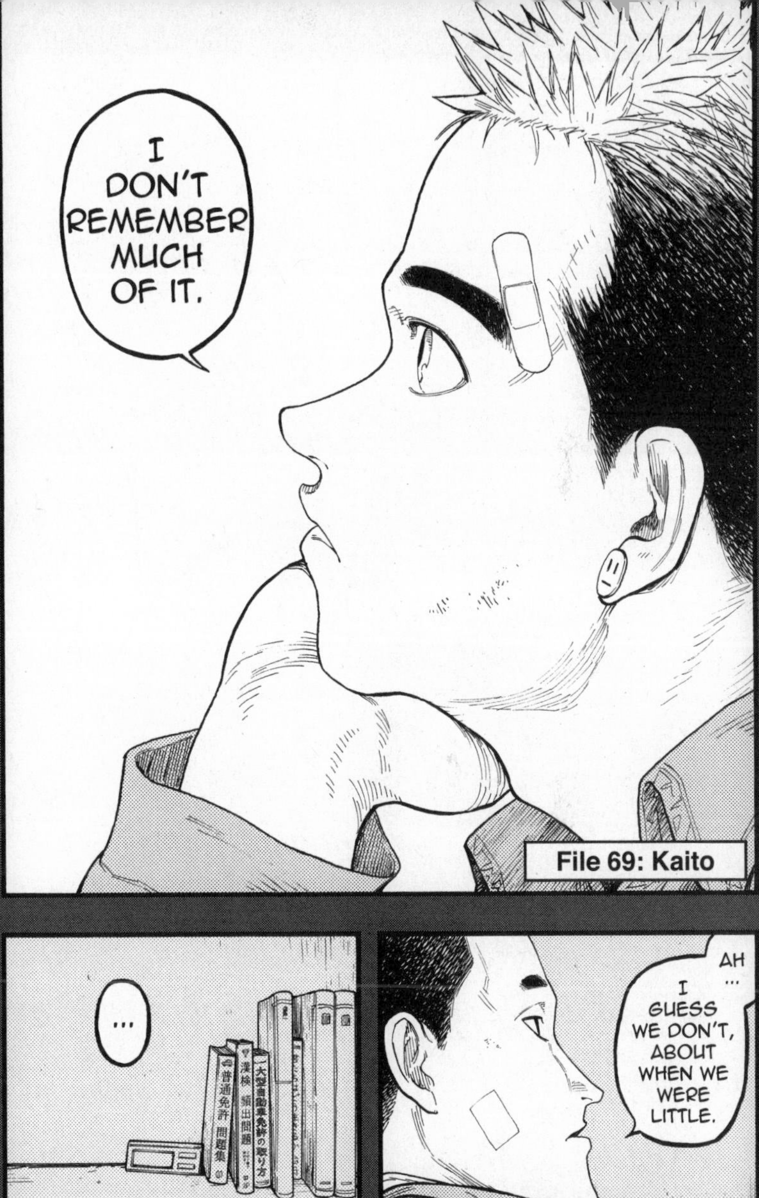
I DON'T REMEMBER MUCH OF IT.
File 69: Kaito
AH ...
I GUESS WE DON'T, ABOUT WHEN WE WERE LITTLE.
...
普通免許 問題集
漢検 頻出問題
大型自動車免許の取り方

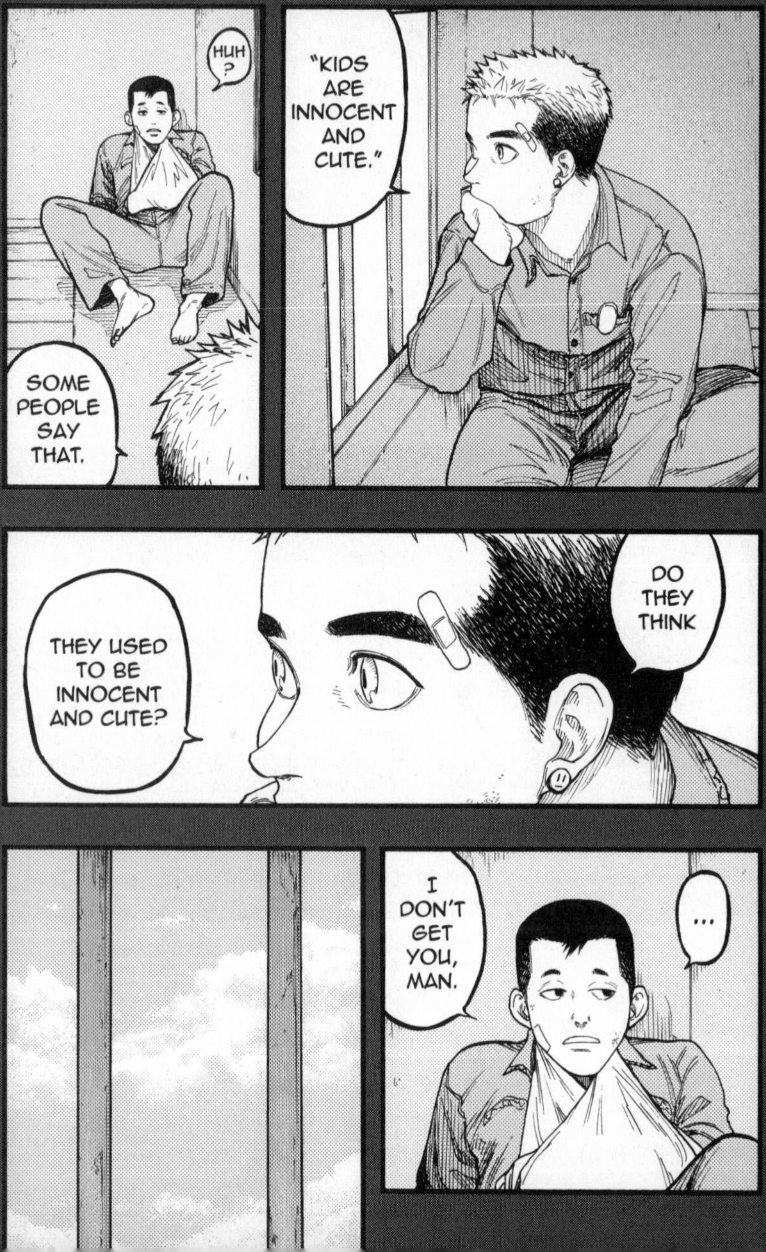
"KIDS ARE INNOCENT AND CUTE."
HUH?
SOME PEOPLE SAY THAT.
DO THEY THINK
THEY USED TO BE INNOCENT AND CUTE?
...
I DON'T GET YOU, MAN.

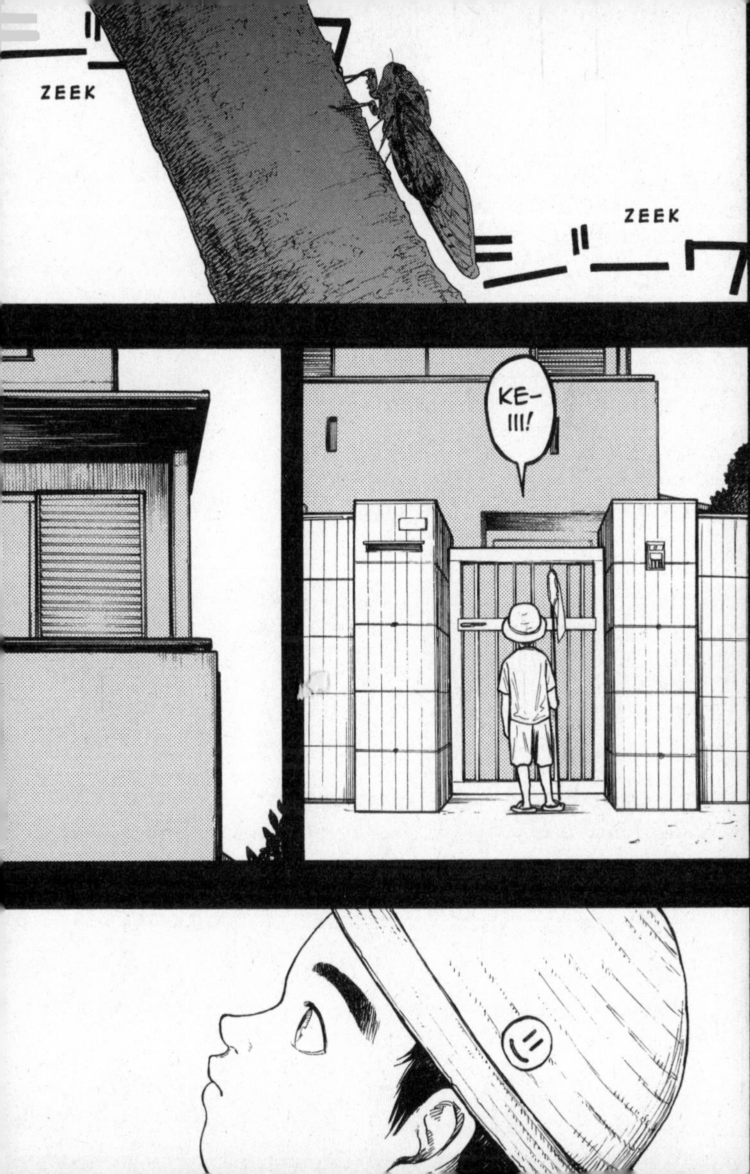
ZEEK
ZEEK
KE-III!

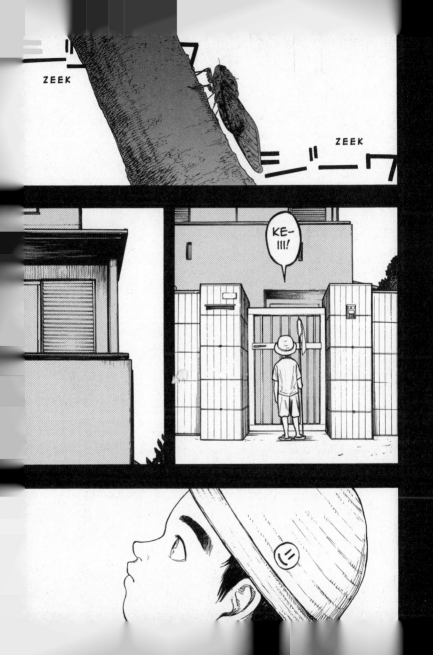

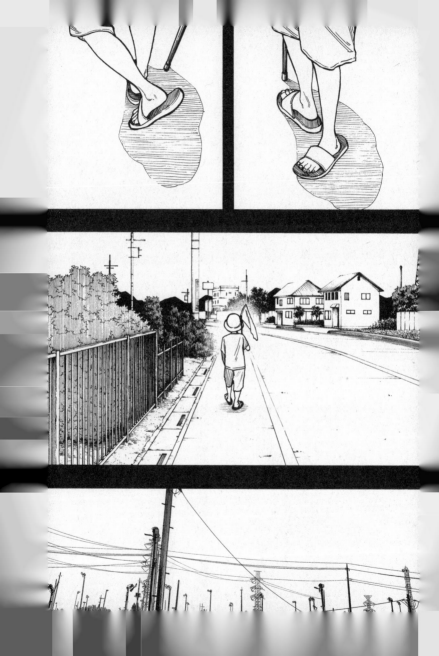

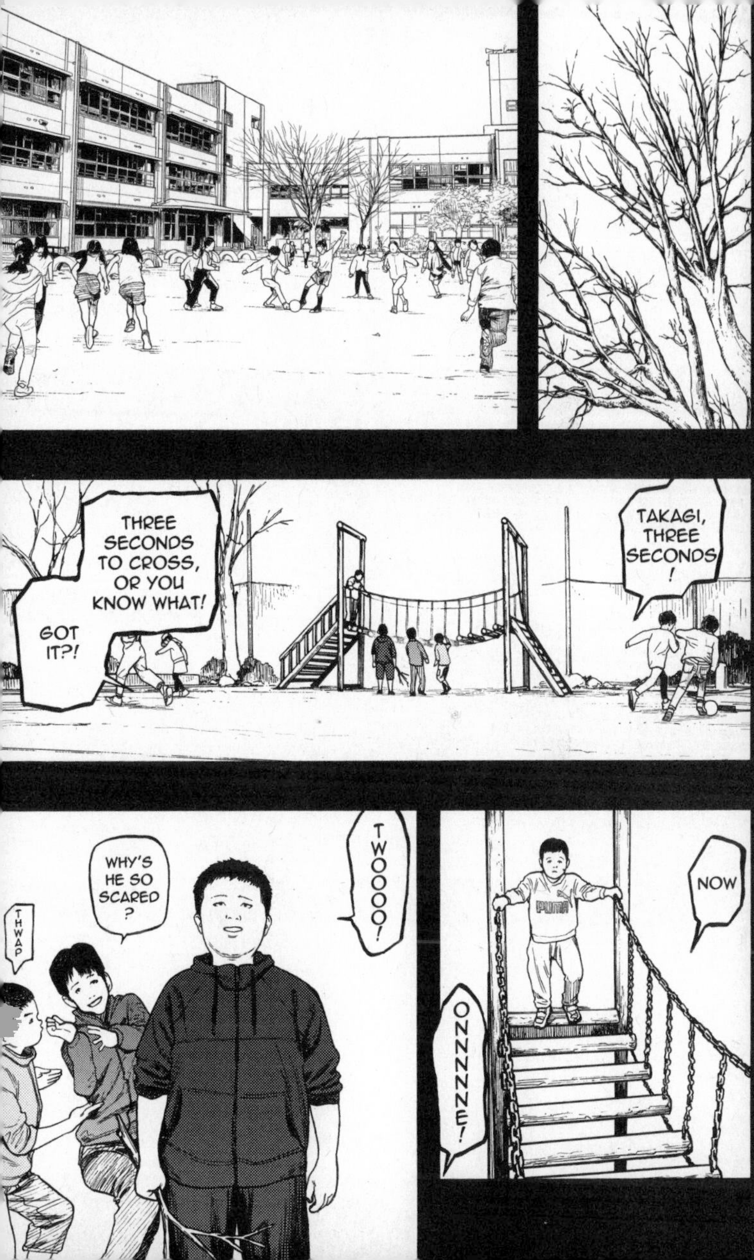
TAKAGI, THREE SECONDS!
THREE SECONDS TO CROSS, OR YOU KNOW WHAT!
GOT IT?!
NOW
ONNNNNE!
TWOOOO!
WHY'S HE SO SCARED?
THWAP

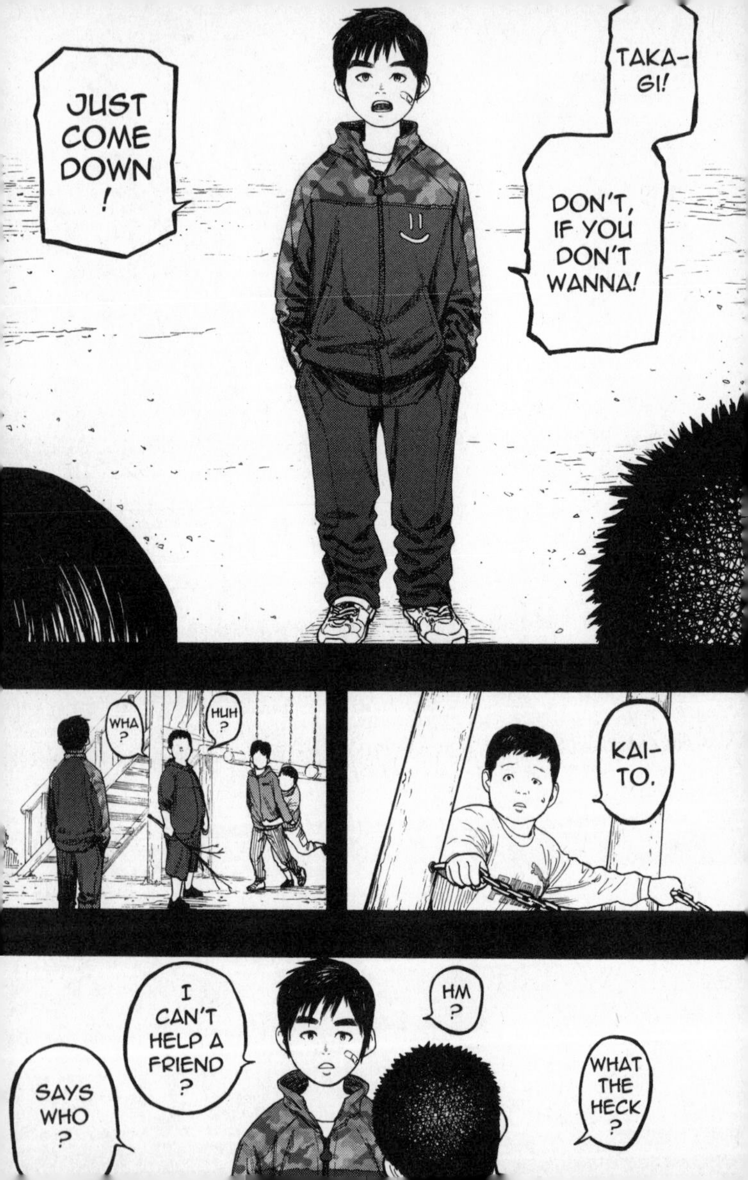
TAKA-GI!
DON'T, IF YOU DON'T WANNA!
JUST COME DOWN!
KAI-TO.
HUH?
WHA?
HM?
WHAT THE HECK?
I CAN'T HELP A FRIEND?
SAYS WHO?

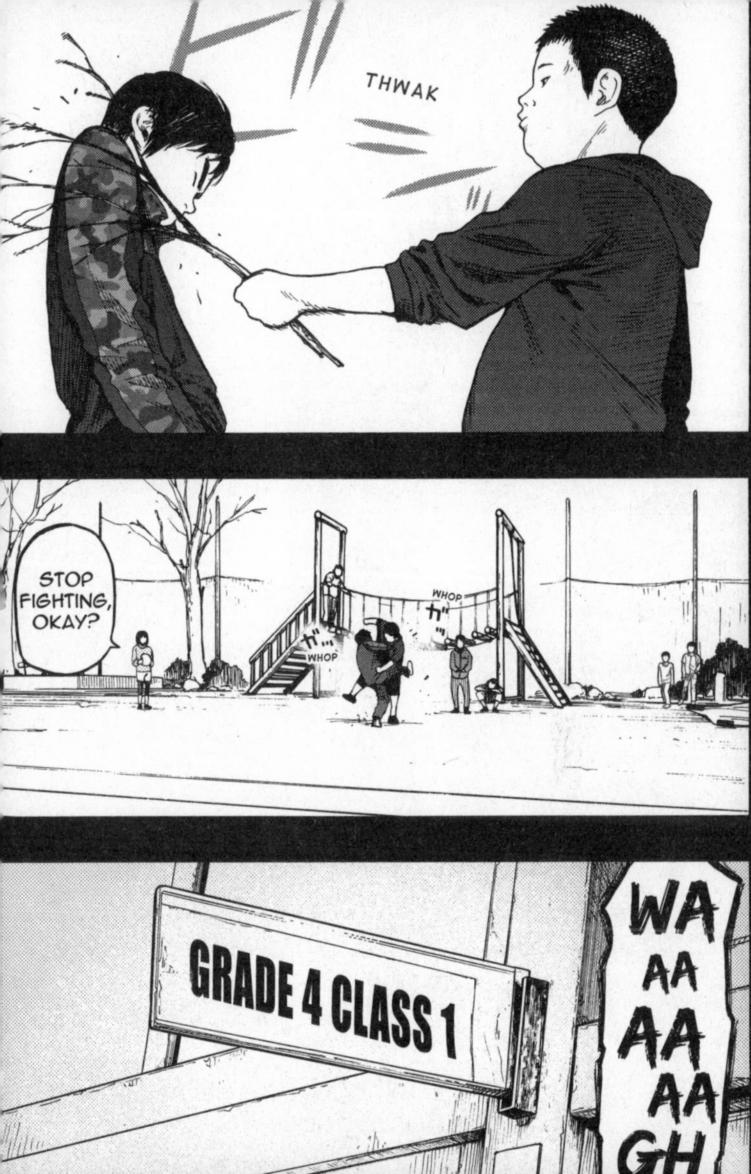
THWAK
WHOP
WHOP
STOP FIGHTING, OKAY?
WAAAAAAAAAGH
GRADE 4 CLASS 1

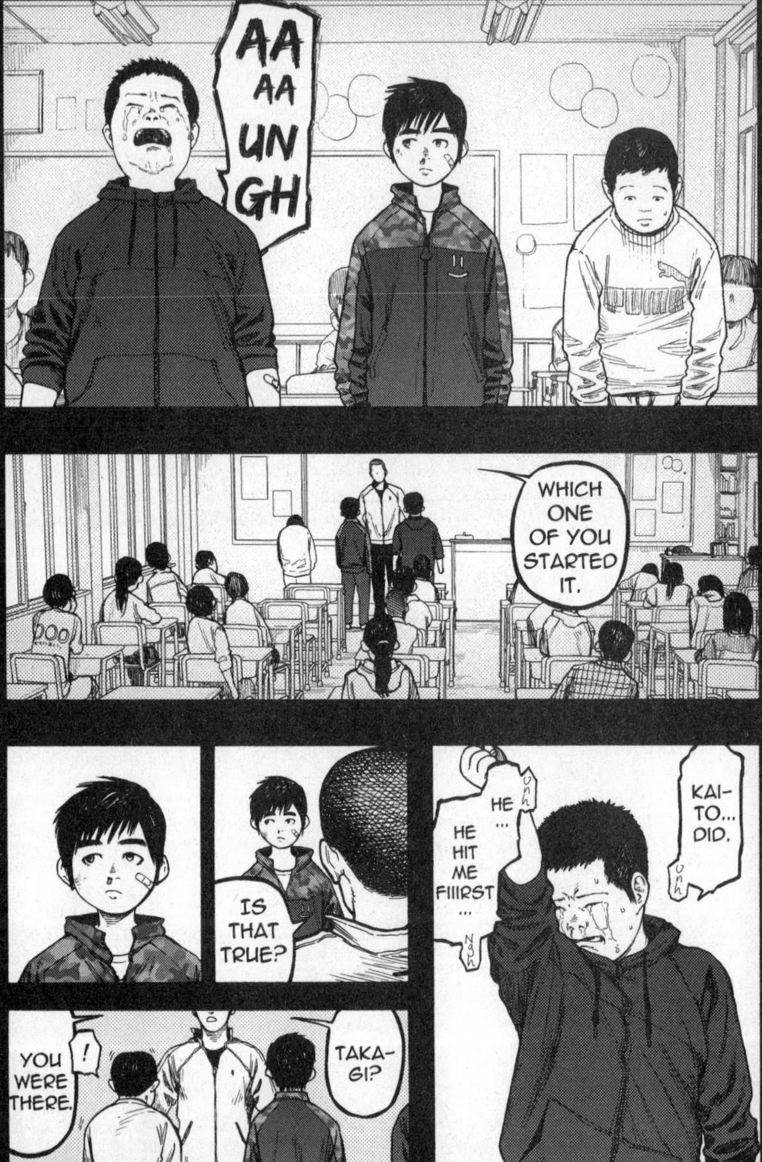
AA
AA
UNGH
WHICH ONE OF YOU STARTED IT.
KAI-TO... DID.
unh
HE ...
unh
HE HIT ME FIIIRST ...
Ngh
IS THAT TRUE?
TAKA-GI?
!
YOU WERE THERE.

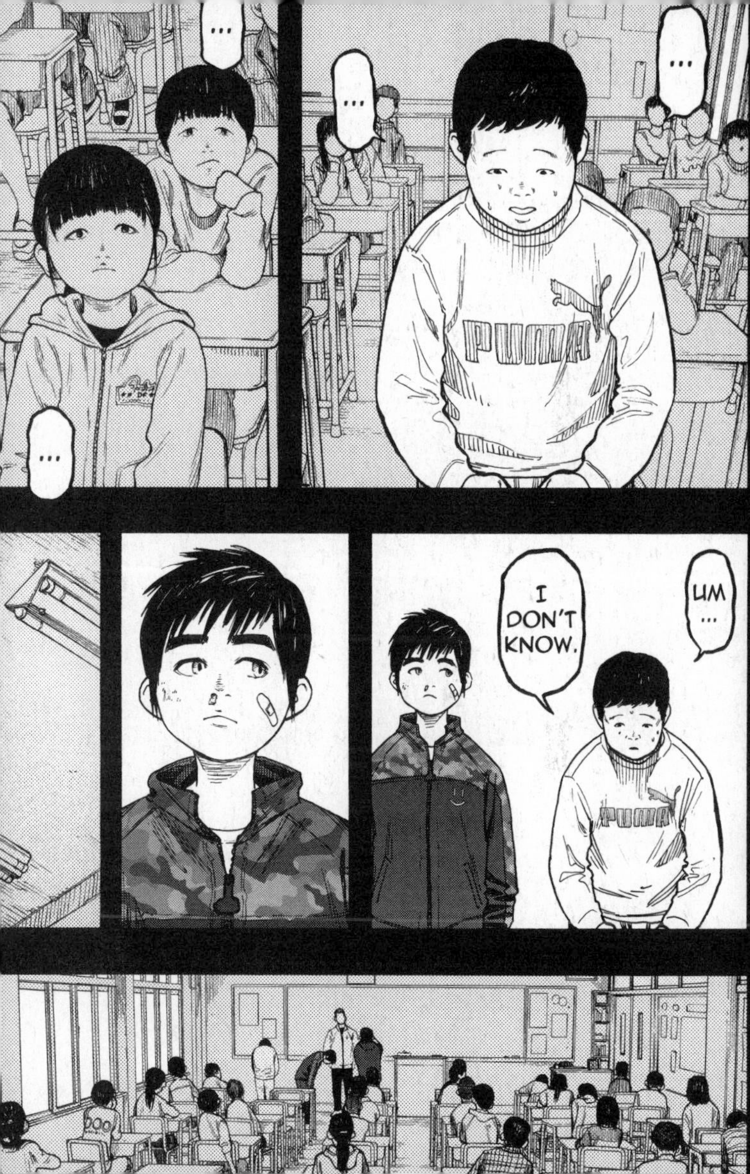
...
...
...
...
UM ...
I DON'T KNOW.

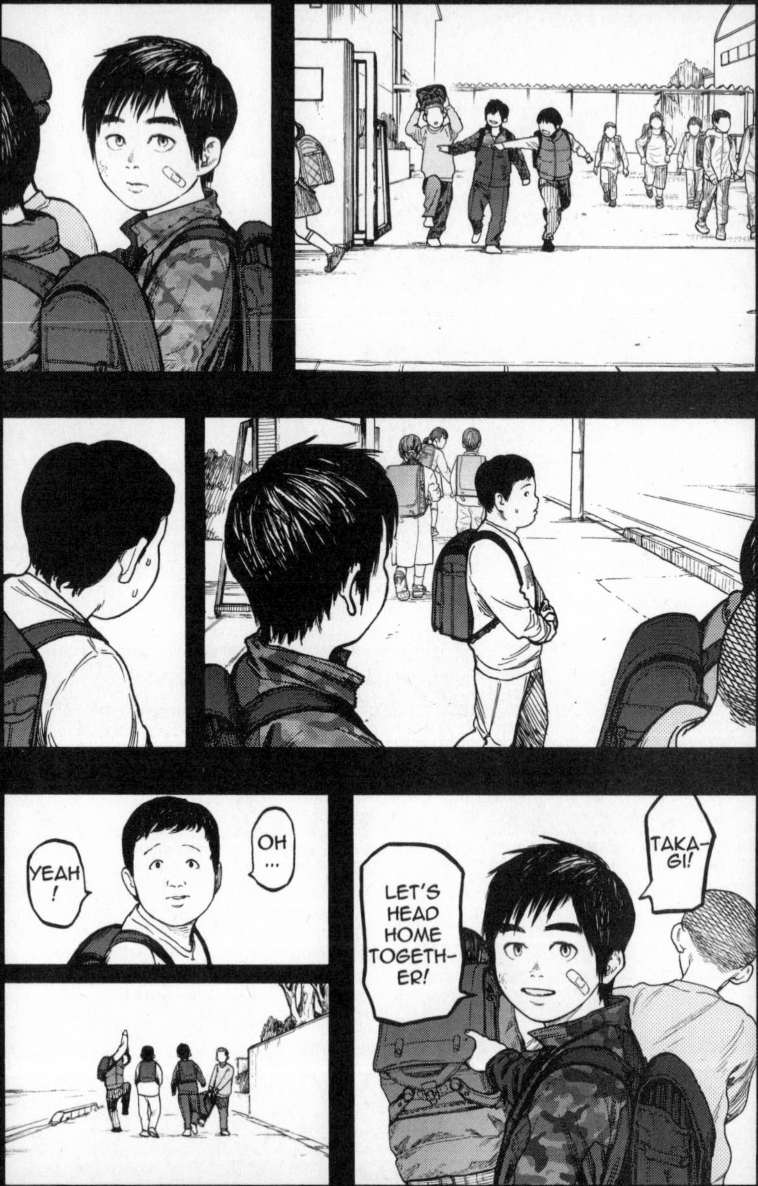
TAKA-GI!
LET'S HEAD HOME TOGETH-ER!
OH ...
YEAH!

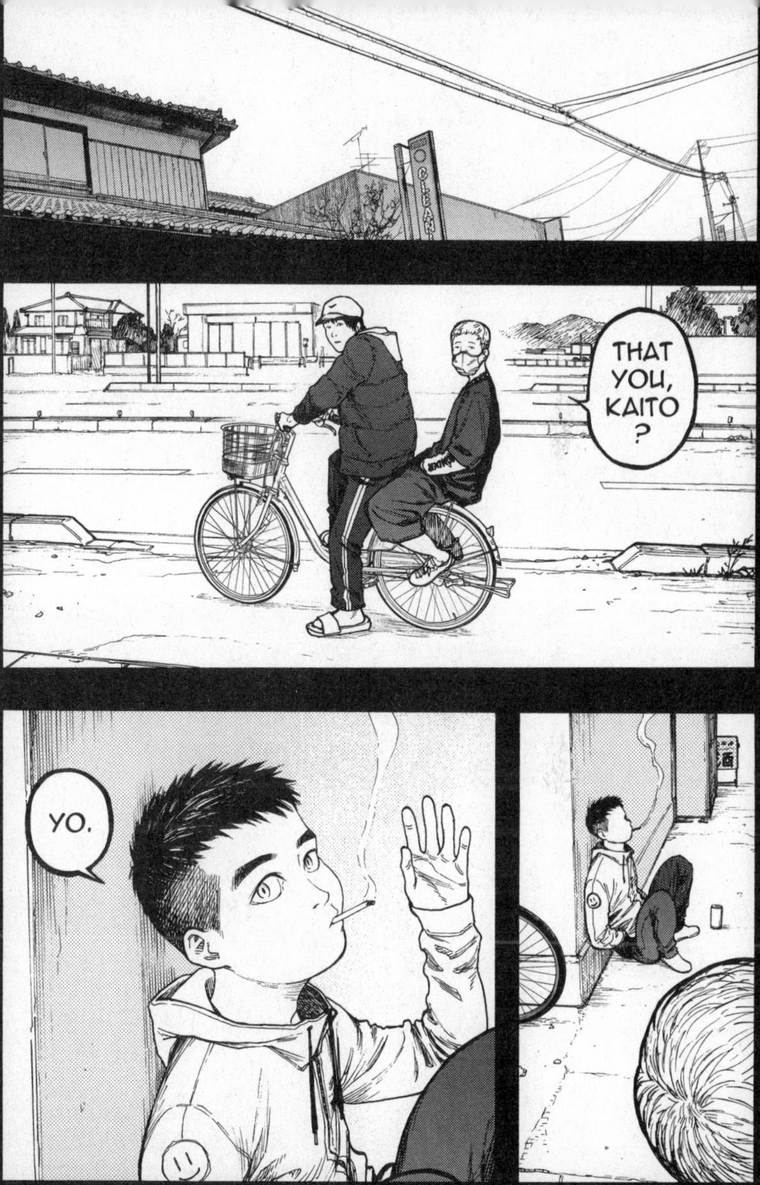
THAT YOU, KAITO?
YO.

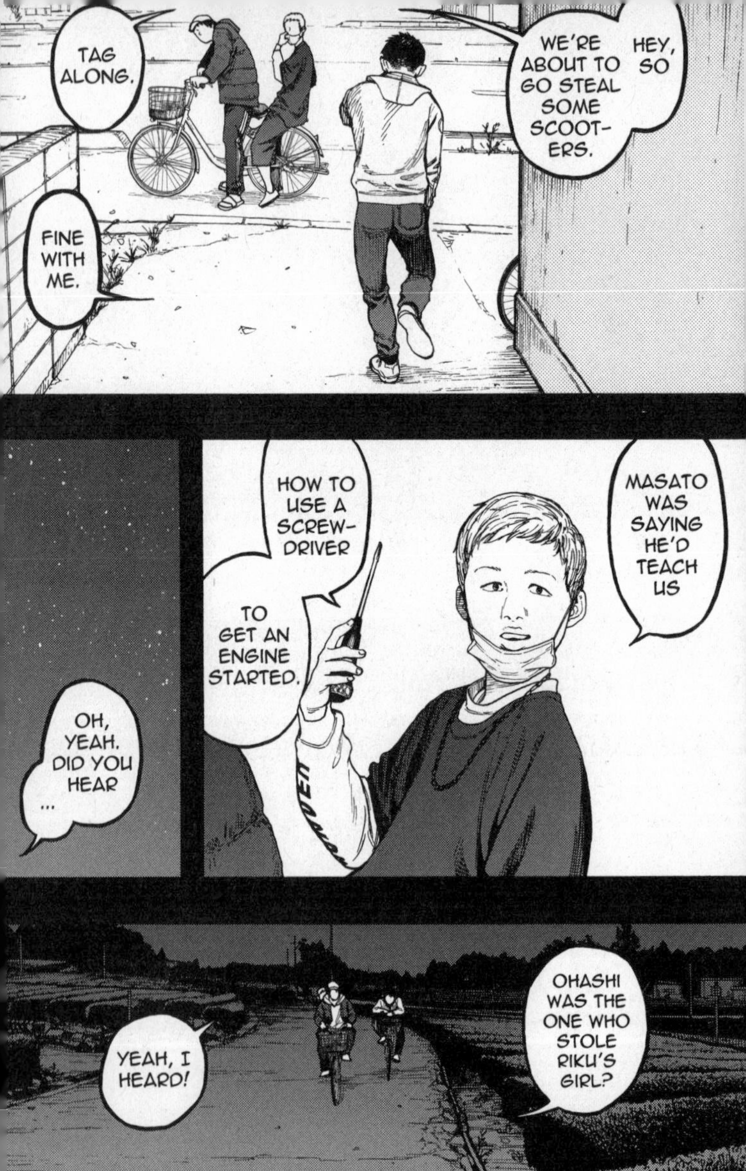
HEY, SO
WE'RE ABOUT TO GO STEAL SOME SCOOT-ERS.
TAG ALONG.
FINE WITH ME.
MASATO WAS SAYING HE'D TEACH US
HOW TO USE A SCREW-DRIVER
TO GET AN ENGINE STARTED.
OH, YEAH. DID YOU HEAR ...
OHASHI WAS THE ONE WHO STOLE RIKU'S GIRL?
YEAH, I HEARD!

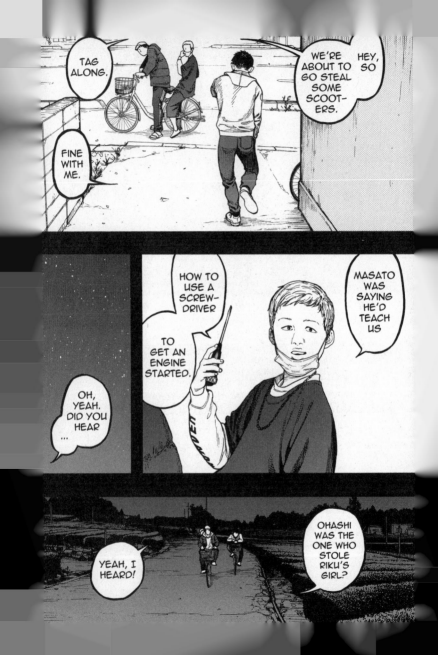

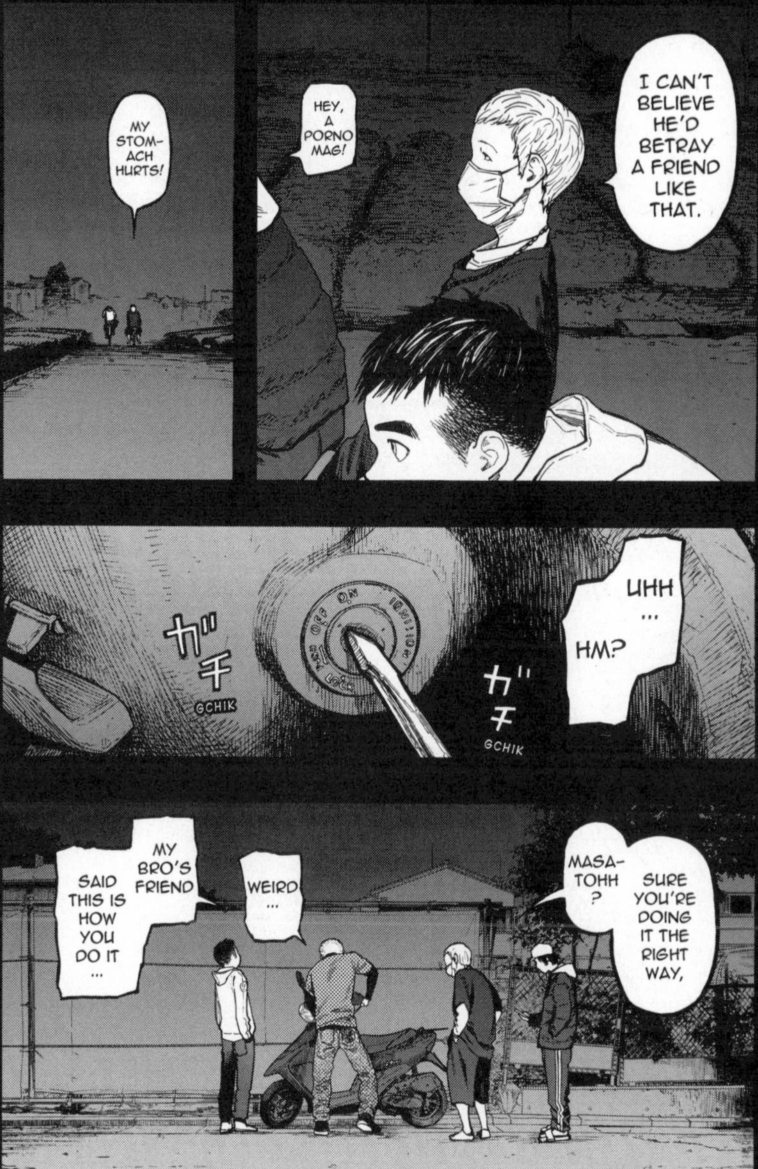
I CAN'T BELIEVE HE'D BETRAY A FRIEND LIKE THAT.
HEY, A PORNO MAG!
MY STOM-ACH HURTS!
UHH ... HM?
ガチ
GCHIK
ガチ
GCHIK
SURE YOU'RE DOING IT THE RIGHT WAY,
MASA-TOHH ?
WEIRD ...
MY BRO'S FRIEND
SAID THIS IS HOW YOU DO IT ...

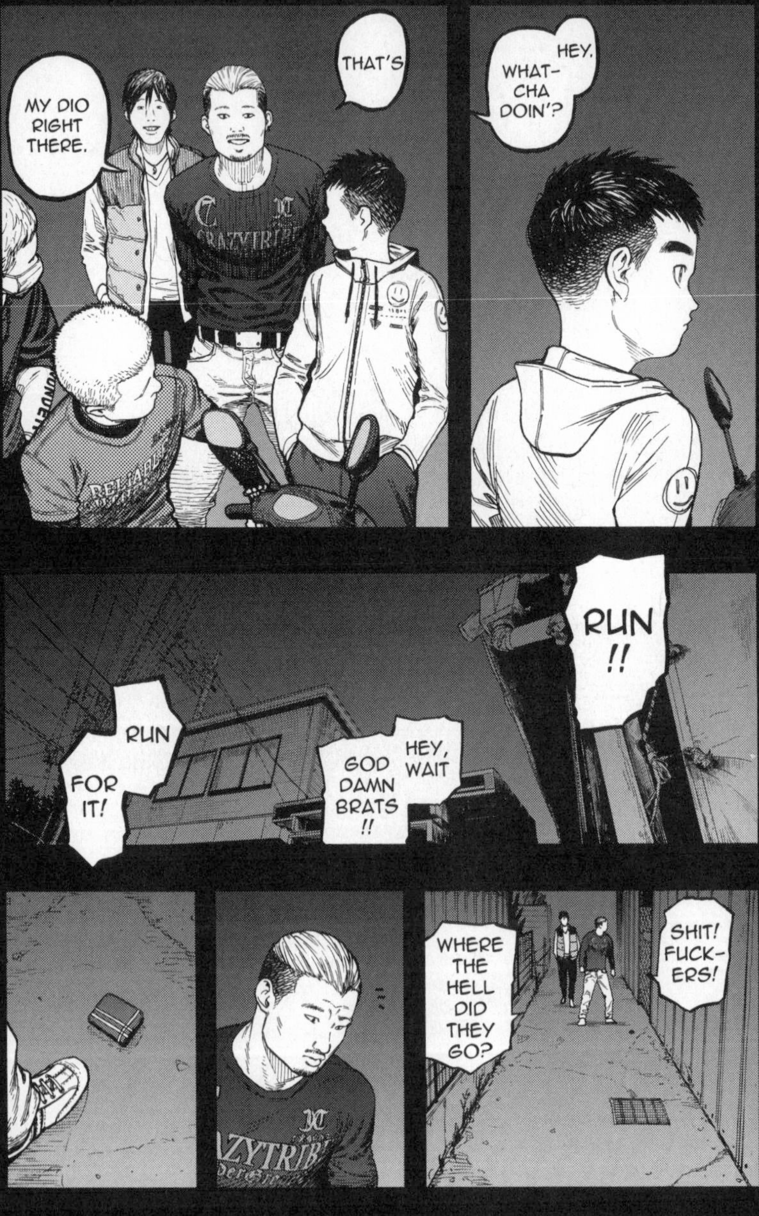
HEY, WHAT-CHA DOIN'?
THAT'S
MY DIO RIGHT THERE.
RUN !!
HEY, WAIT
GOD DAMN BRATS !!
RUN
FOR IT!
SHIT! FUCK-ERS!
WHERE THE HELL DID THEY GO?

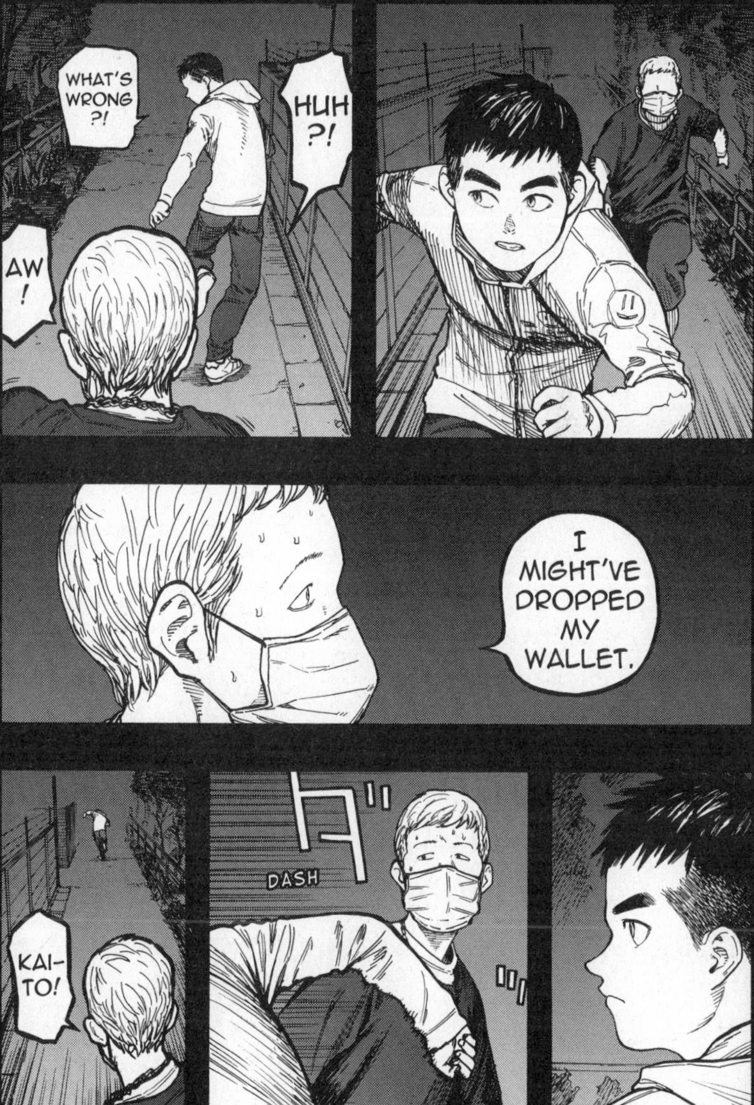
HUH ?!
WHAT'S WRONG ?!
AW !
I MIGHT'VE DROPPED MY WALLET.
DASH
KAI-TO!

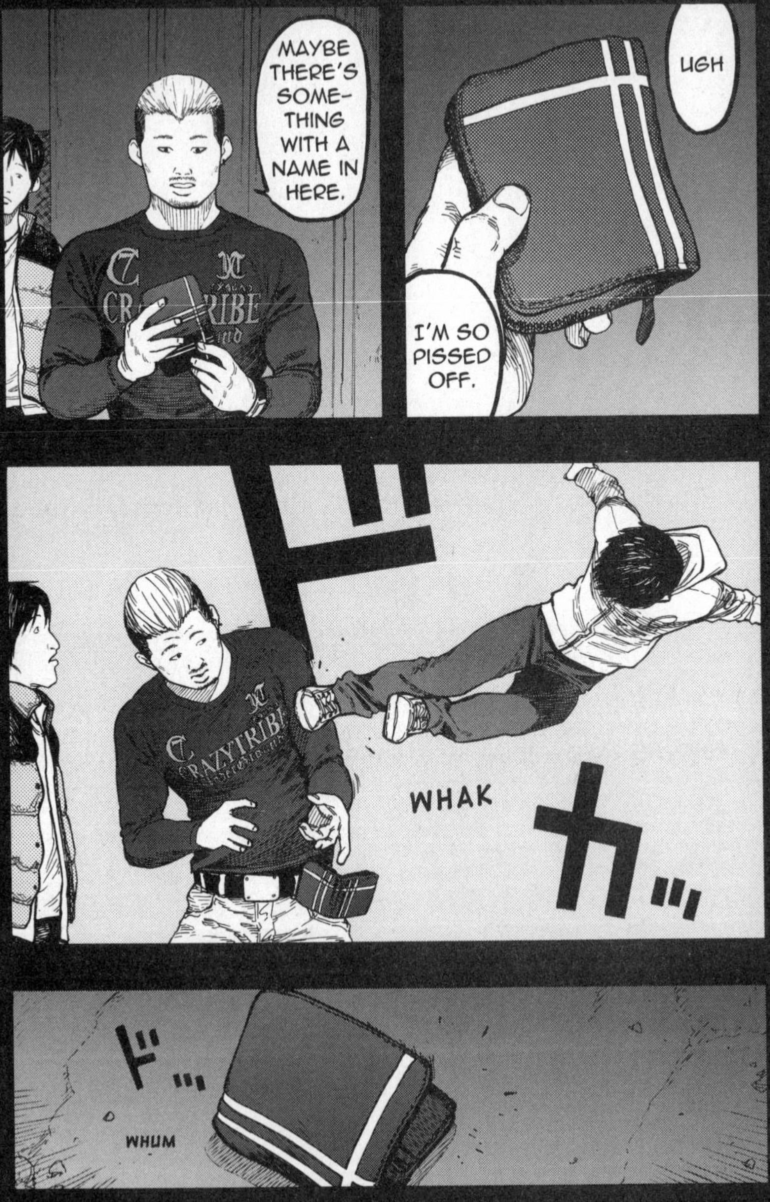
UGH
I'M SO PISSED OFF.
MAYBE THERE'S SOME-THING WITH A NAME IN HERE.
ド
WHAK
カッ
ドッ
WHUM

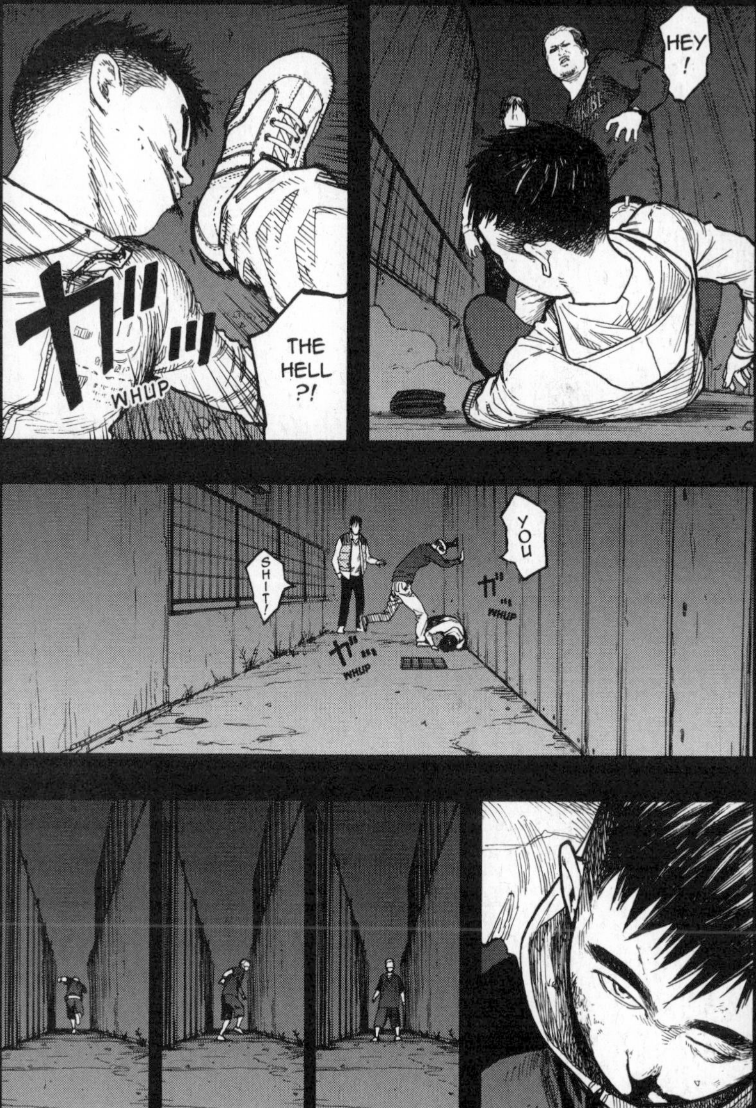
HEY!
ガッ
WHUP
THE HELL?!
YOU
ガッ
WHUP
SHIT!
ガッ
WHUP

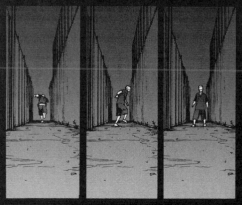

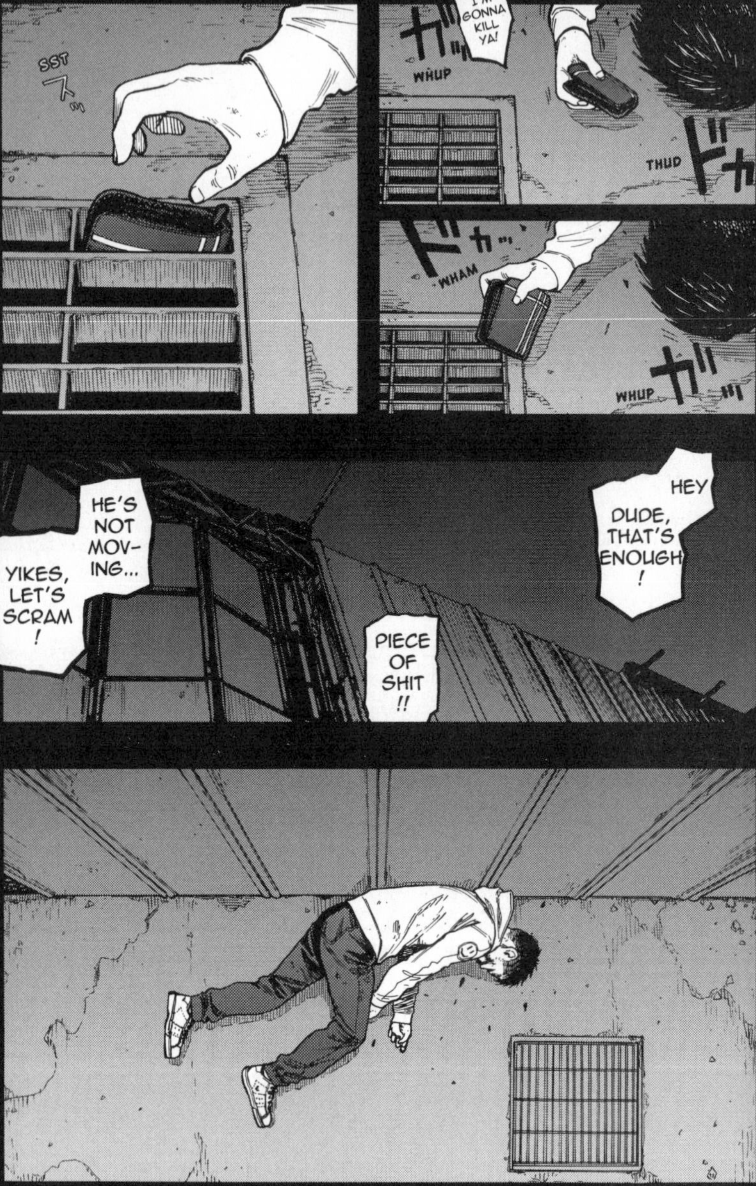
I'M GONNA KILL YA!
WHUP
THUD
WHAM
WHUP
SST
HEY DUDE, THAT'S ENOUGH!
PIECE OF SHIT!!
HE'S NOT MOVING...
YIKES, LET'S SCRAM!

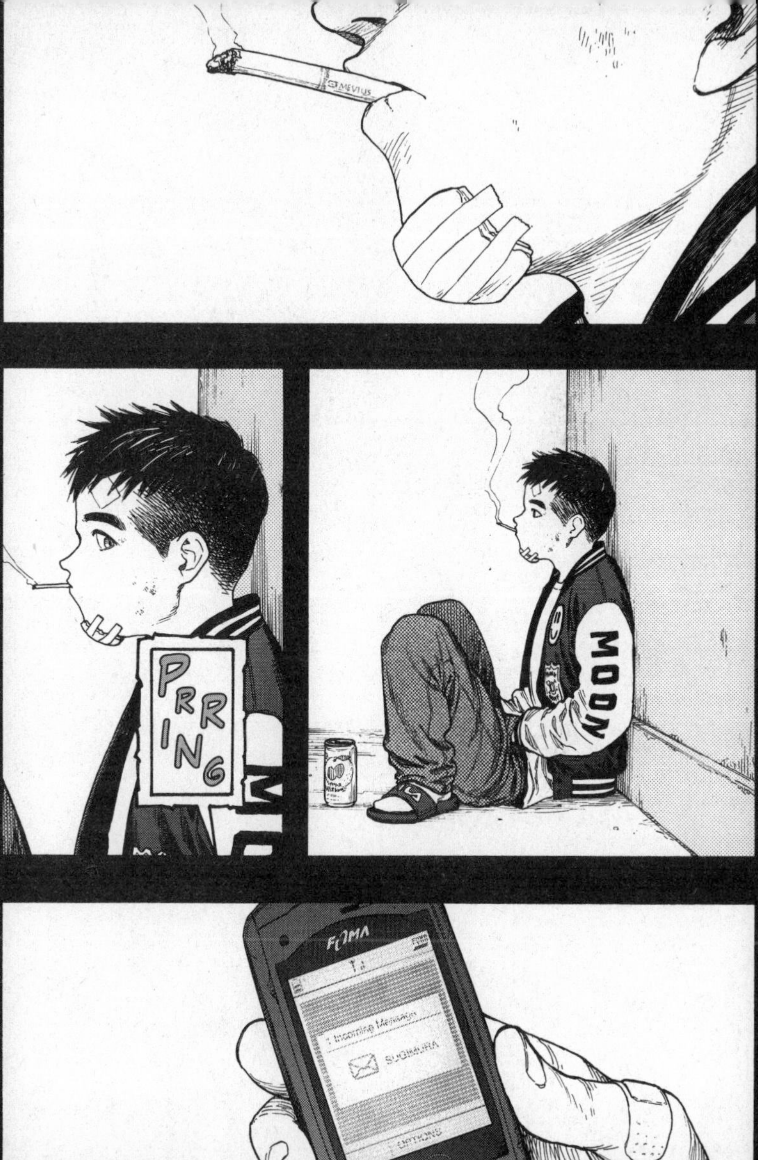
MEVIUS
MOON
PRRING
FOMA
1 Incoming Message
SUGIMURA

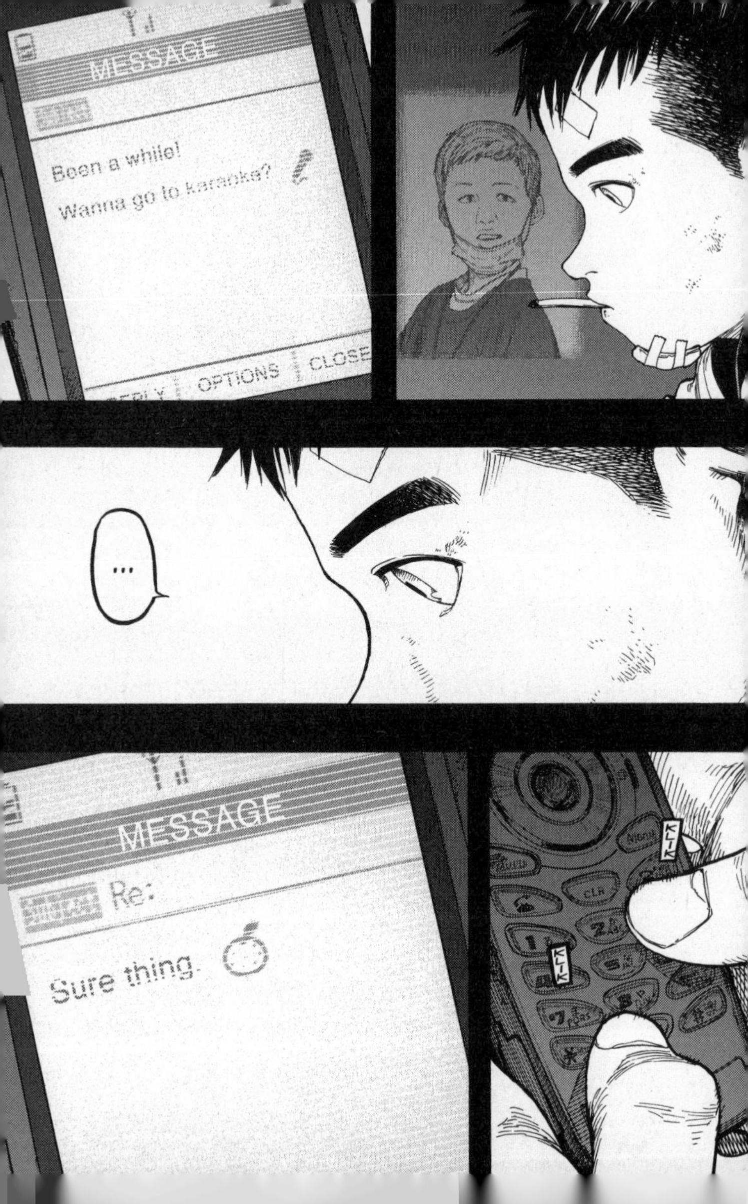
MESSAGE
Been a while!
Wanna go to karaoke?
OPTIONS
CLOSE
...
KLIK
KLIK
MESSAGE
Re:
Sure thing.

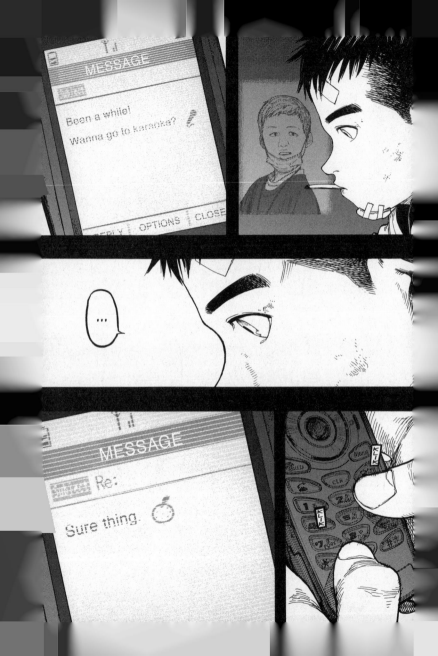

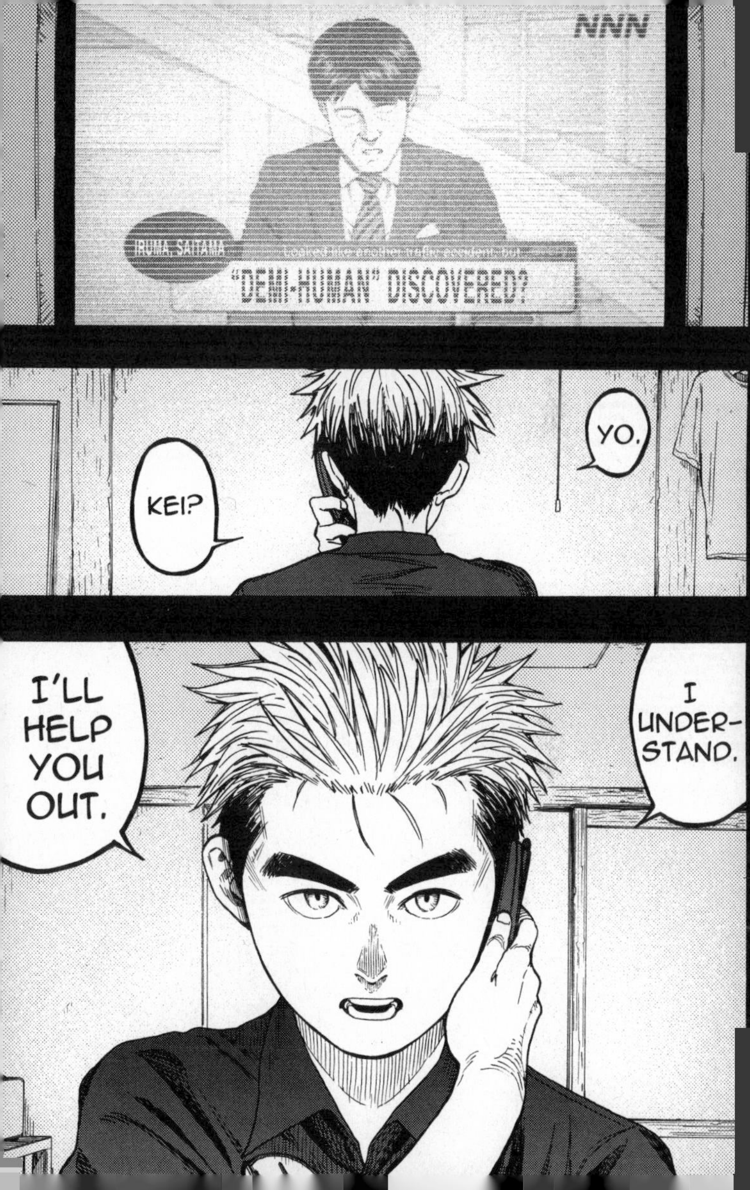
NNN
IRUMA, SAITAMA
"DEMI-HUMAN" DISCOVERED?
YO.
KEI?
I UNDERSTAND.
I'LL HELP YOU OUT.

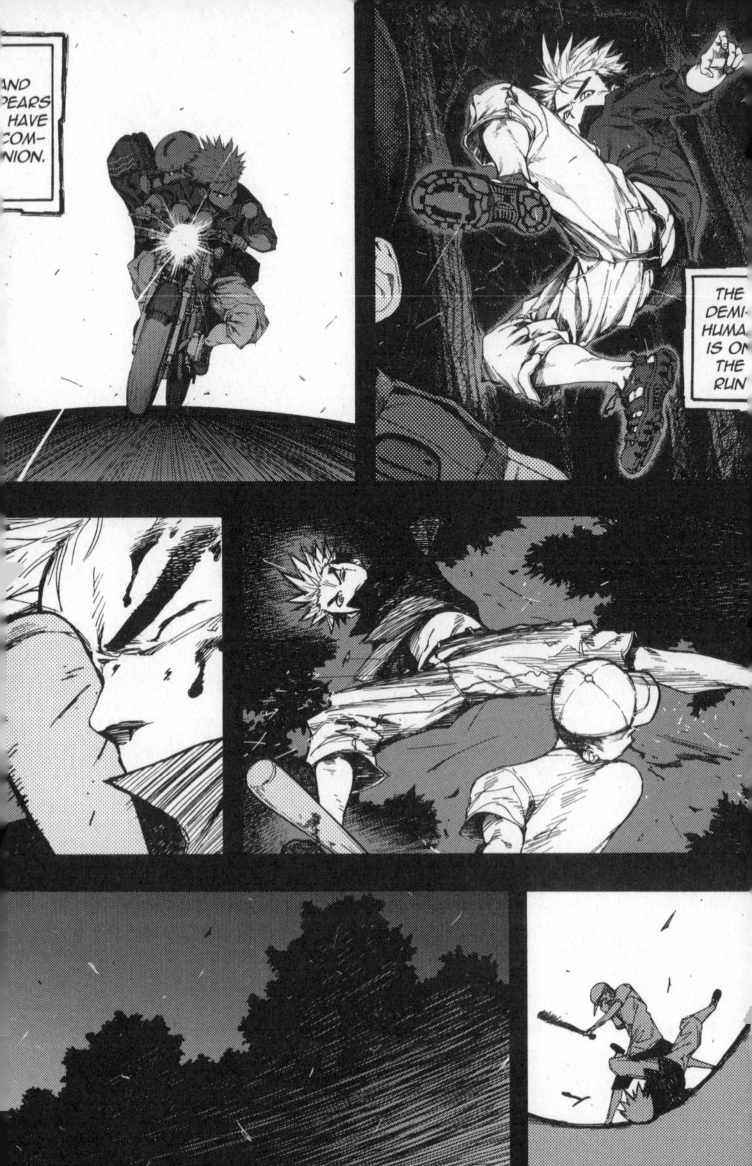
THE DEMI- HUMA IS ON THE RUN
AND PEARS HAVE COM- NION.

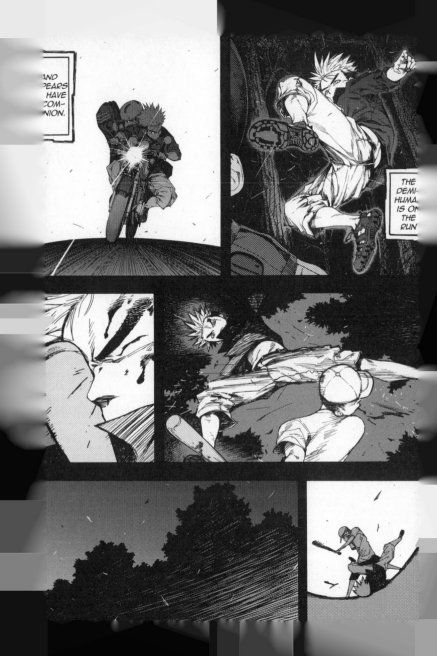

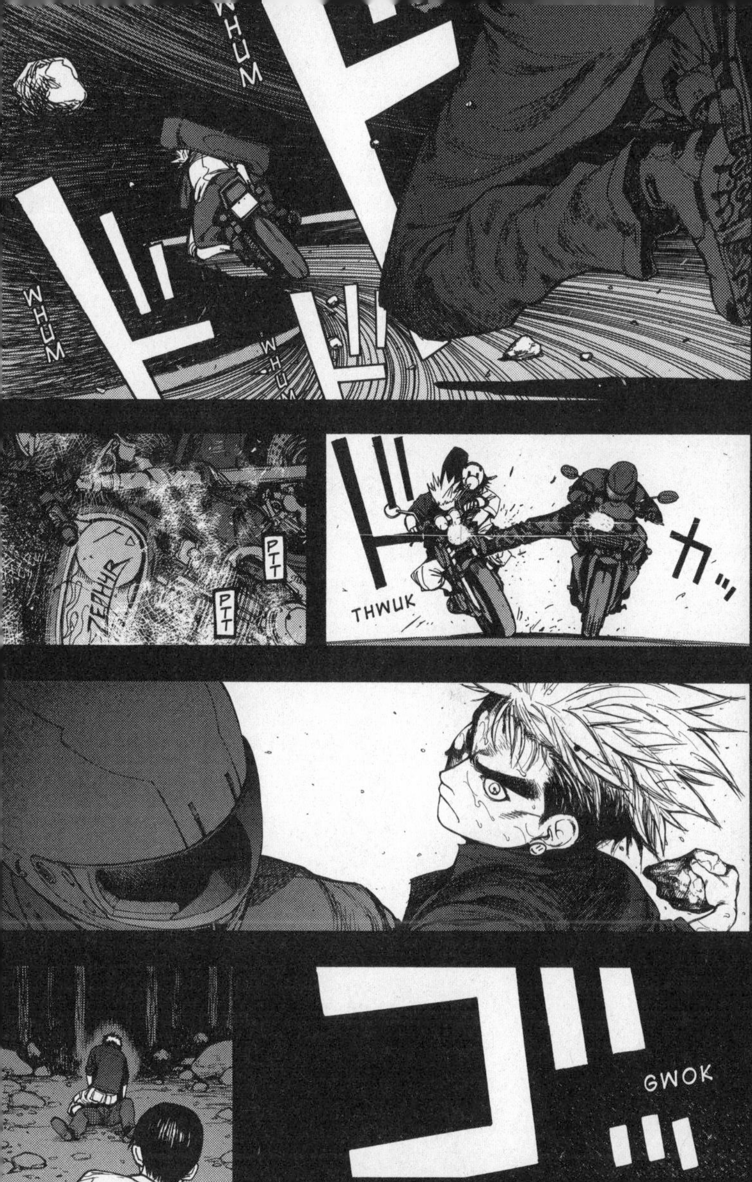
WHUM
WHUM
WHUM
THWUK
カッ
PTT
PTT
ZEPHYR
GWOK
ゴッ

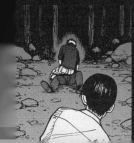

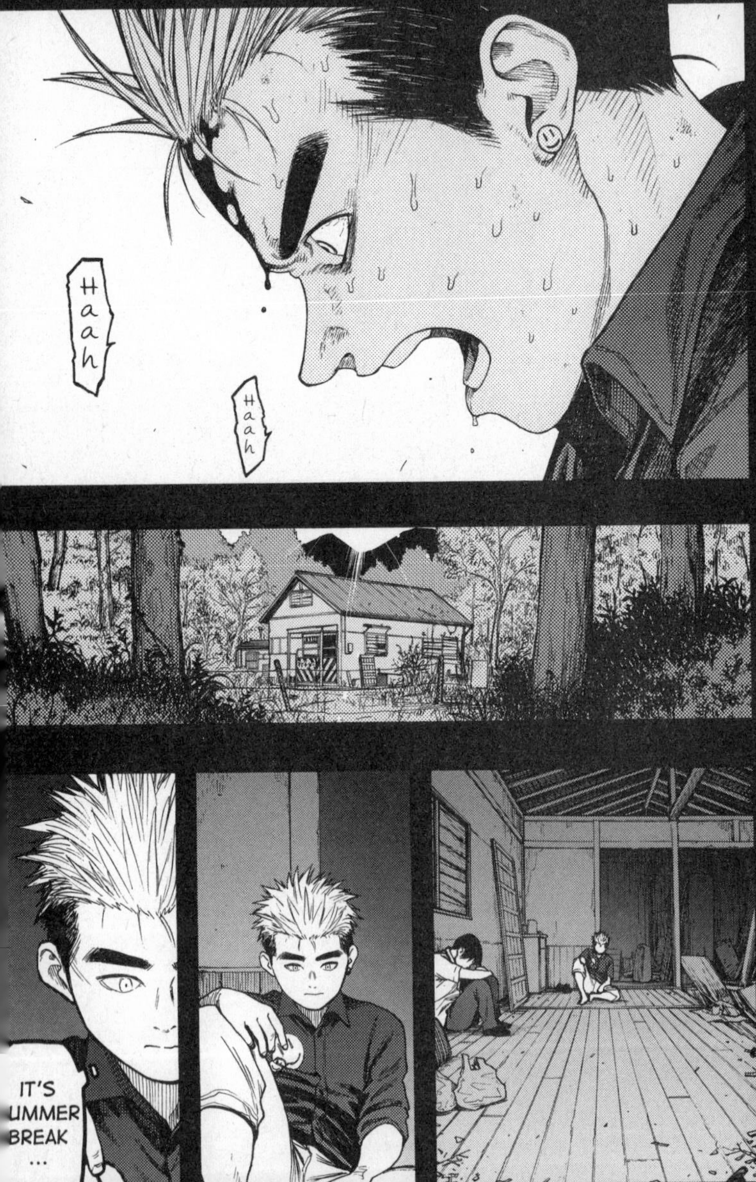
Haah
Haah
IT'S
UMMER
BREAK
...

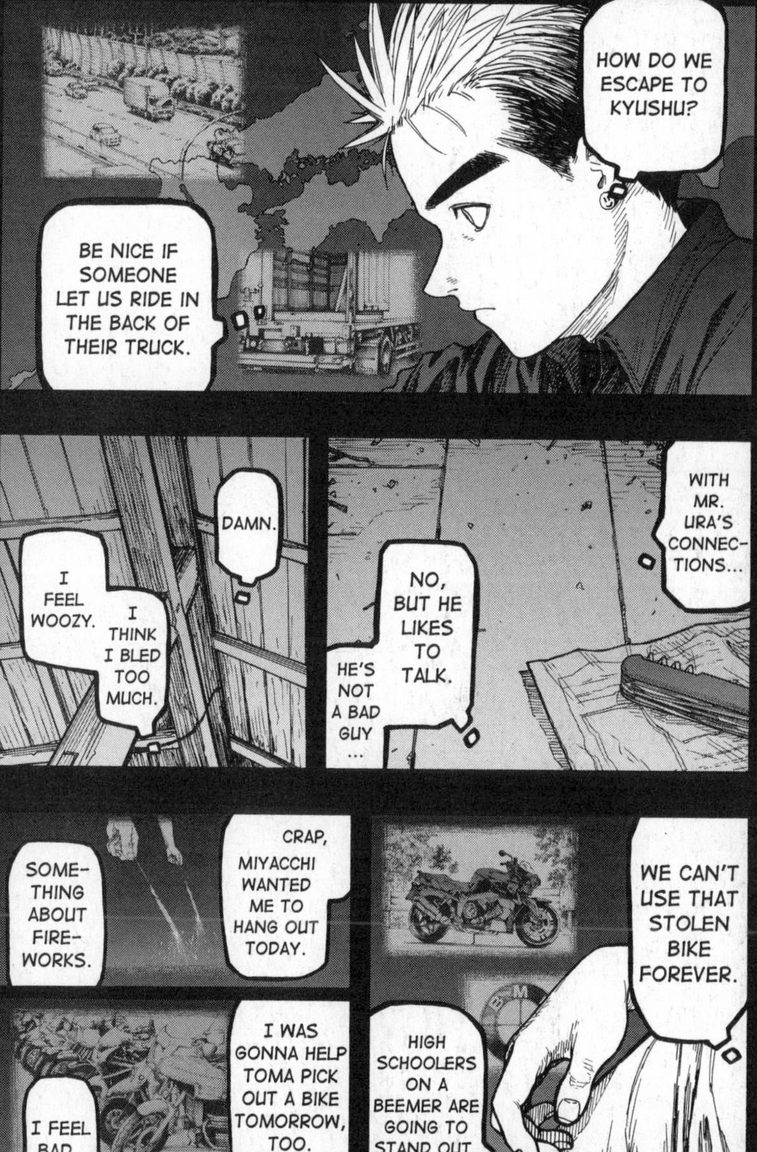

HOW DO WE ESCAPE TO KYUSHU?
BE NICE IF SOMEONE LET US RIDE IN THE BACK OF THEIR TRUCK.
WITH MR. URA'S CONNEC-TIONS...
NO, BUT HE LIKES TO TALK.
HE'S NOT A BAD GUY ...
DAMN.
I FEEL WOOZY.
I THINK I BLED TOO MUCH.
WE CAN'T USE THAT STOLEN BIKE FOREVER.
HIGH SCHOOLERS ON A BEEMER ARE GOING TO STAND OUT.
CRAP, MIYACCHI WANTED ME TO HANG OUT TODAY.
SOME-THING ABOUT FIRE-WORKS.
I WAS GONNA HELP TOMA PICK OUT A BIKE TOMORROW, TOO.
I FEEL BAD...

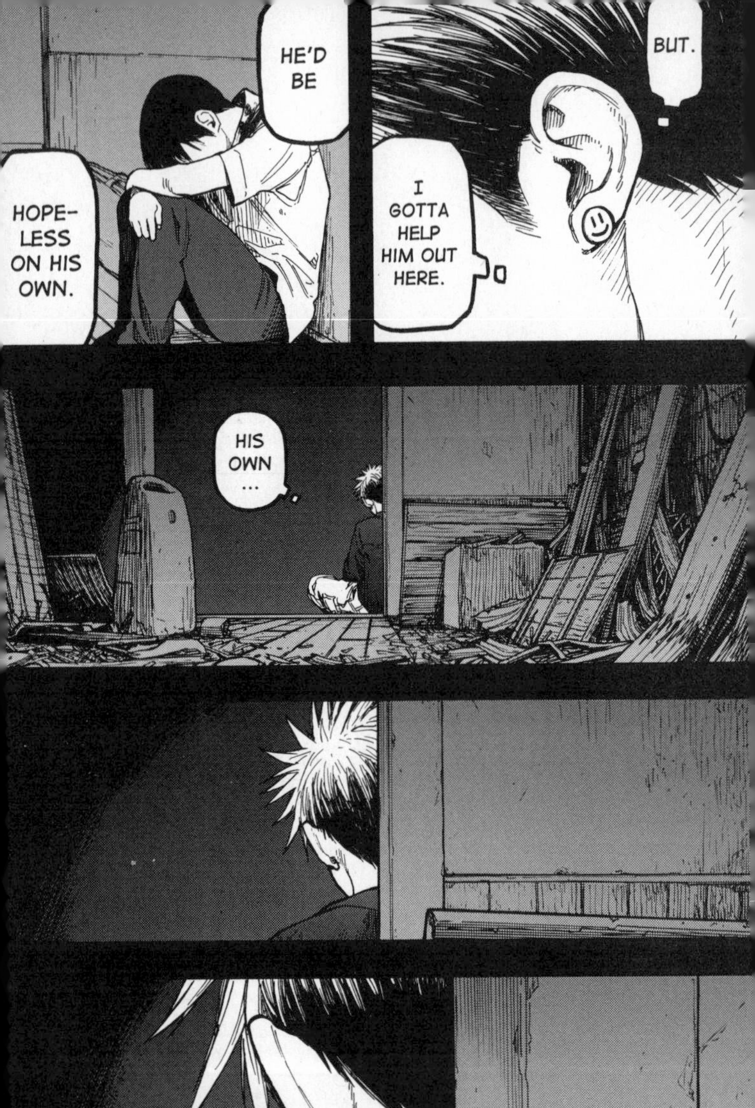
BUT.
I GOTTA HELP HIM OUT HERE.
HE'D BE
HOPE-LESS ON HIS OWN.
HIS OWN ...

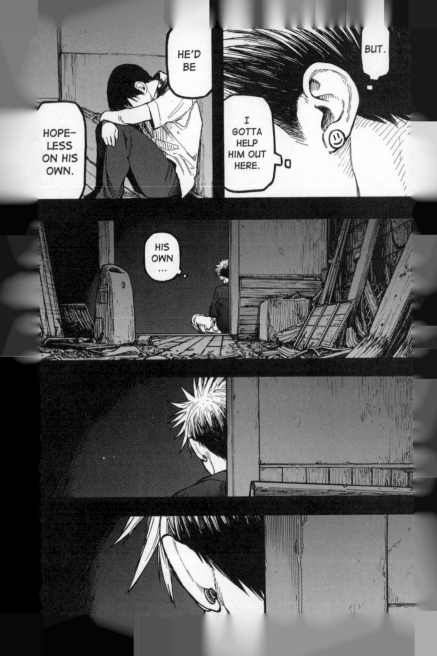

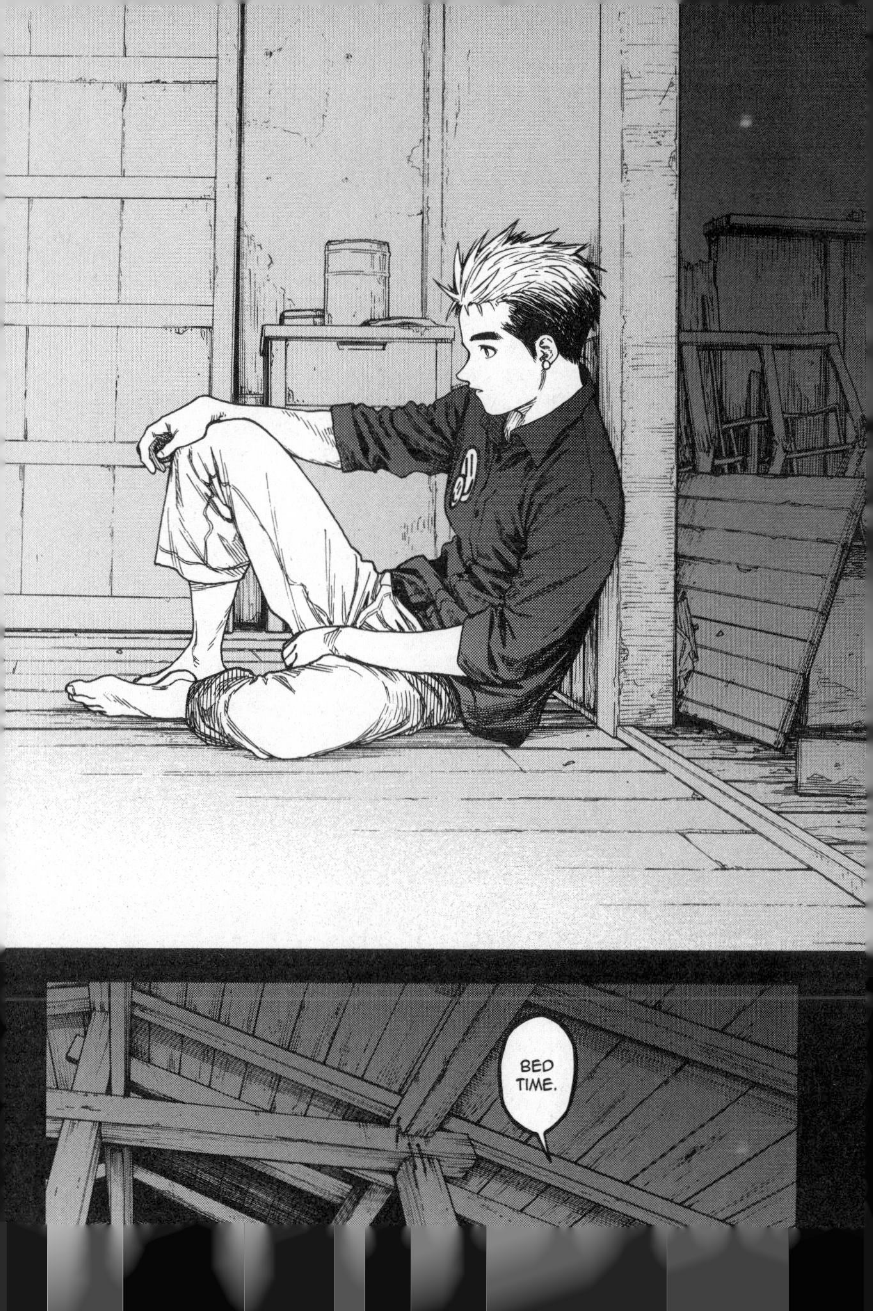
BED TIME.

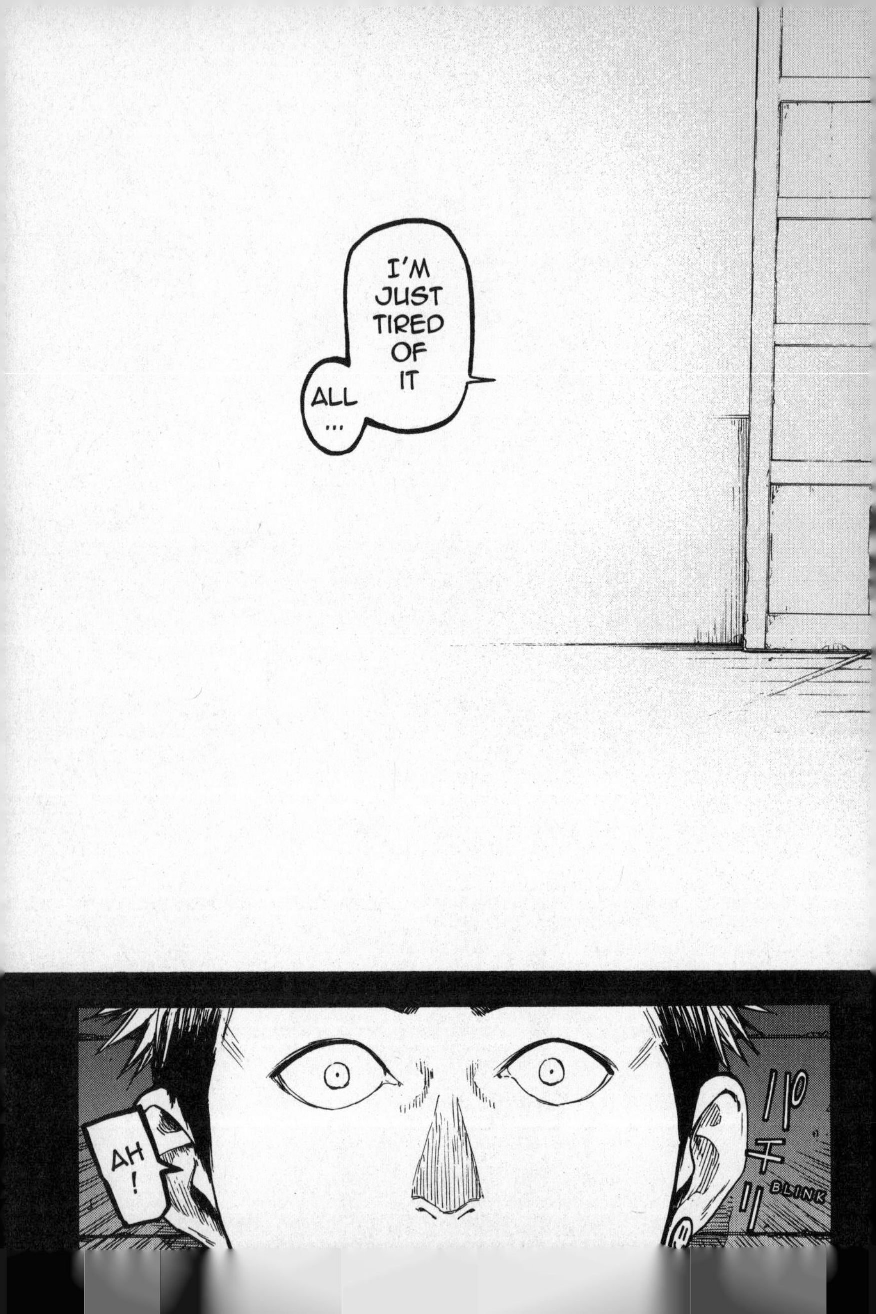
I'M JUST TIRED OF IT ALL ...
BLINK
AH!

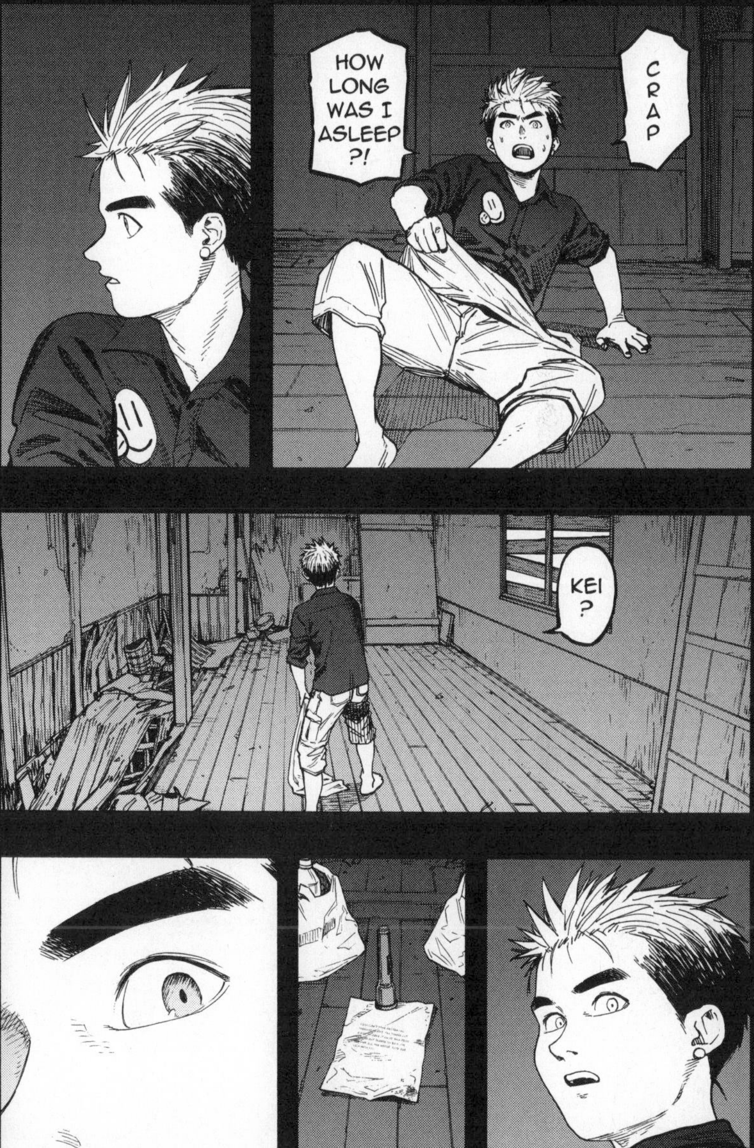
CRAP
HOW LONG WAS I ASLEEP?!
KEI?

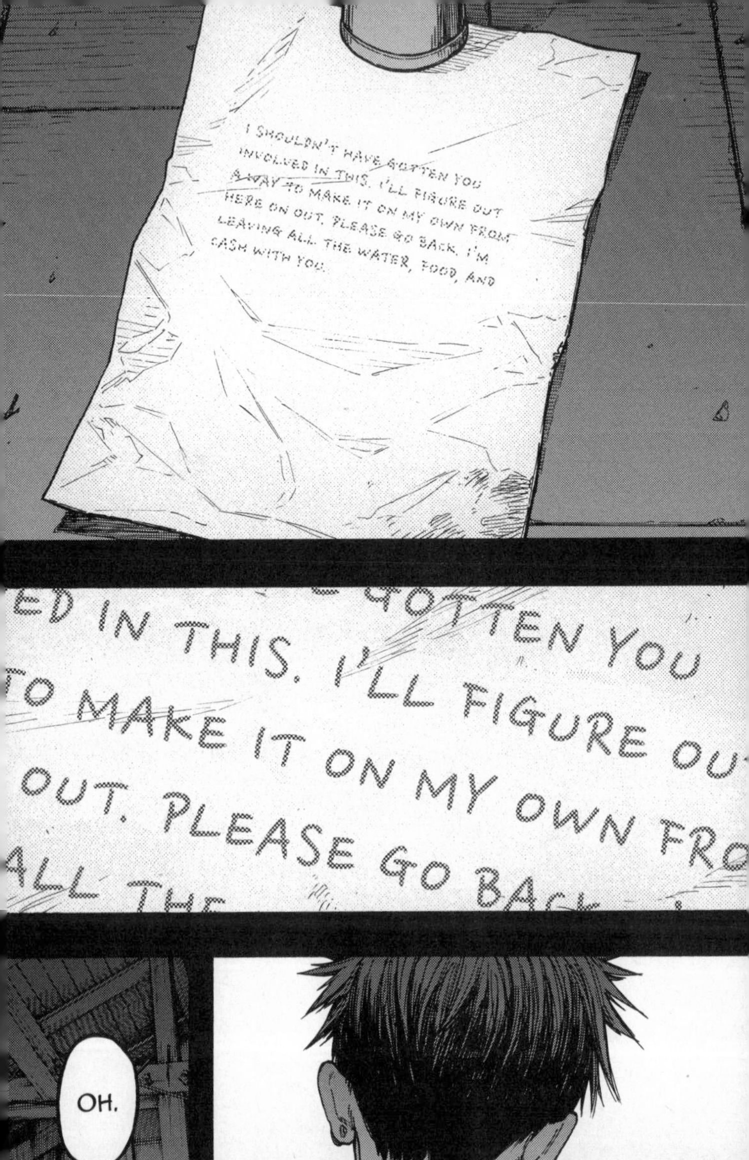
I SHOULDN'T HAVE GOTTEN YOU
INVOLVED IN THIS. I'LL FIGURE OUT
A WAY TO MAKE IT ON MY OWN FROM
HERE ON OUT. PLEASE GO BACK. I'M
LEAVING ALL THE WATER, FOOD, AND
CASH WITH YOU.
GOTTEN YOU
ED IN THIS. I'LL FIGURE OU
TO MAKE IT ON MY OWN FRO
OUT. PLEASE GO BACK.
ALL THE
OH.

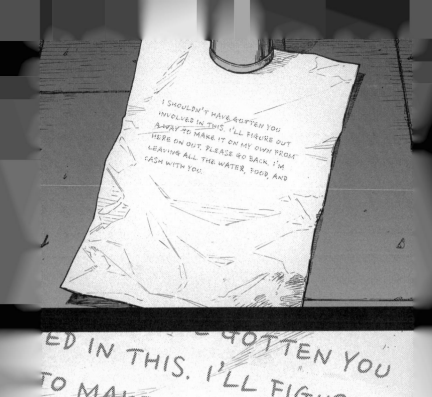

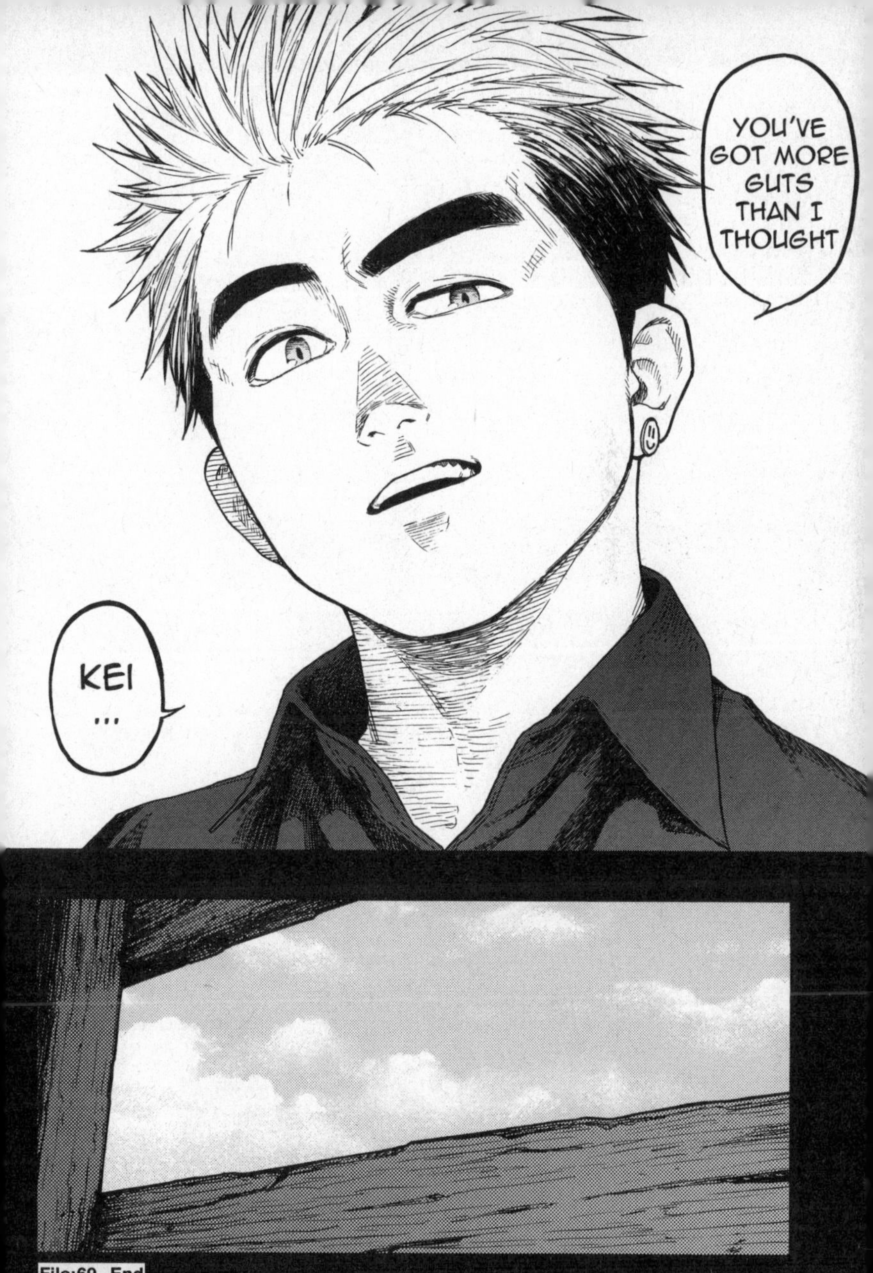
YOU'VE GOT MORE GUTS THAN I THOUGHT
KEI ...

File:69 End

File 70: Dedication

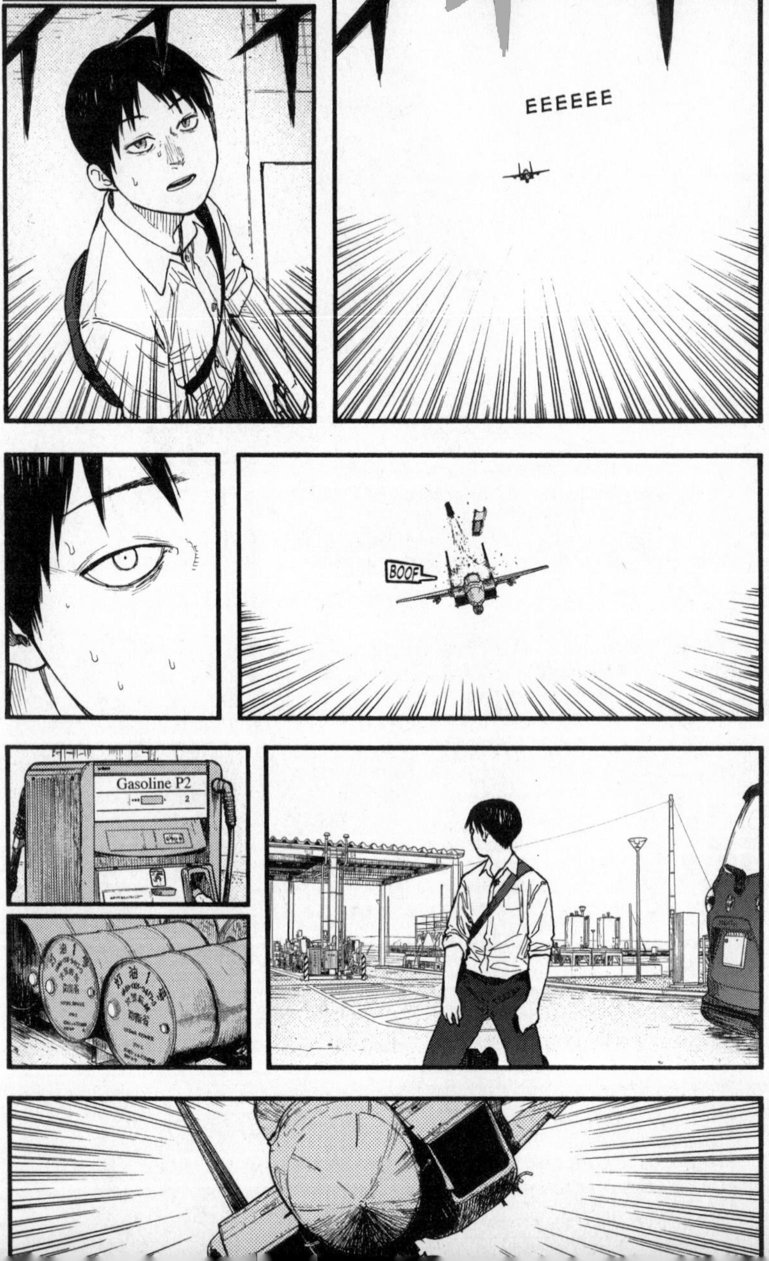

EEEEEE
BOOF
Gasoline P2

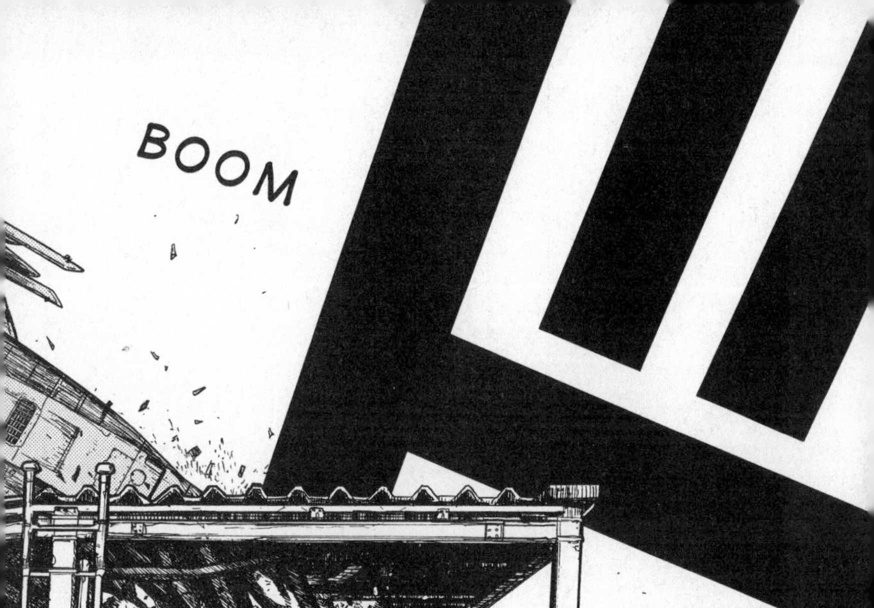
BOOM
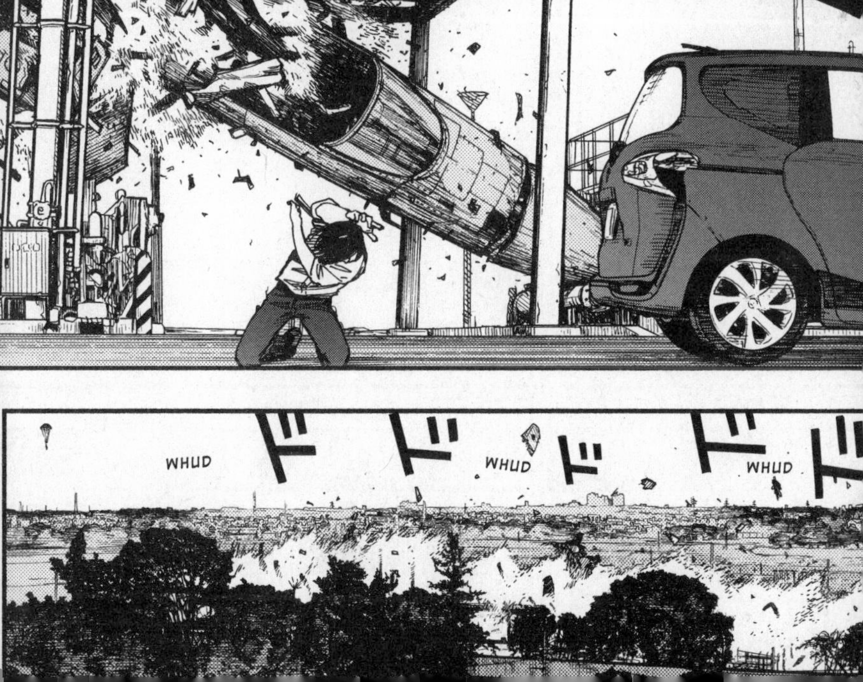
ド
WHUD
ド
ド
WHUD
ド
ド
WHUD

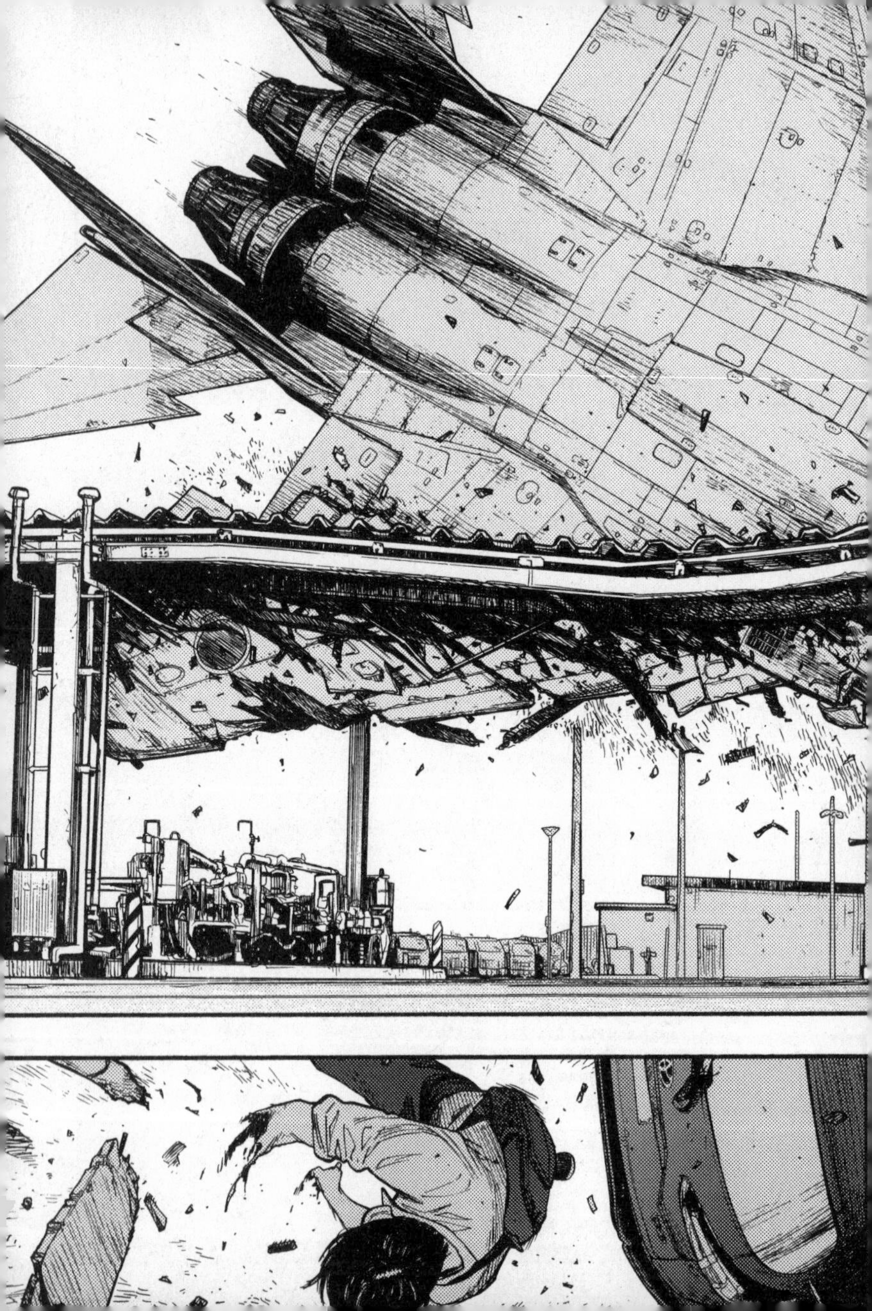

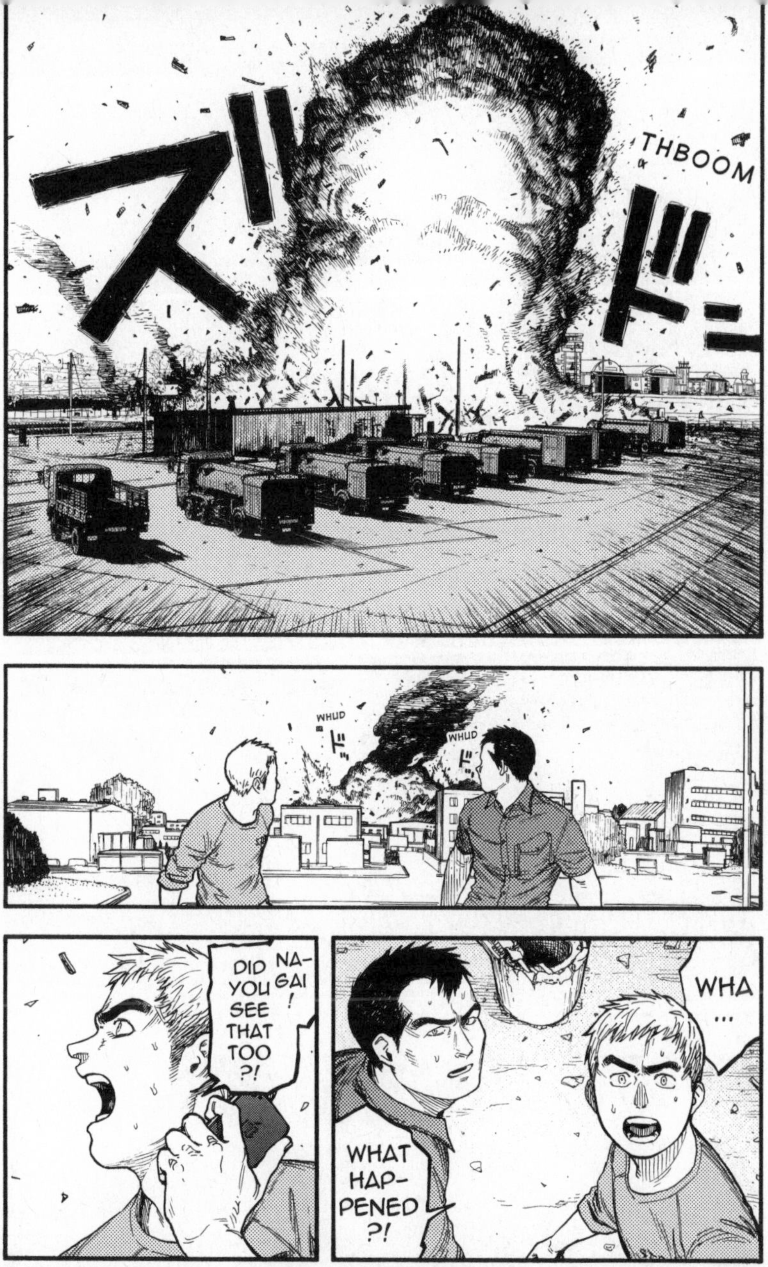
THBOOM
ズドー
WHUD
ド
WHUD
ド
WHA...
WHAT HAPPENED?!
NAGAI!
DID YOU SEE THAT TOO?!

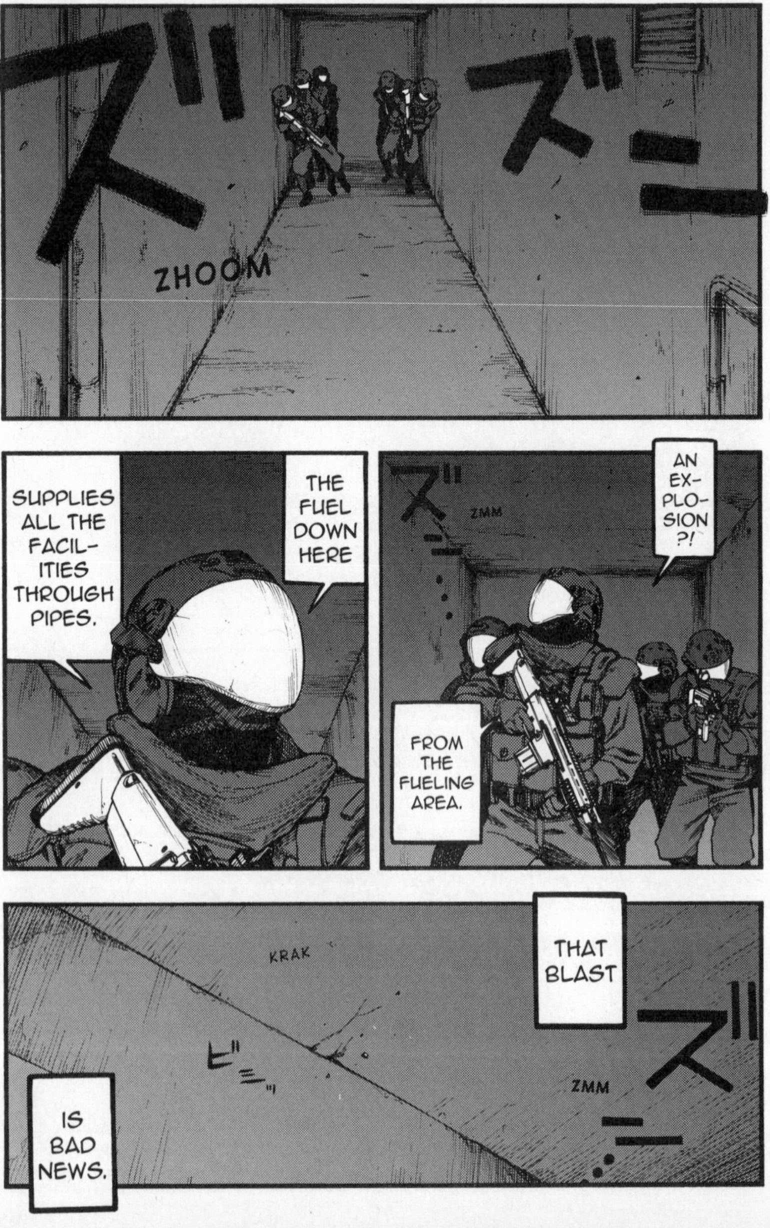

ズズーー
ZHOOM
AN EX-PLO-SION?!
ズー
ZMM
FROM THE FUELING AREA.
THE FUEL DOWN HERE
SUPPLIES ALL THE FACIL-ITIES THROUGH PIPES.
THAT BLAST
ズー
ZMM
KRAK
ビー
IS BAD NEWS.

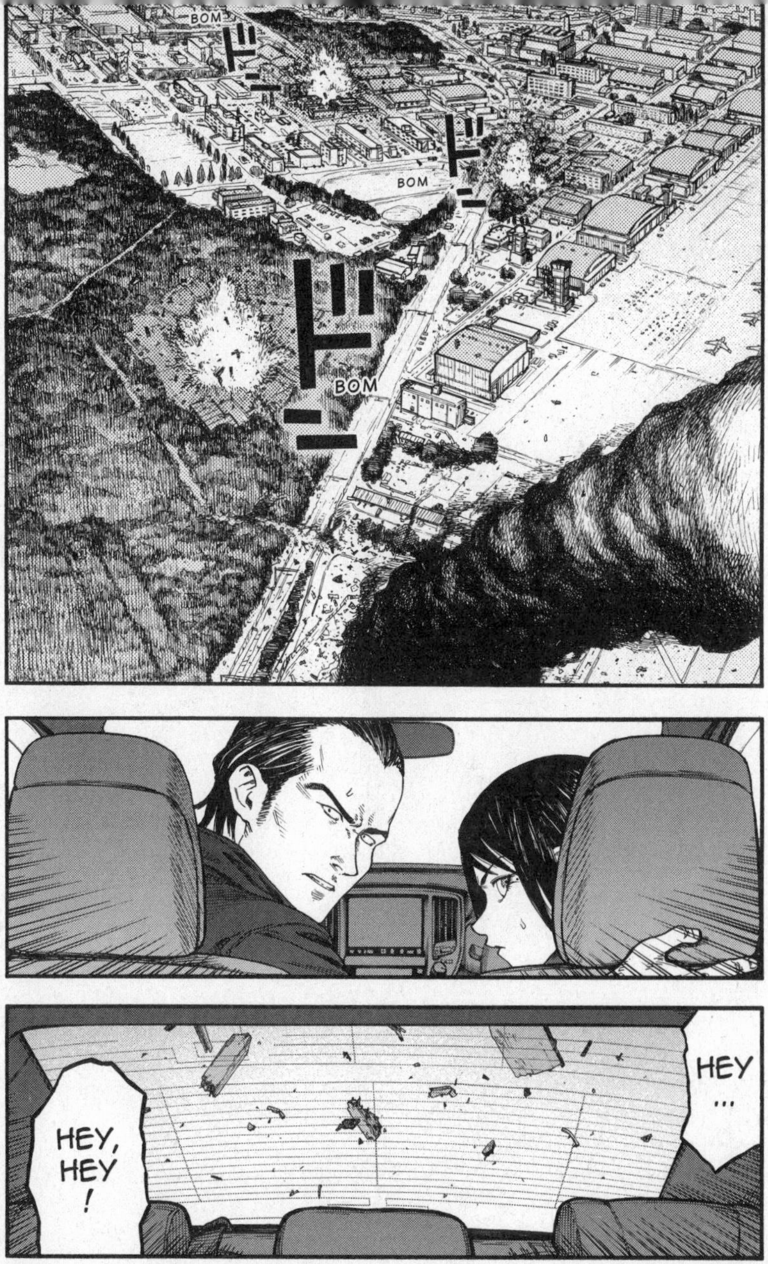
BOM
ドー
ドー
BOM
BOM
ドー
HEY ...
HEY, HEY !

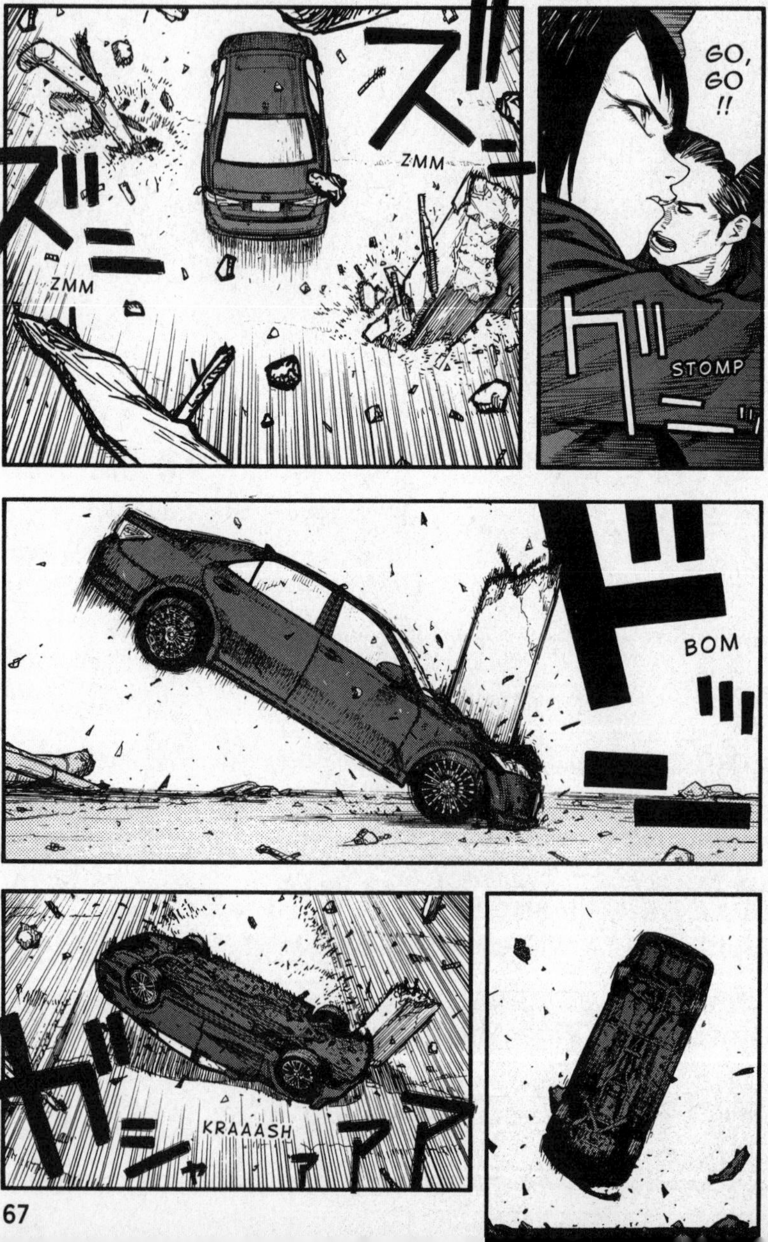
GO, GO !!
STOMP
ZMM
ZMM
BOM
KRAASH

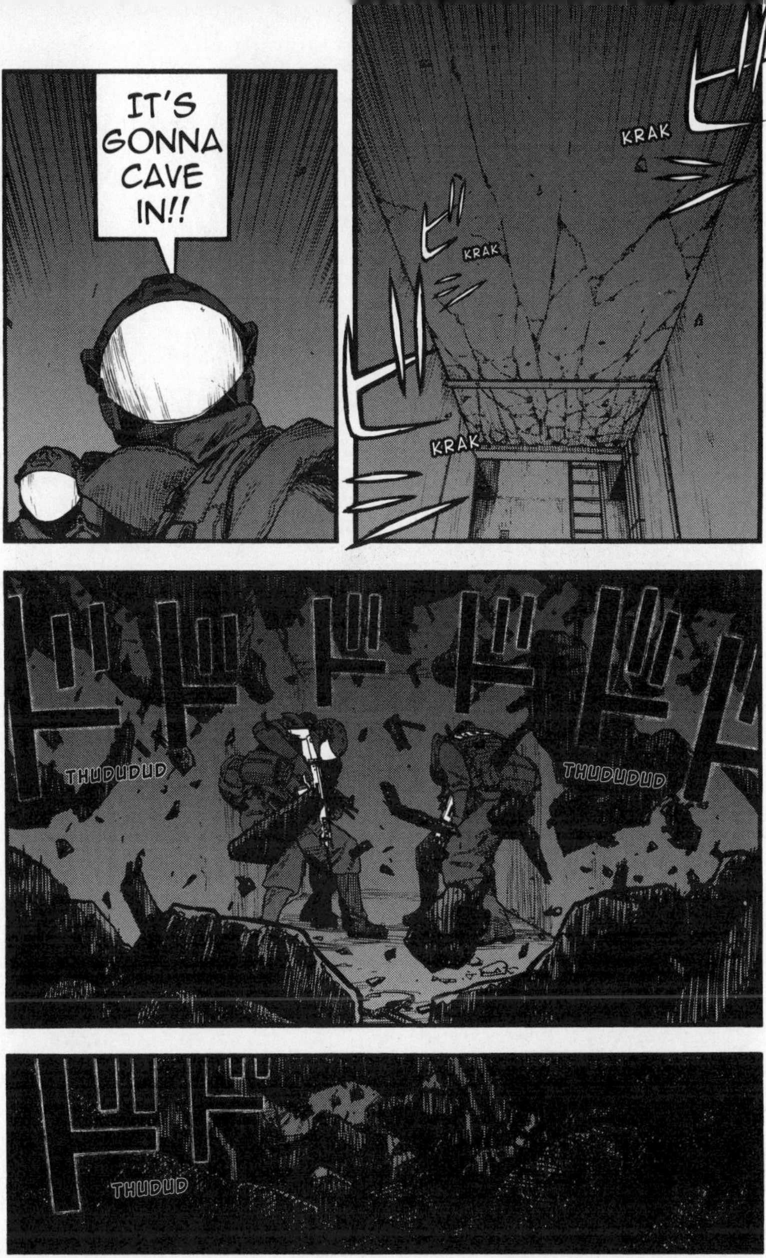
KRAK
KRAK
KRAK
IT'S GONNA CAVE IN!!
THUDUDUD
THUDUDUD
THUDUD

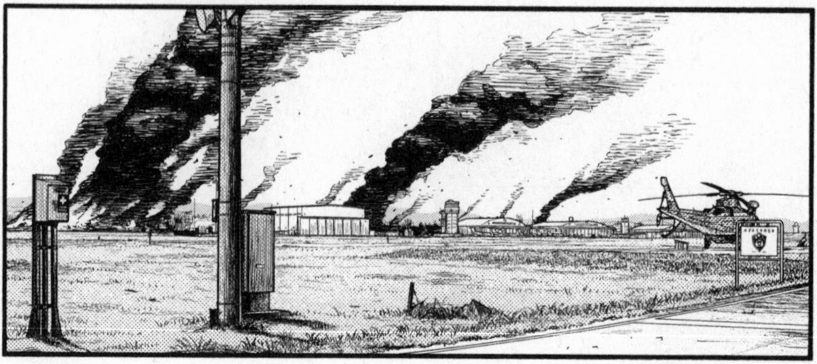

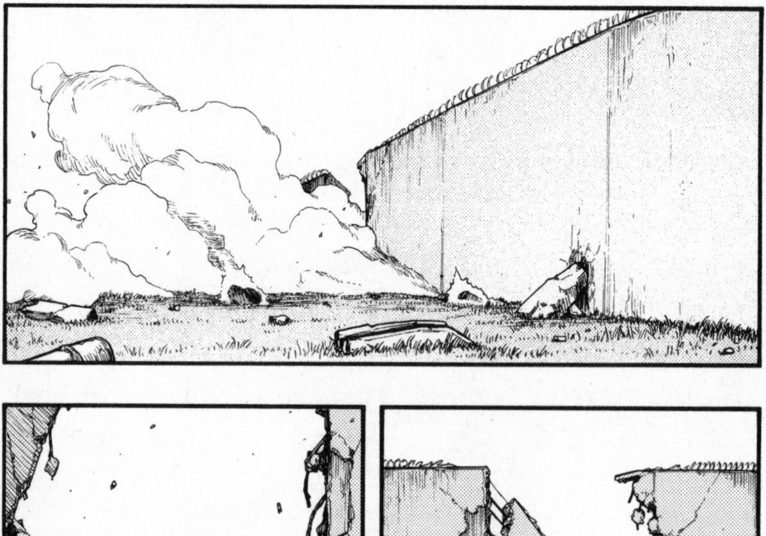

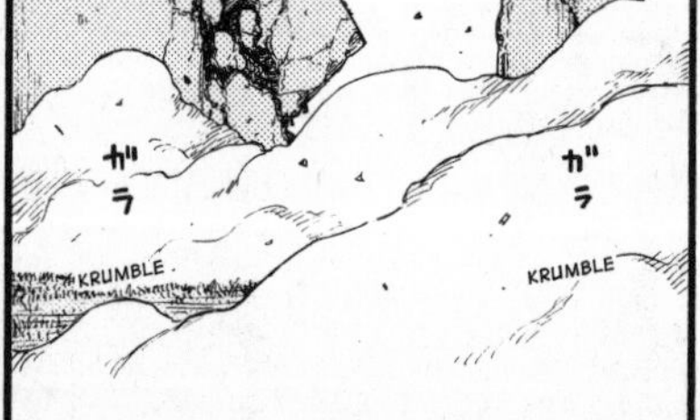
ガラ
KRUMBLE
ガラ
KRUMBLE

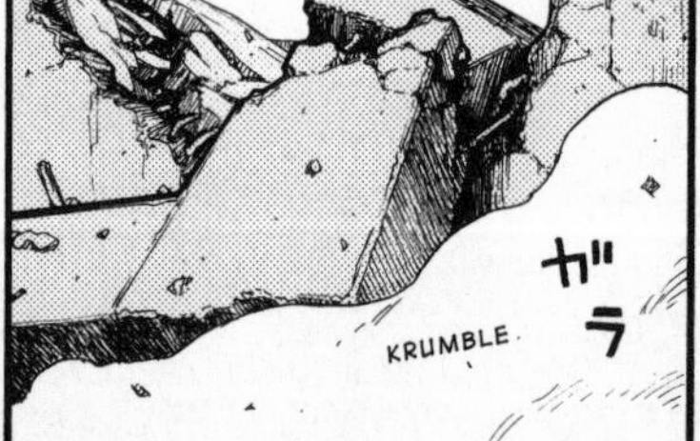
ガラ
KRUMBLE

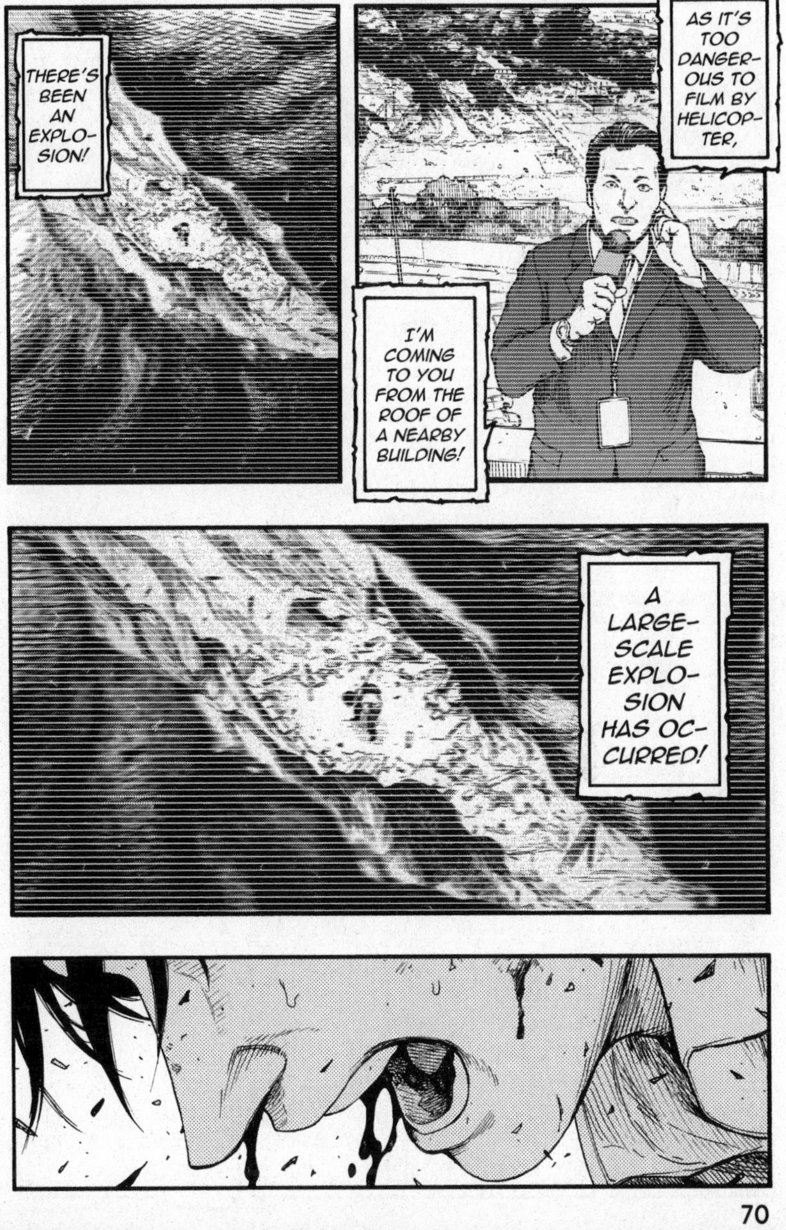
AS IT'S TOO DANGER-OUS TO FILM BY HELICOP-TER,
I'M COMING TO YOU FROM THE ROOF OF A NEARBY BUILDING!
THERE'S BEEN AN EXPLO-SION!
A LARGE-SCALE EXPLO-SION HAS OC-CURRED!

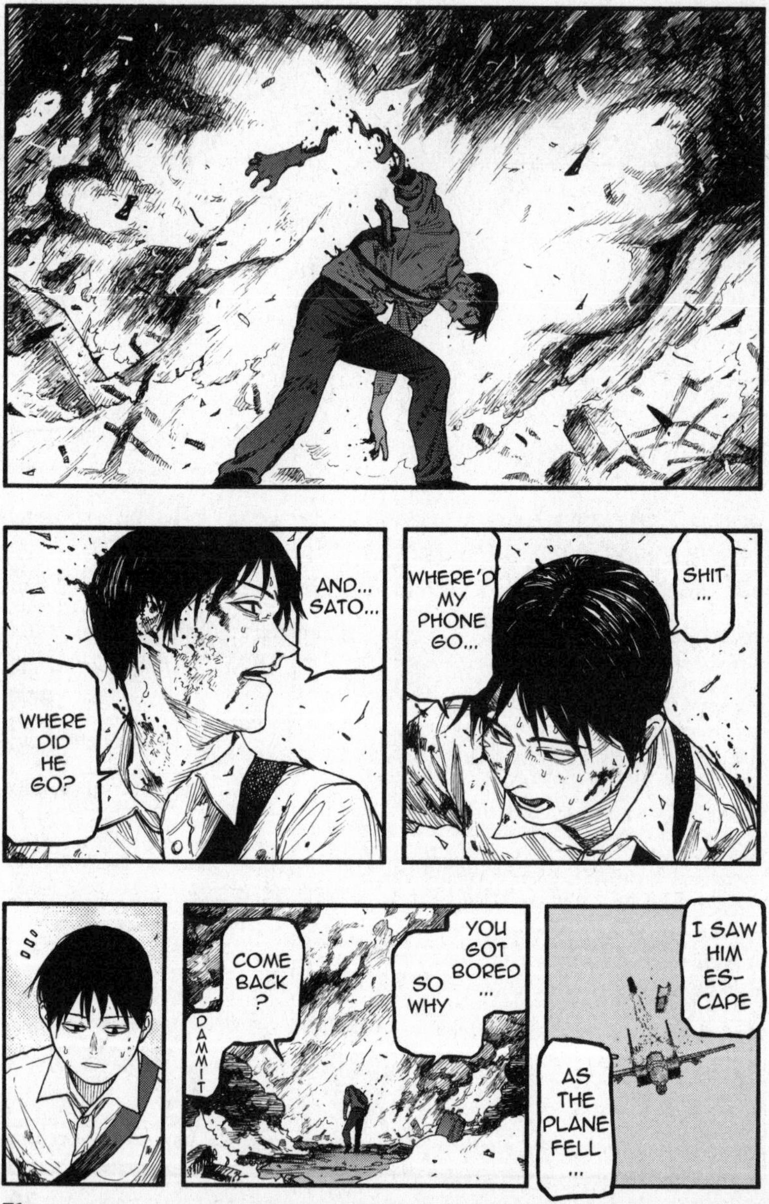
SHIT...
WHERE'D MY PHONE GO...
AND... SATO...
WHERE DID HE GO?
I SAW HIM ES-CAPE
AS THE PLANE FELL...
YOU GOT BORED...
SO WHY
COME BACK?
DAMMIT

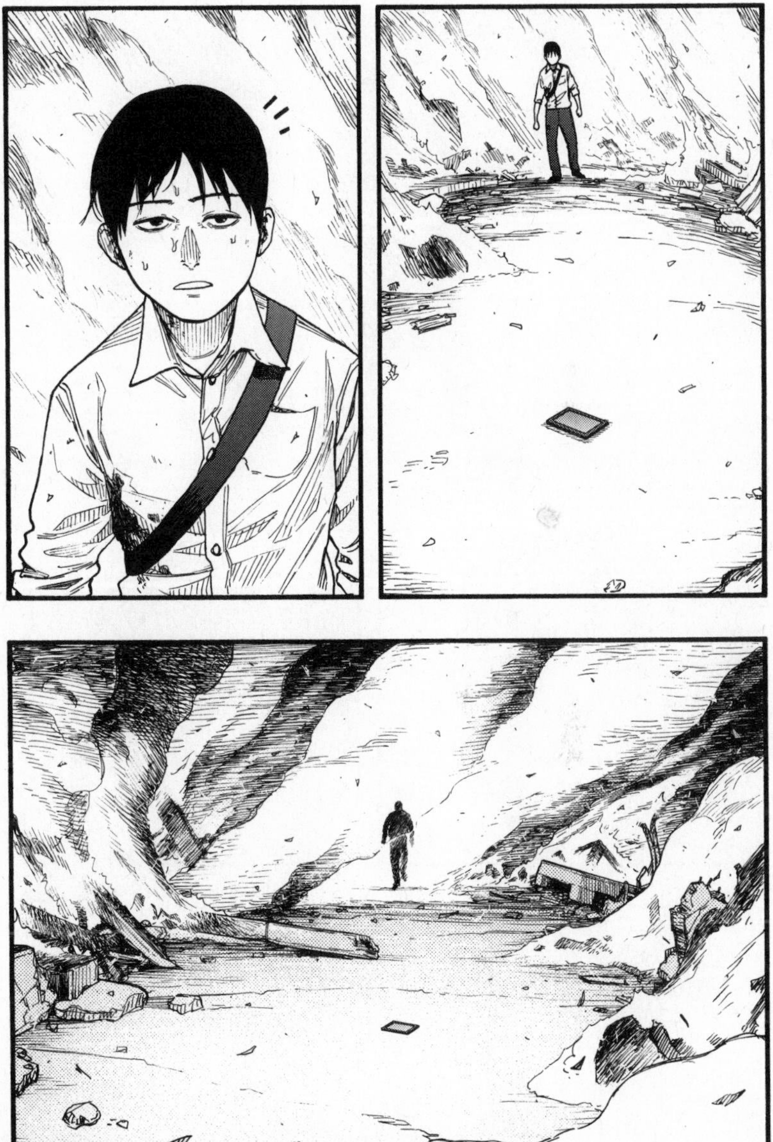

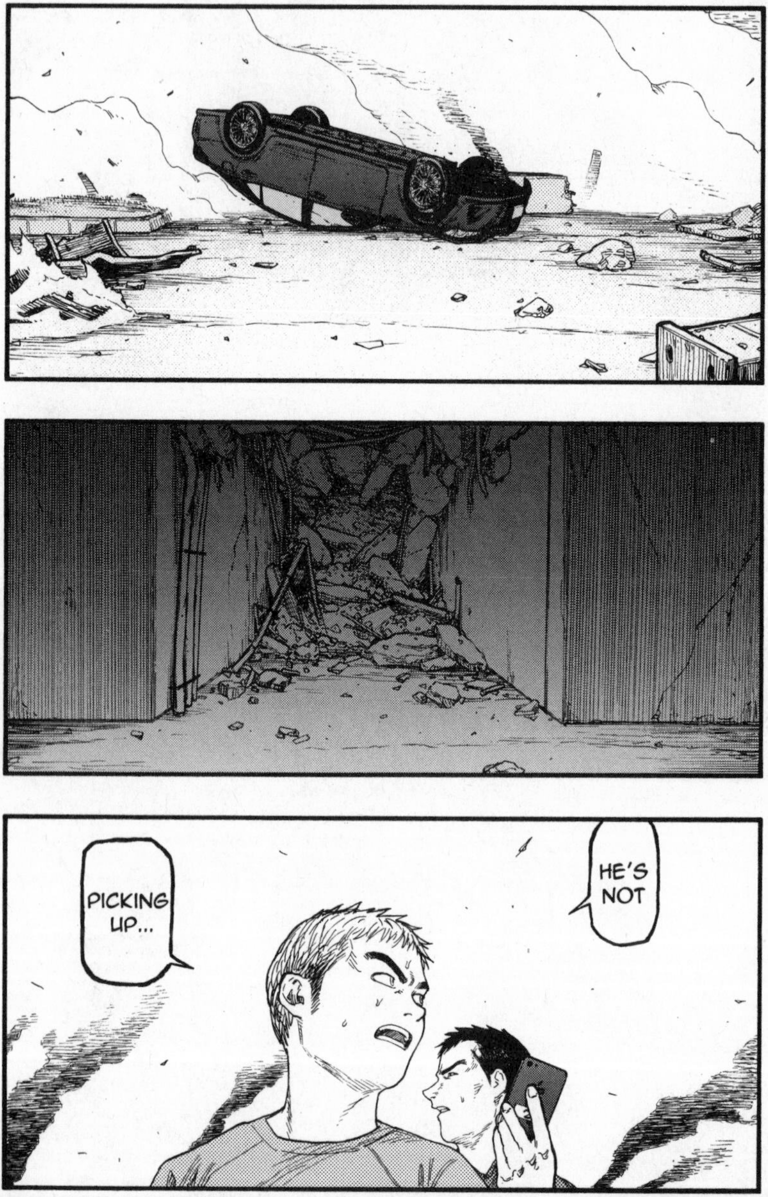
HE'S NOT
PICKING UP...

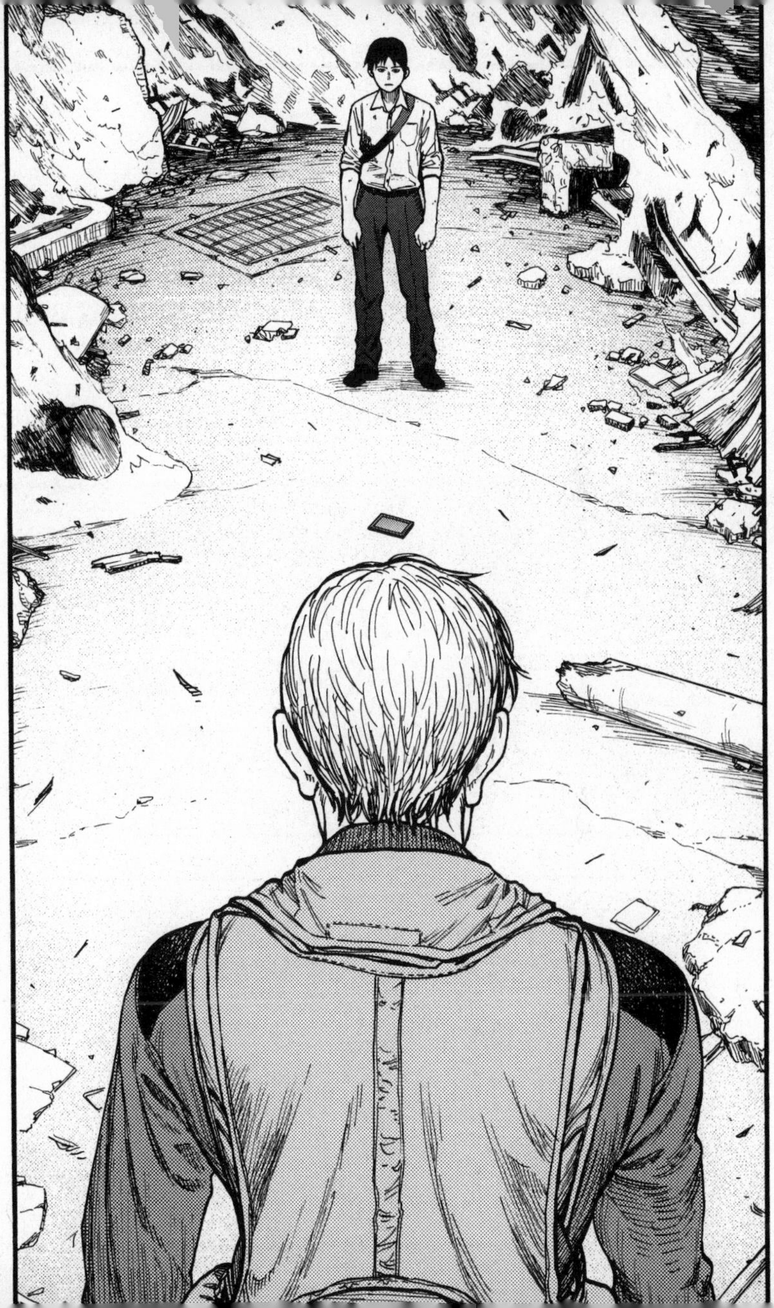

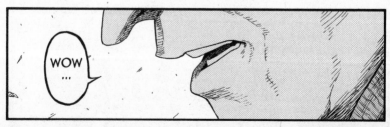

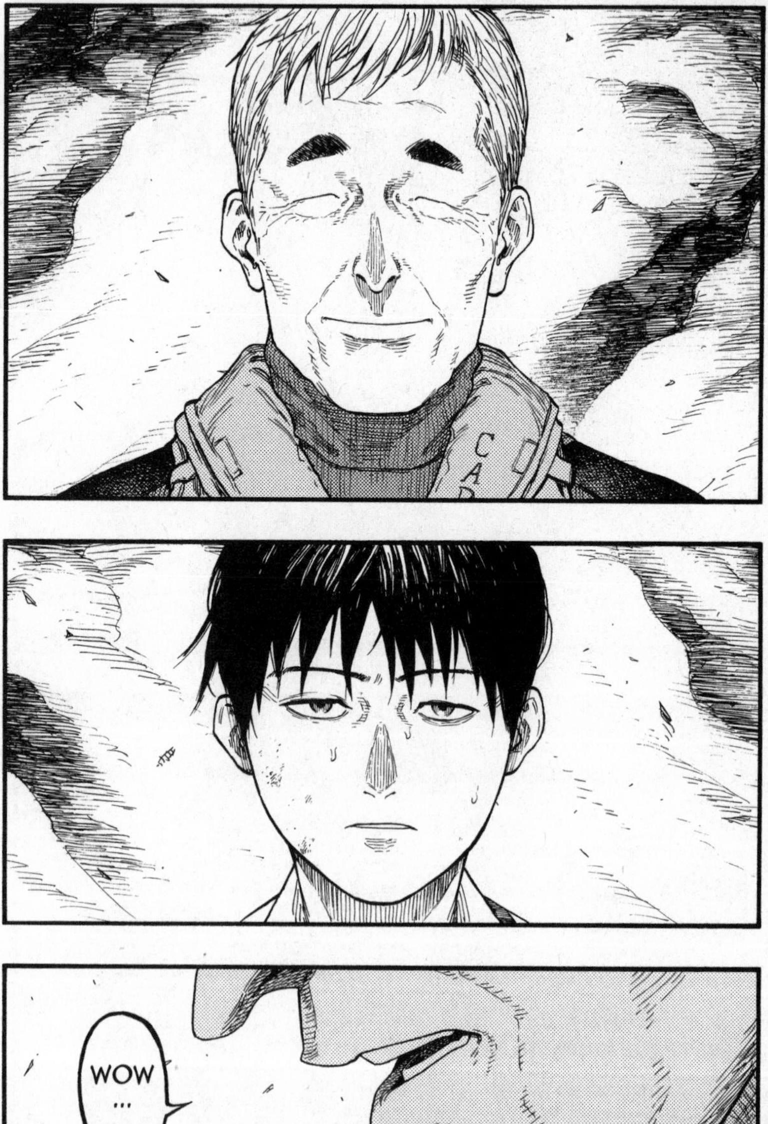
WOW
...

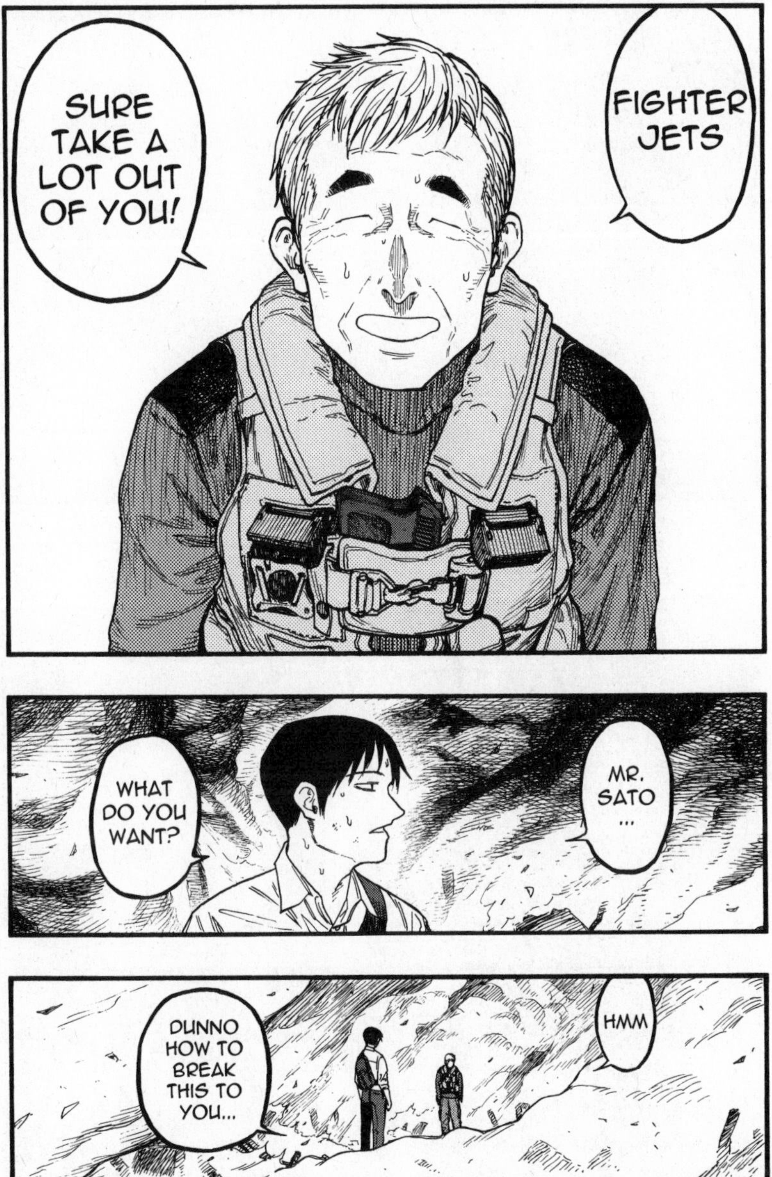
FIGHTER JETS
SURE TAKE A LOT OUT OF YOU!
MR. SATO ...
WHAT DO YOU WANT?
HMM
DUNNO HOW TO BREAK THIS TO YOU...

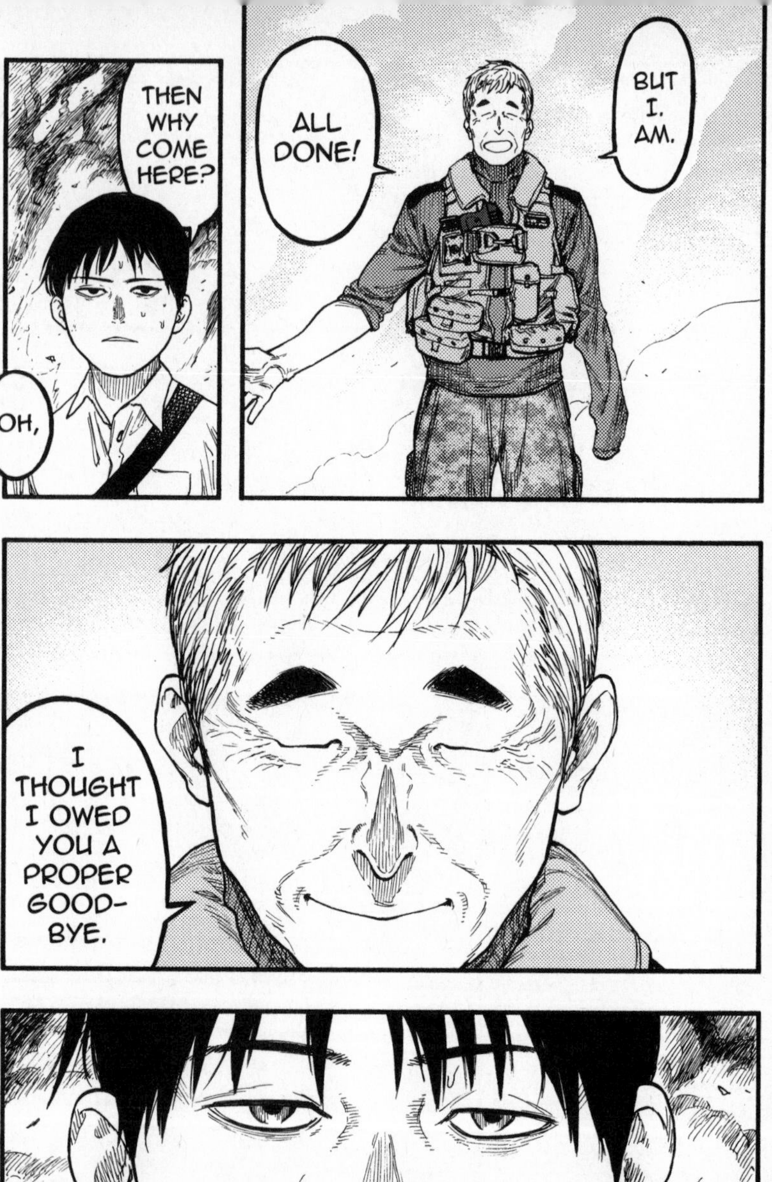
BUT I. AM.
ALL DONE!
THEN WHY COME HERE?
OH,
I THOUGHT I OWED YOU A PROPER GOOD-BYE.

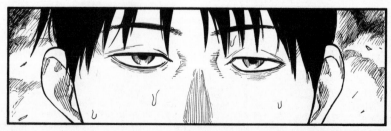

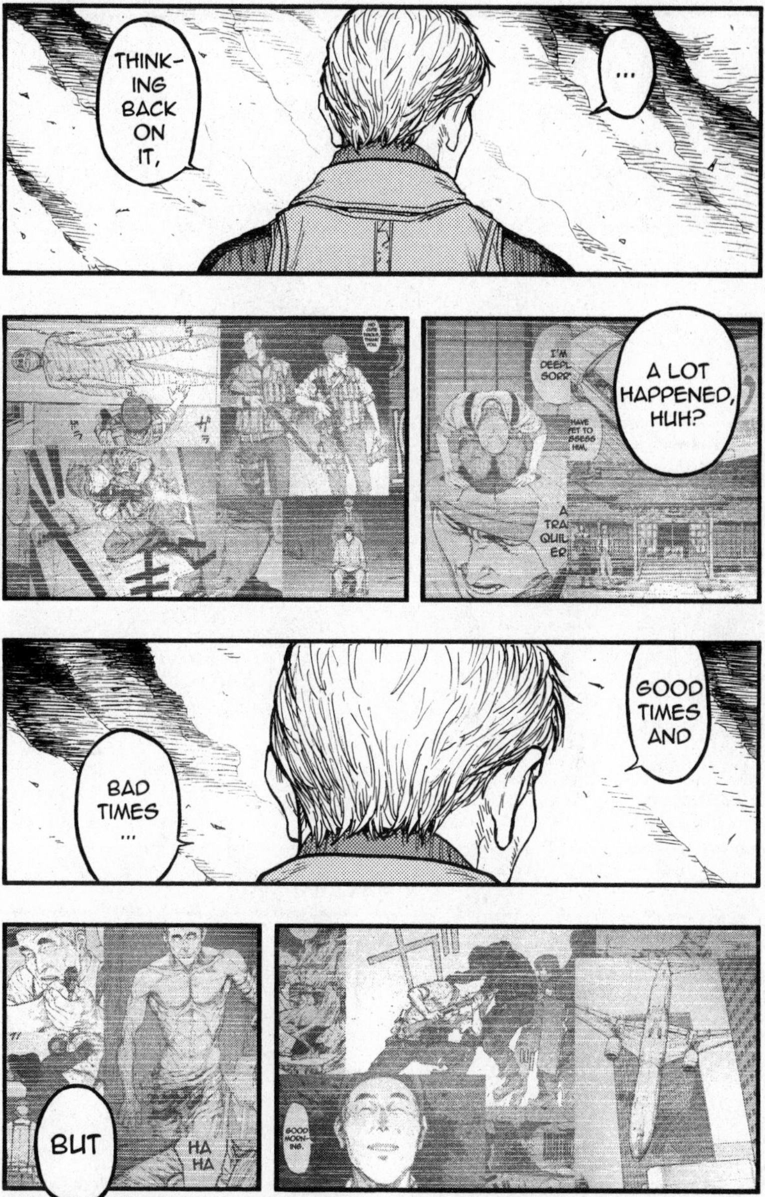
...
THINKING-ING BACK ON IT,
A LOT HAPPENED, HUH?
GOOD TIMES AND
BAD TIMES ...
GOOD MORNING.
BUT
HA HA

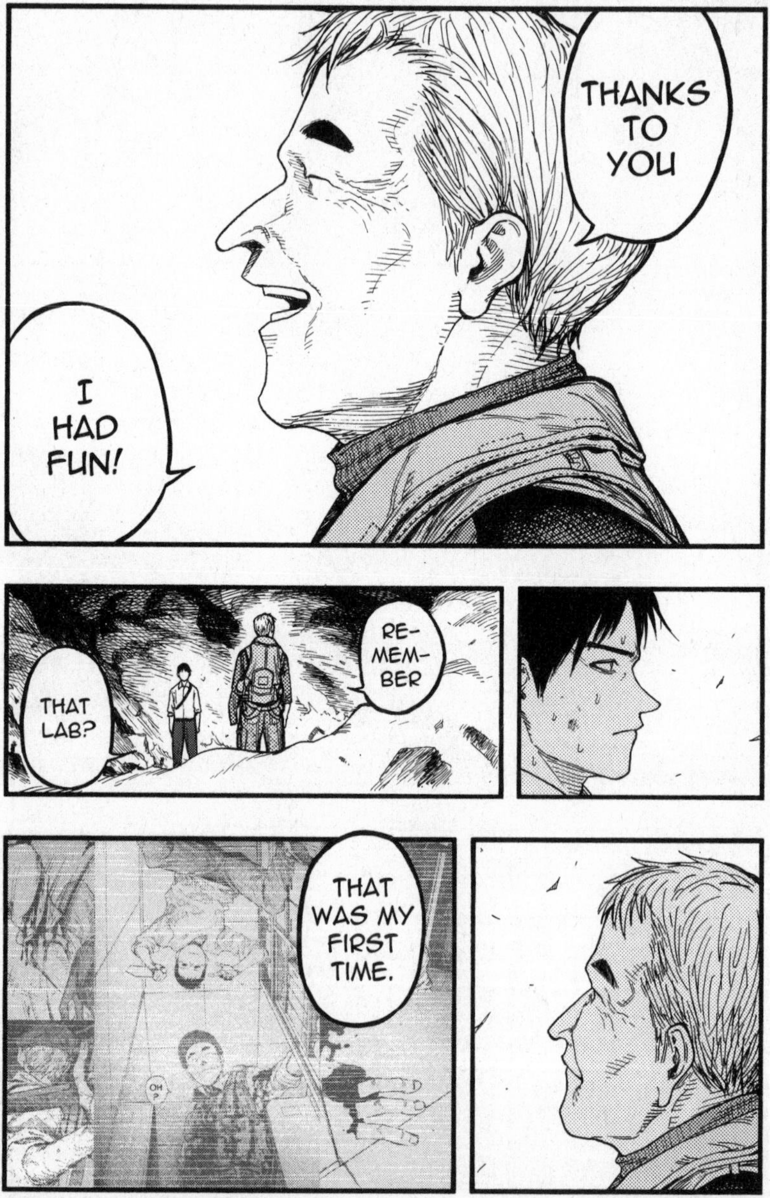
THANKS TO YOU
I HAD FUN!
RE-MEM-BER
THAT LAB?
THAT WAS MY FIRST TIME.
OH?

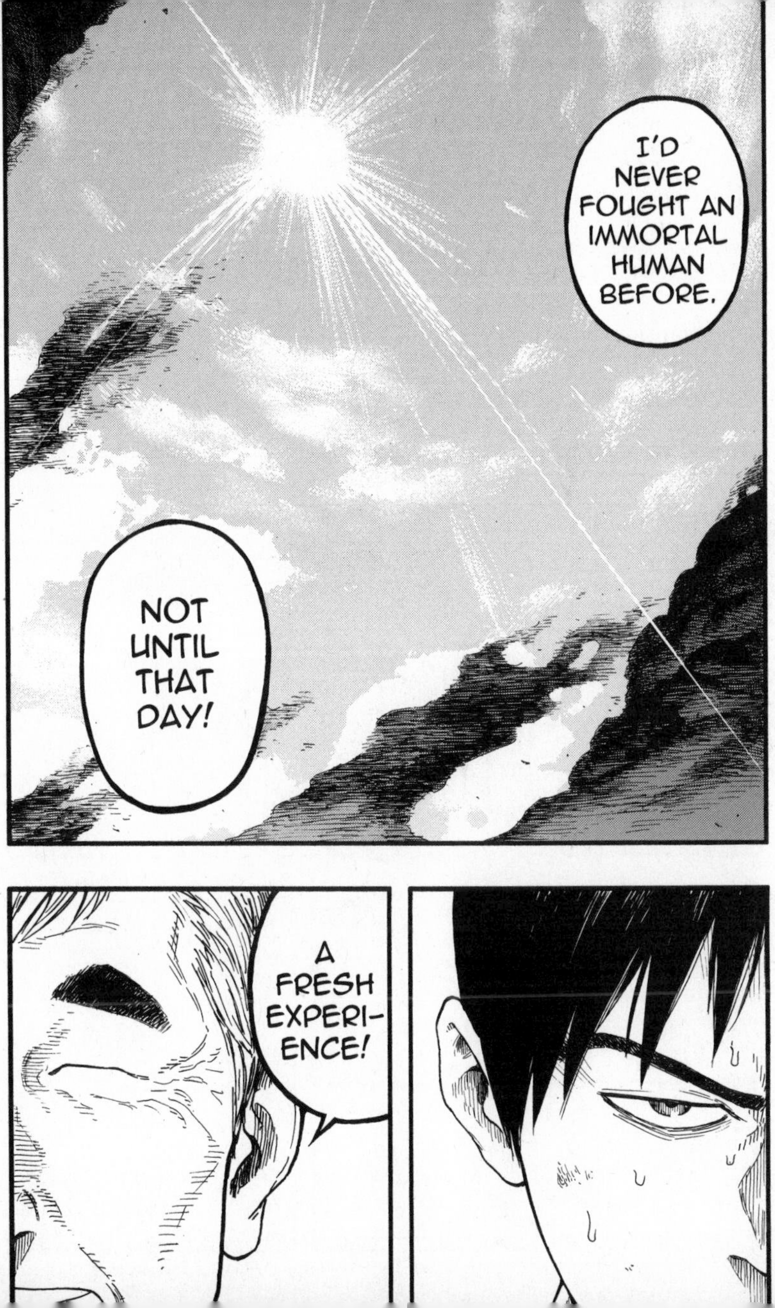
I'D NEVER FOUGHT AN IMMORTAL HUMAN BEFORE.
NOT UNTIL THAT DAY!
A FRESH EXPERI-ENCE!

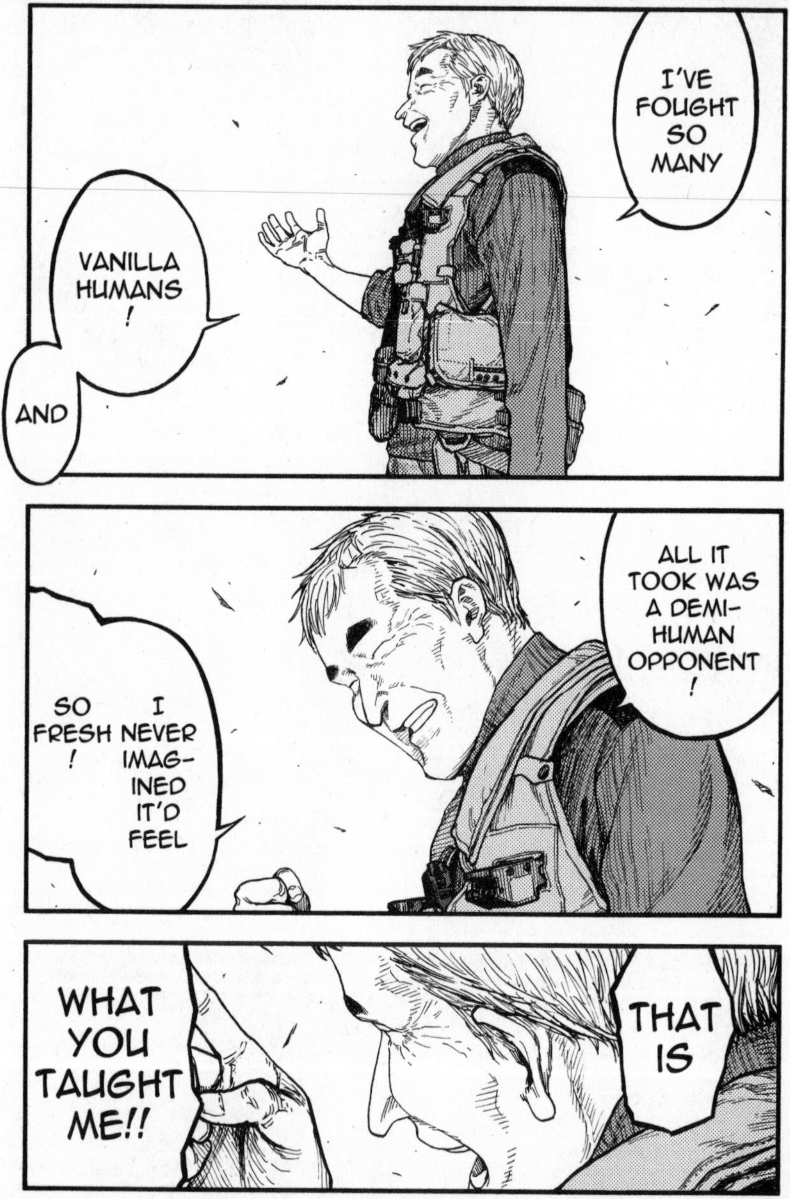
I'VE FOUGHT SO MANY
VANILLA HUMANS!
AND
ALL IT TOOK WAS A DEMI-HUMAN OPPONENT!
I NEVER IMAGINED IT'D FEEL
SO FRESH!
THAT IS
WHAT YOU TAUGHT ME!!

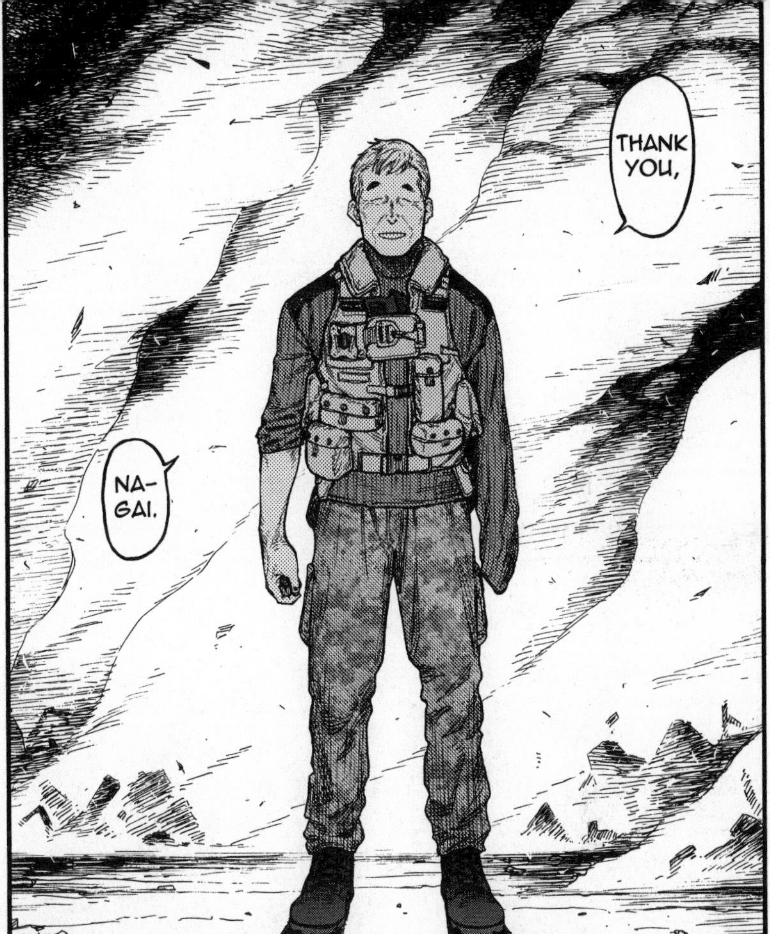
THANK YOU,
NA-GAI.
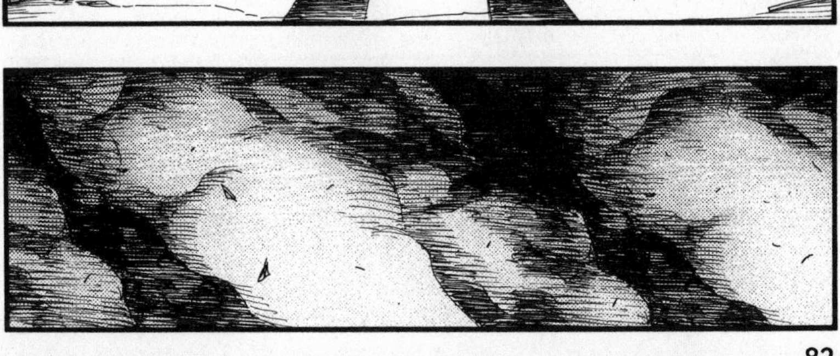

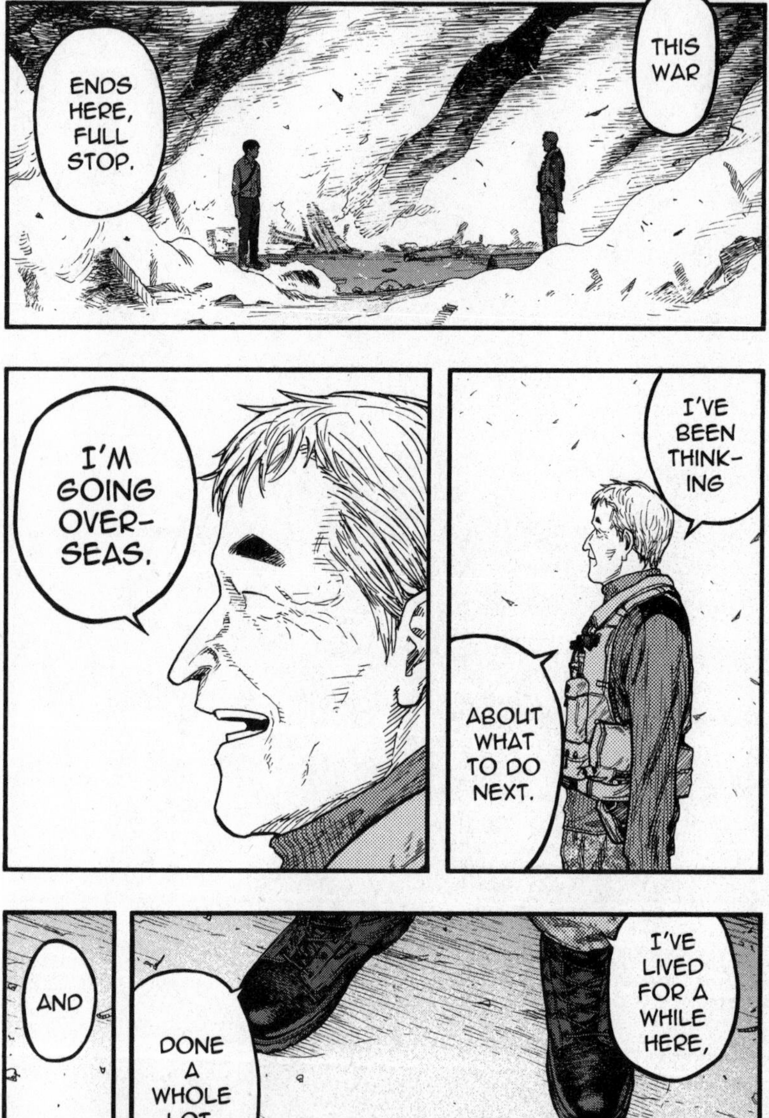
THIS WAR
ENDS HERE, FULL STOP.
I'VE BEEN THINKING
ABOUT WHAT TO DO NEXT.
I'M GOING OVERSEAS.
I'VE LIVED FOR A WHILE HERE,
DONE A WHOLE LOT.
AND

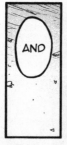

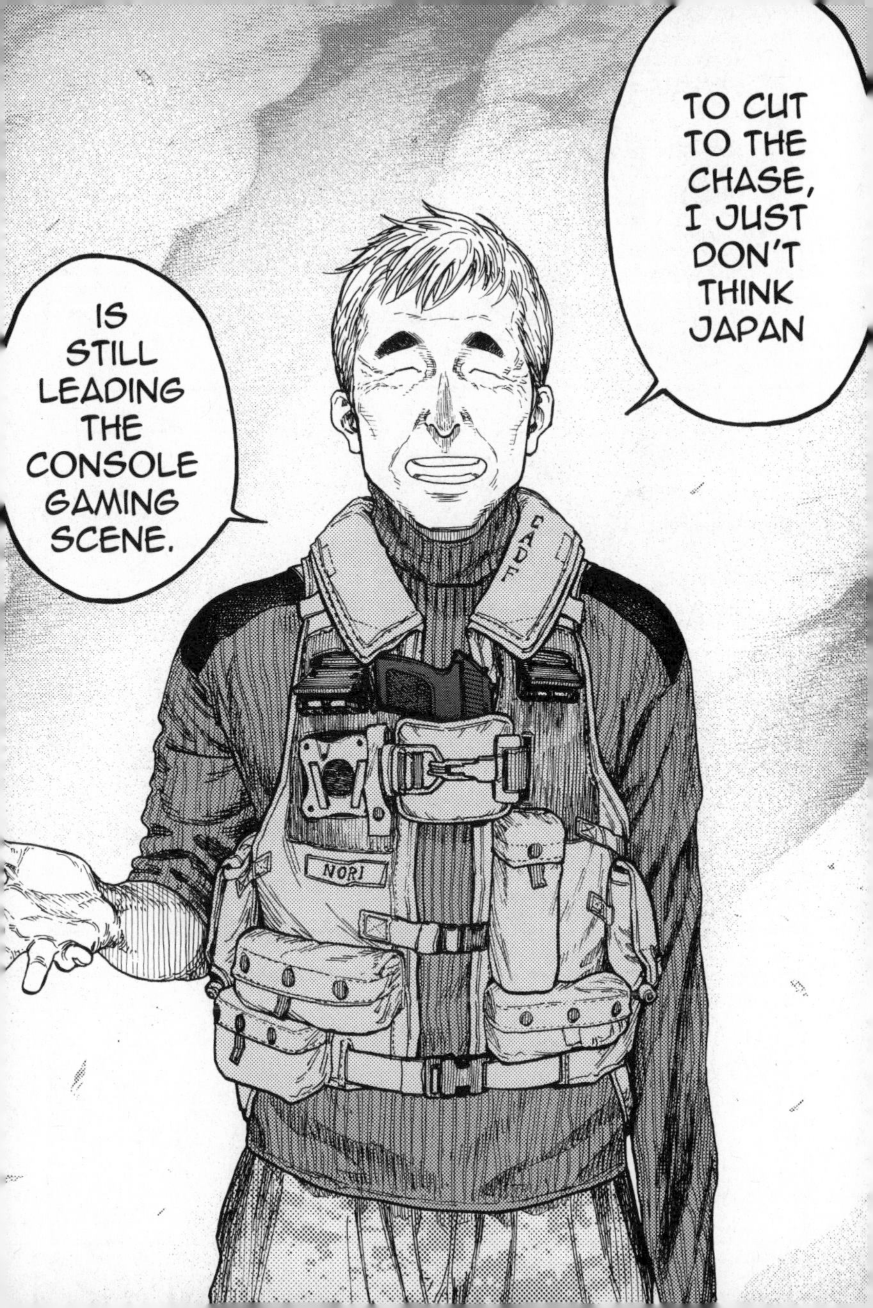
TO CUT TO THE CHASE, I JUST DON'T THINK JAPAN
IS STILL LEADING THE CONSOLE GAMING SCENE.
NORI

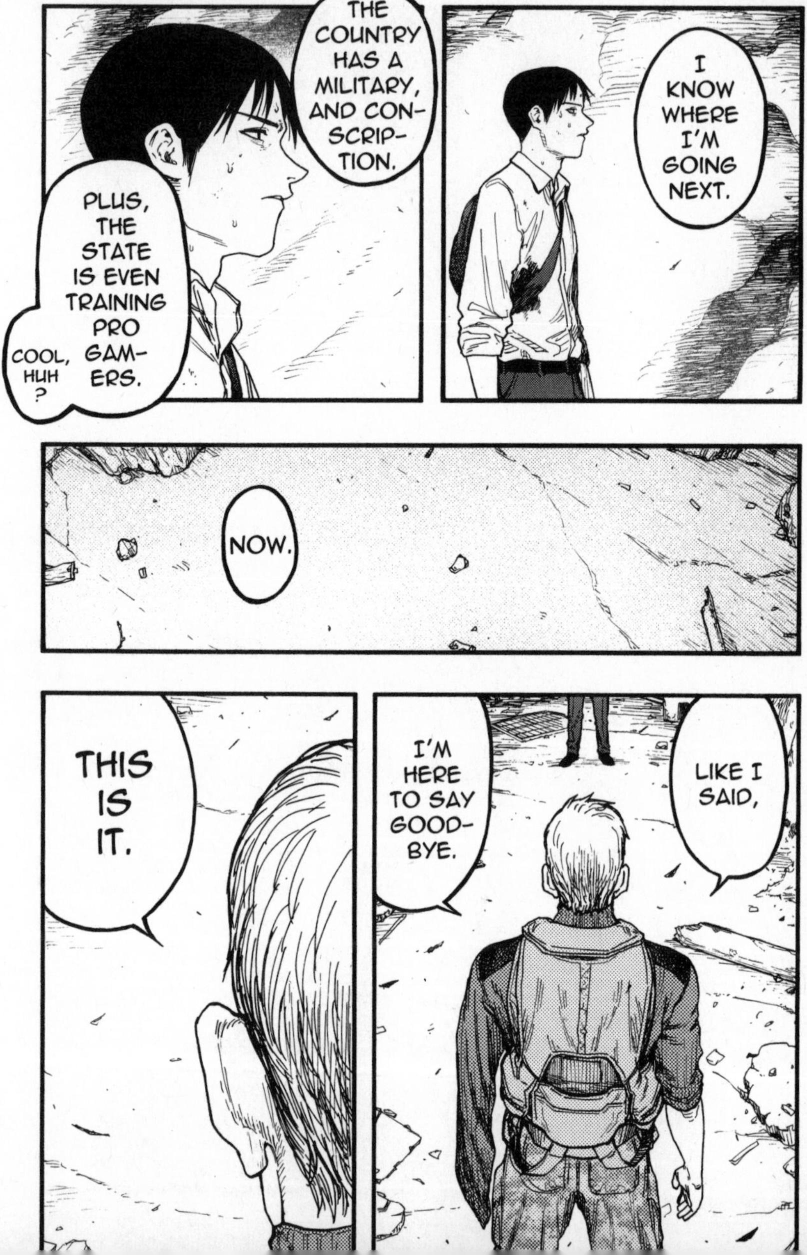
I KNOW WHERE I'M GOING NEXT.
THE COUNTRY HAS A MILITARY, AND CON-SCRIPTION.
PLUS, THE STATE IS EVEN TRAINING PRO GAM-ERS.
COOL, HUH?
NOW.
LIKE I SAID,
I'M HERE TO SAY GOOD-BYE.
THIS IS IT.

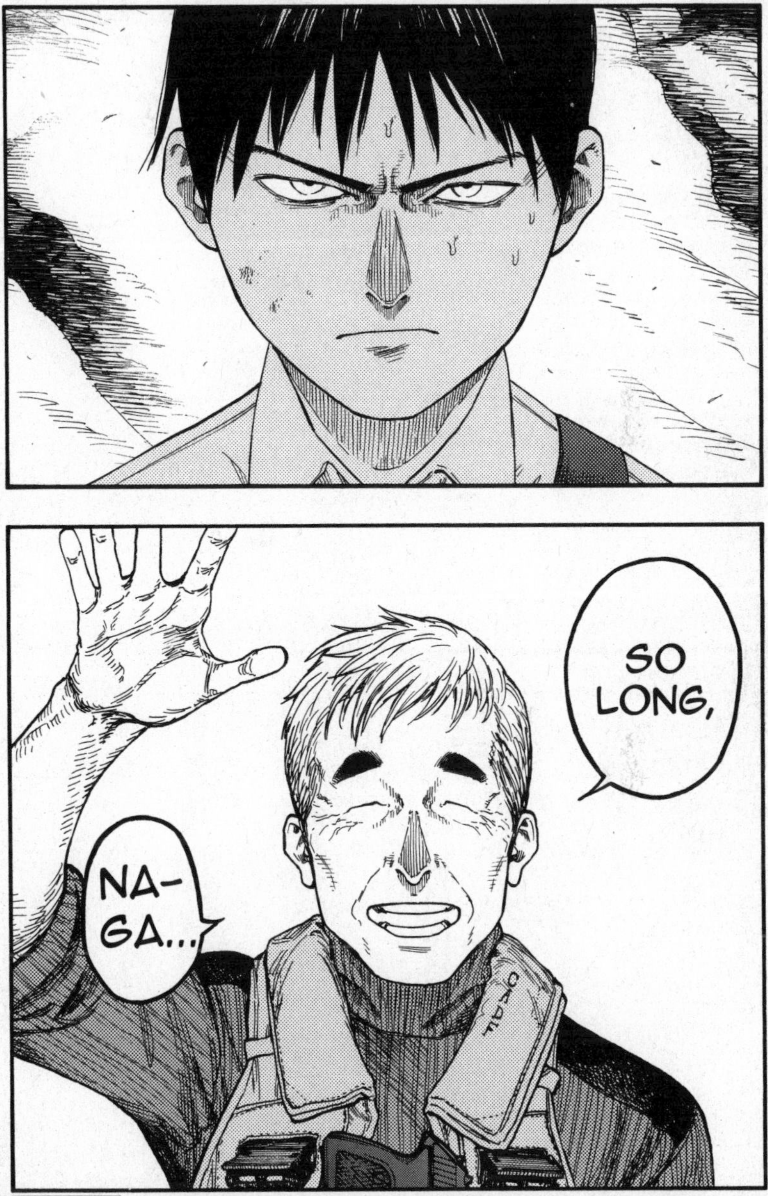
SO LONG,
NA-GA...

File:70 End

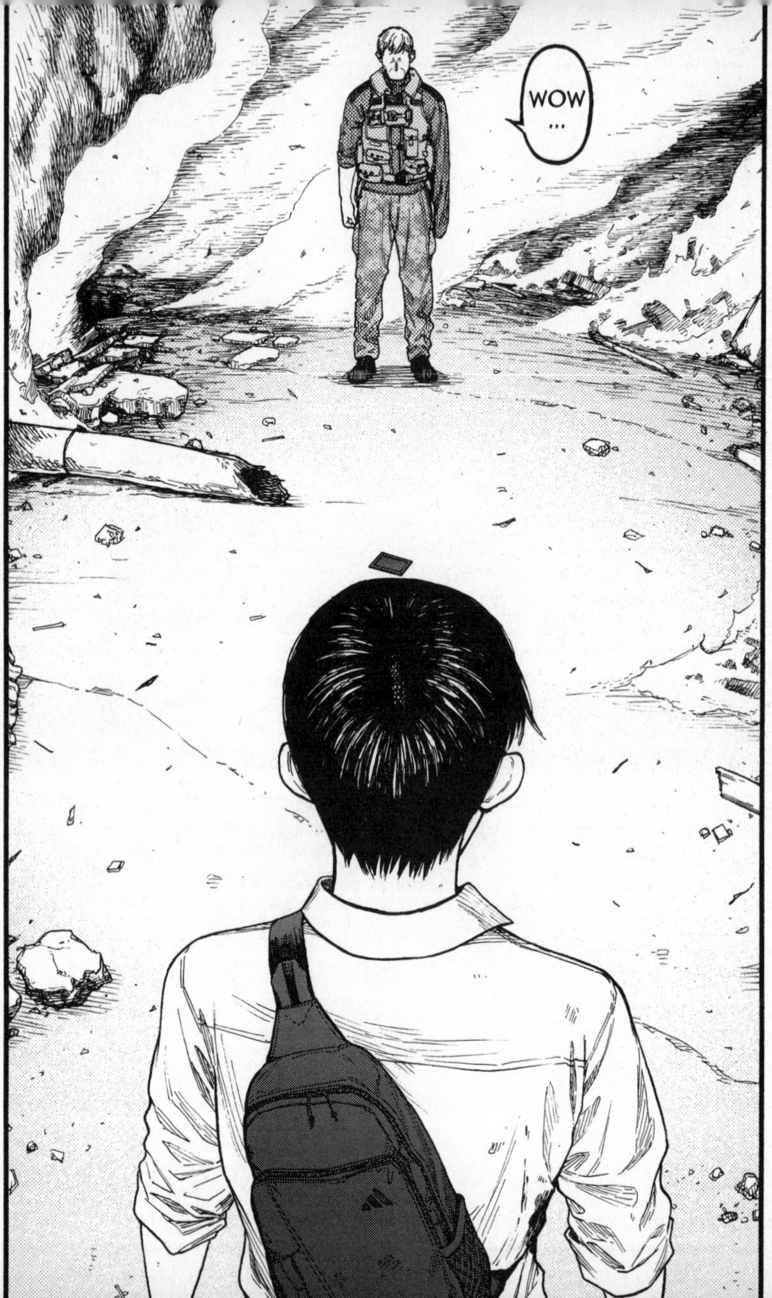
WOW
...

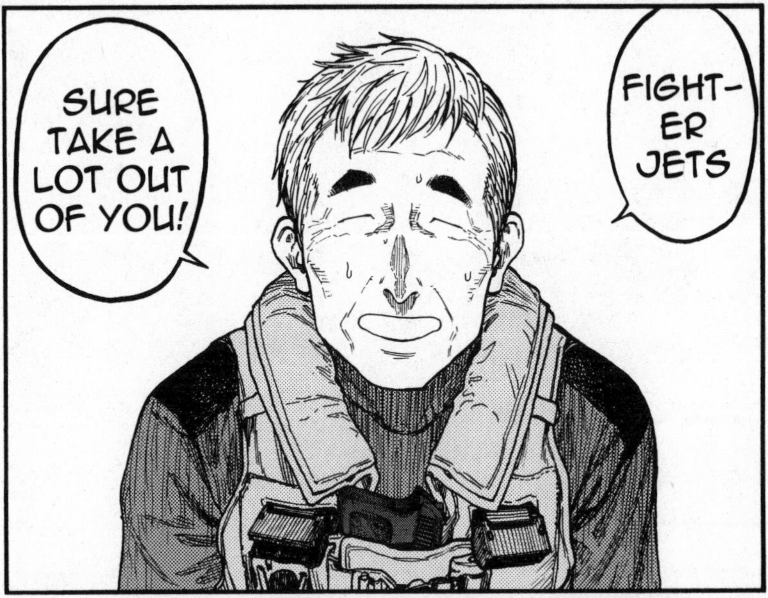
FIGHT-ER JETS
SURE TAKE A LOT OUT OF YOU!

A FEW MINUTES AGO

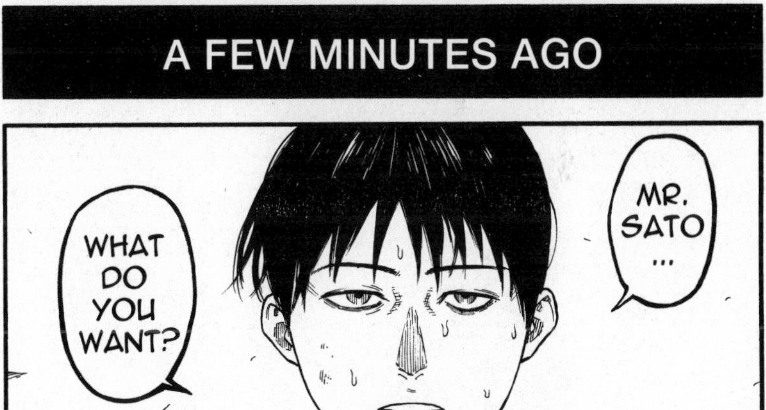
MR. SATO ...
WHAT DO YOU WANT?

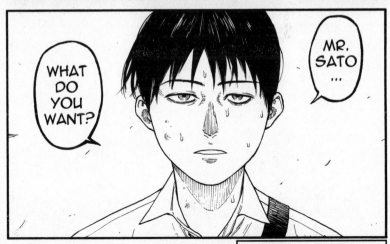

File 71: Deliberation

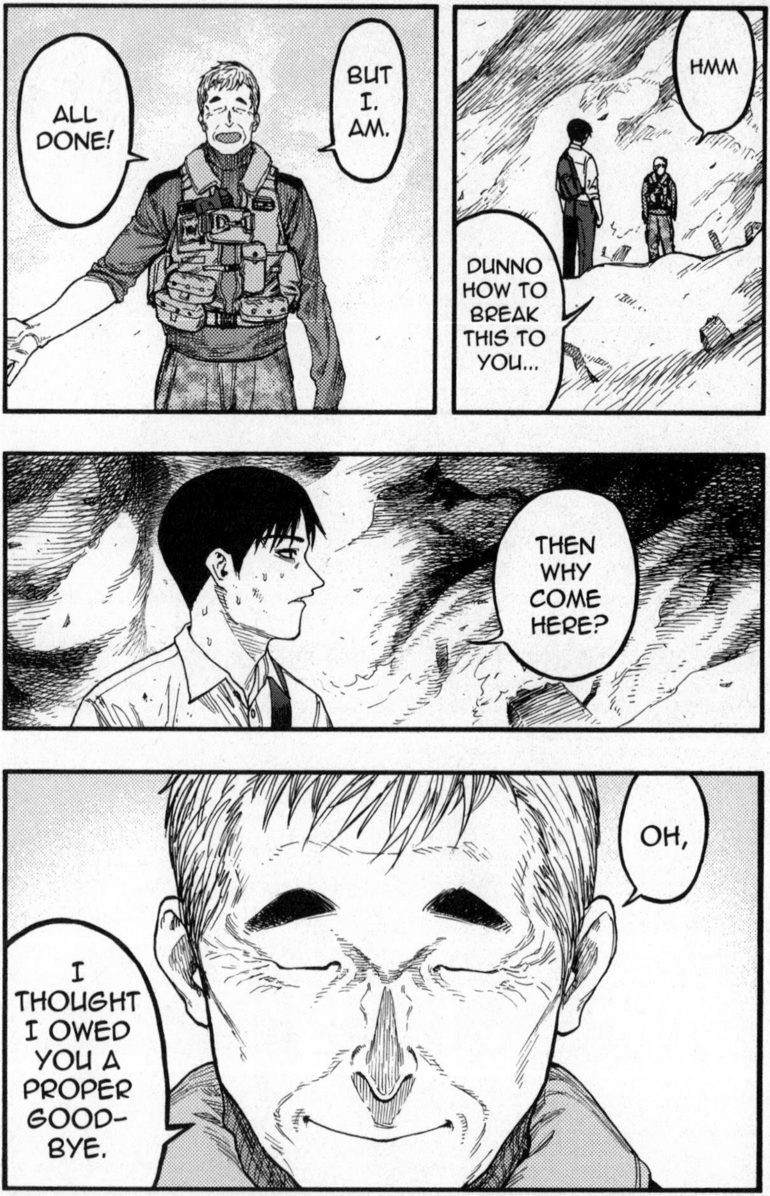
HMM
DUNNO HOW TO BREAK THIS TO YOU...
BUT I. AM.
ALL DONE!
THEN WHY COME HERE?
OH,
I THOUGHT I OWED YOU A PROPER GOOD-BYE.

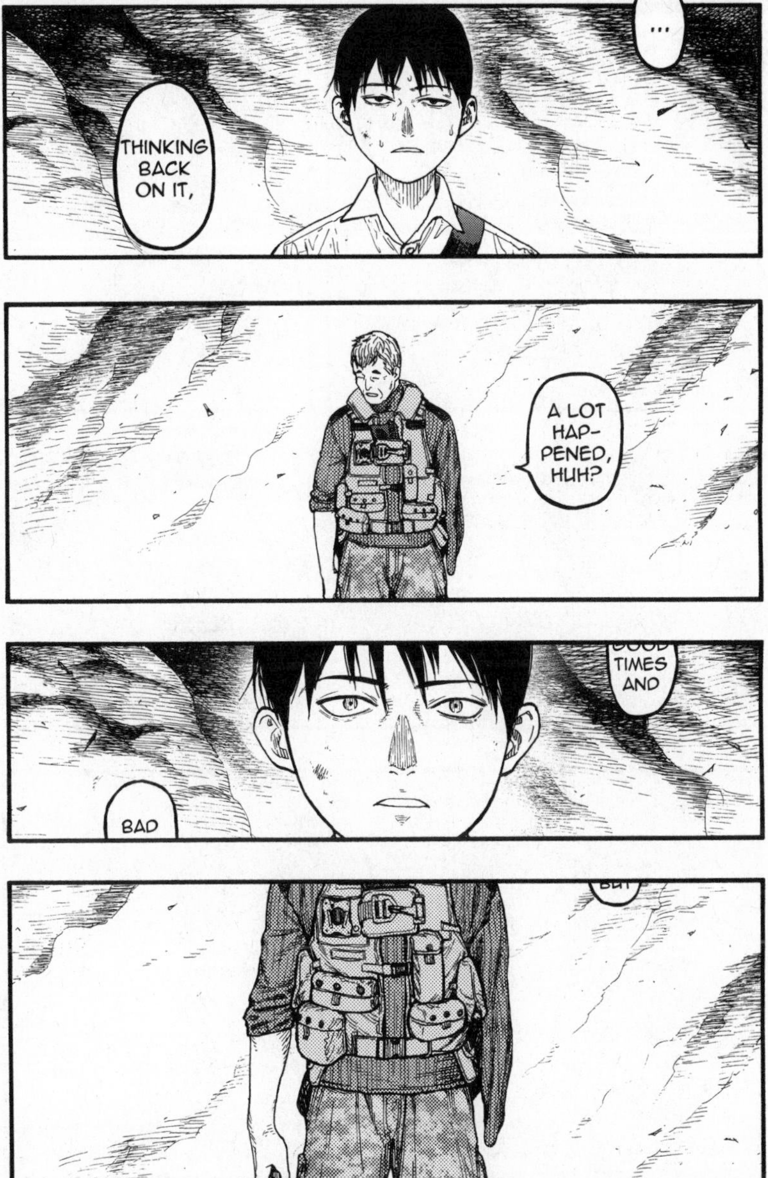
...
THINKING BACK ON IT,
A LOT HAP-PENED, HUH?
TIMES AND
BAD

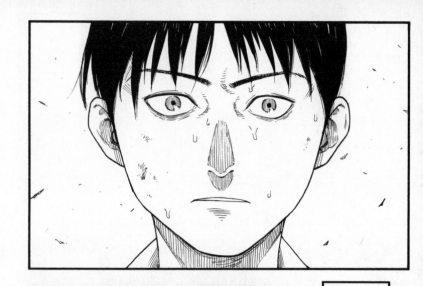

ISN'T

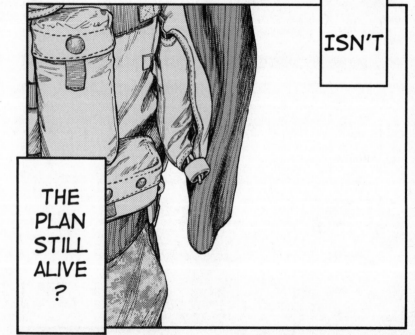

THE
PLAN
STILL
ALIVE
?

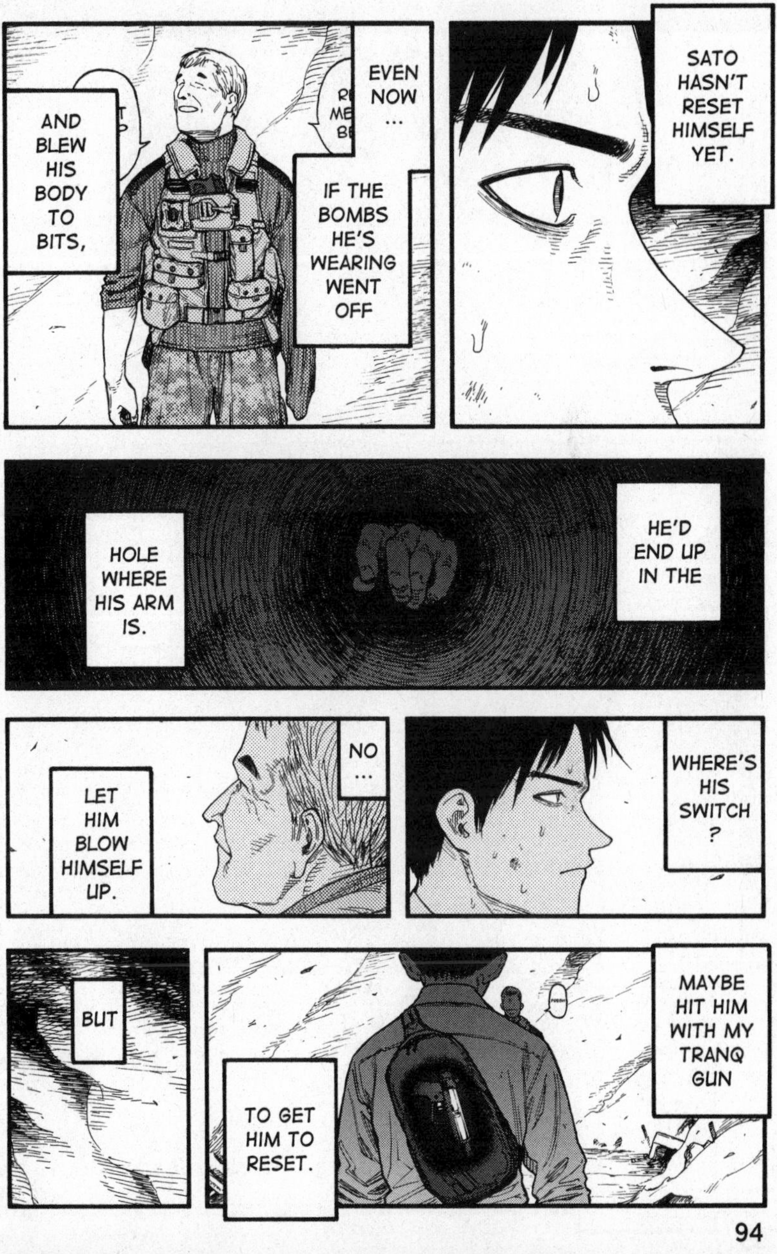
SATO HASN'T RESET HIMSELF YET.
EVEN NOW ...
IF THE BOMBS HE'S WEARING WENT OFF
AND BLEW HIS BODY TO BITS,
HE'D END UP IN THE
HOLE WHERE HIS ARM IS.
WHERE'S HIS SWITCH ?
NO ...
LET HIM BLOW HIMSELF UP.
MAYBE HIT HIM WITH MY TRANQ GUN
TO GET HIM TO RESET.
BUT

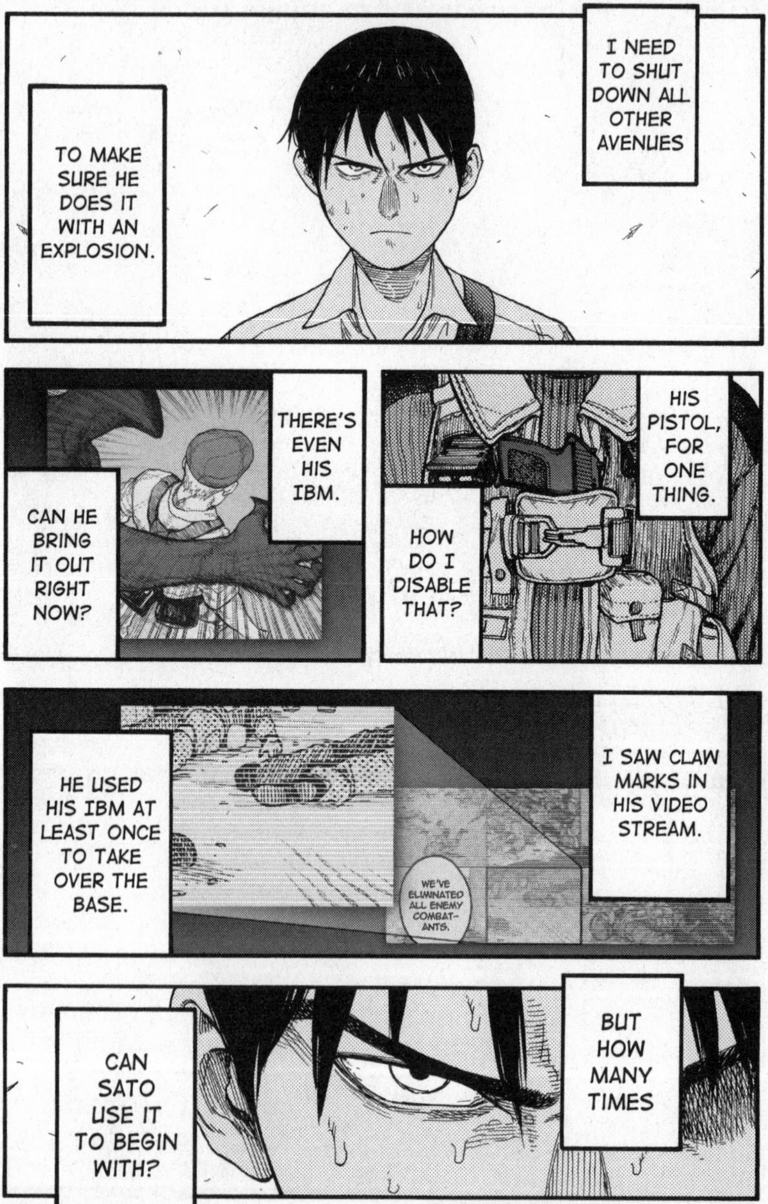
I NEED TO SHUT DOWN ALL OTHER AVENUES
TO MAKE SURE HE DOES IT WITH AN EXPLOSION.
HIS PISTOL, FOR ONE THING.
HOW DO I DISABLE THAT?
THERE'S EVEN HIS IBM.
CAN HE BRING IT OUT RIGHT NOW?
I SAW CLAW MARKS IN HIS VIDEO STREAM.
WE'VE ELIMINATED ALL ENEMY COMBAT-ANTS.
HE USED HIS IBM AT LEAST ONCE TO TAKE OVER THE BASE.
BUT HOW MANY TIMES
CAN SATO USE IT TO BEGIN WITH?

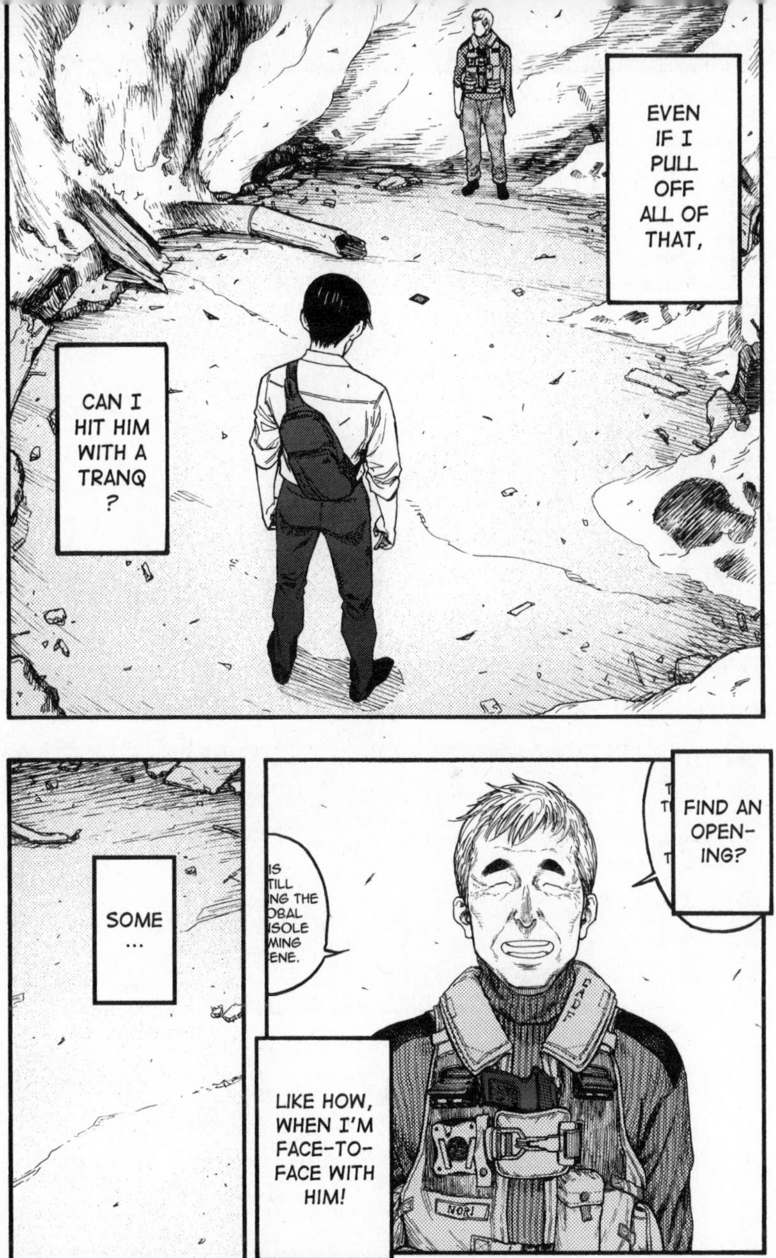
EVEN IF I PULL OFF ALL OF THAT,
CAN I HIT HIM WITH A TRANQ?
FIND AN OPEN-ING?
LIKE HOW, WHEN I'M FACE-TO-FACE WITH HIM!
SOME ...
NORI

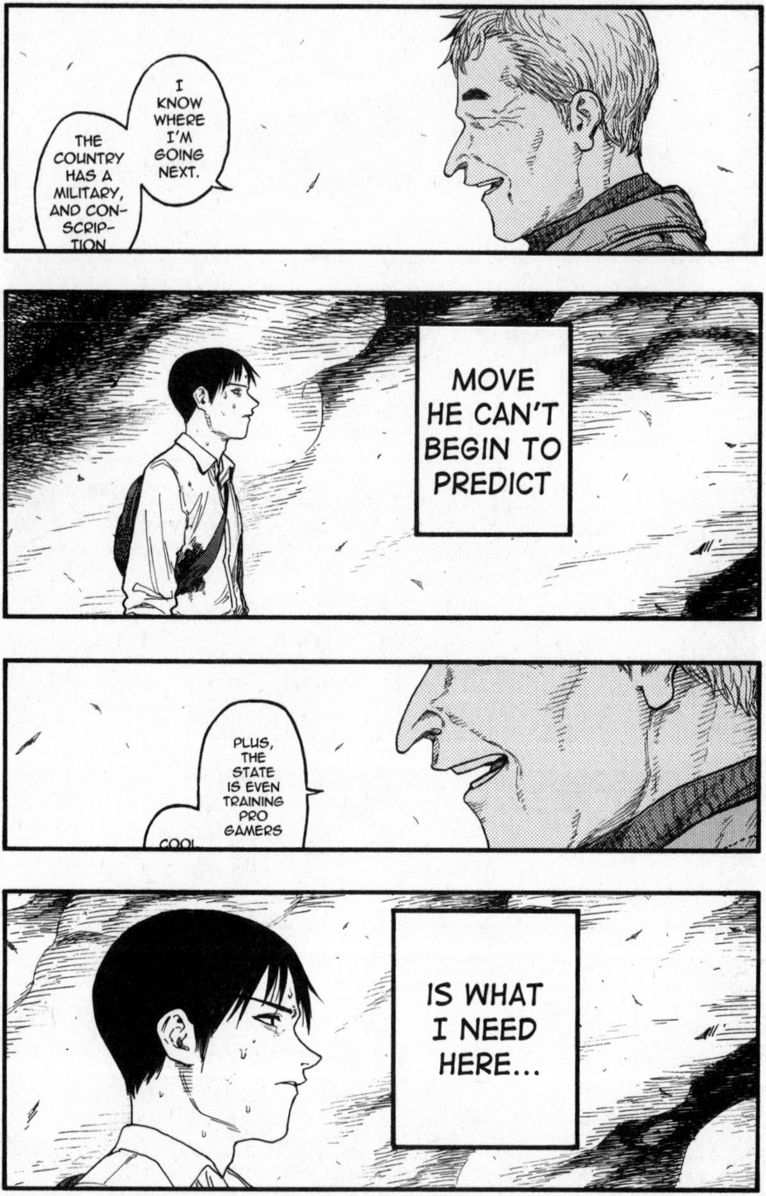
I KNOW WHERE I'M GOING NEXT.
THE COUNTRY HAS A MILITARY, AND CON-SCRIP-TION
MOVE HE CAN'T BEGIN TO PREDICT
PLUS, THE STATE IS EVEN TRAINING PRO GAMERS
COOL
IS WHAT I NEED HERE...

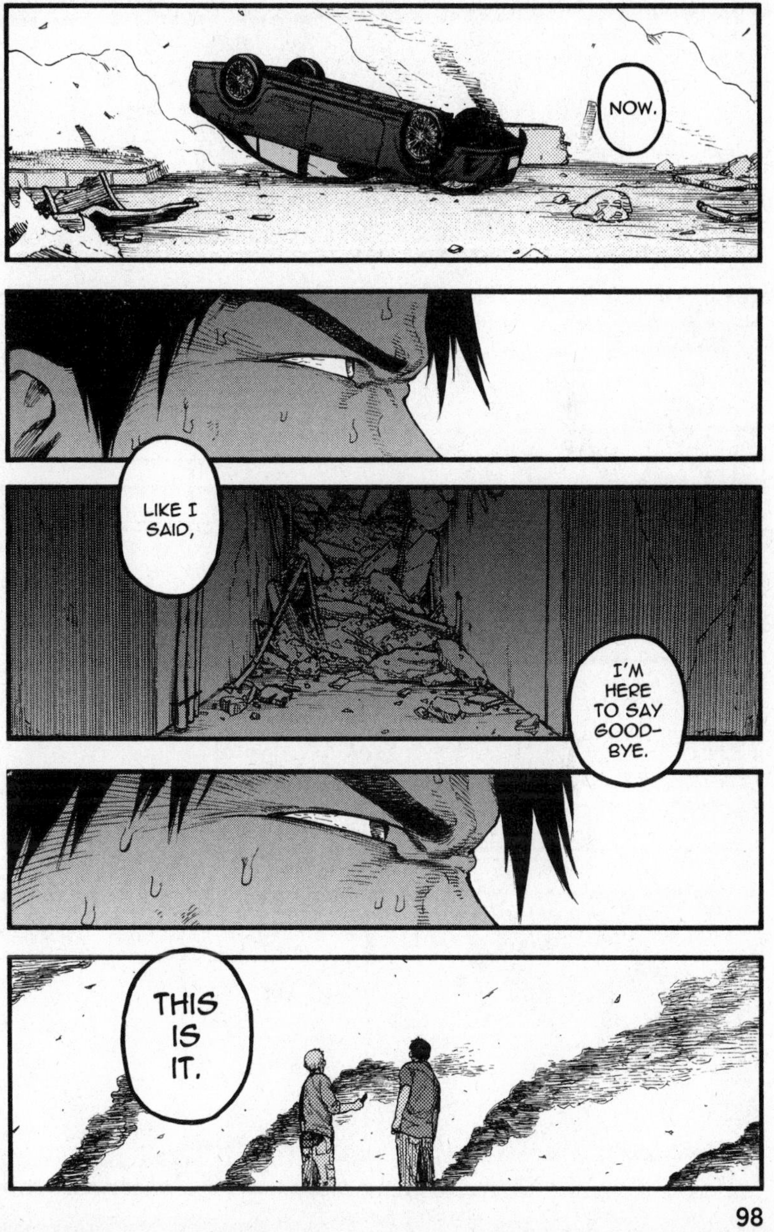
NOW.
LIKE I SAID,
I'M HERE TO SAY GOOD-BYE.
THIS IS IT.

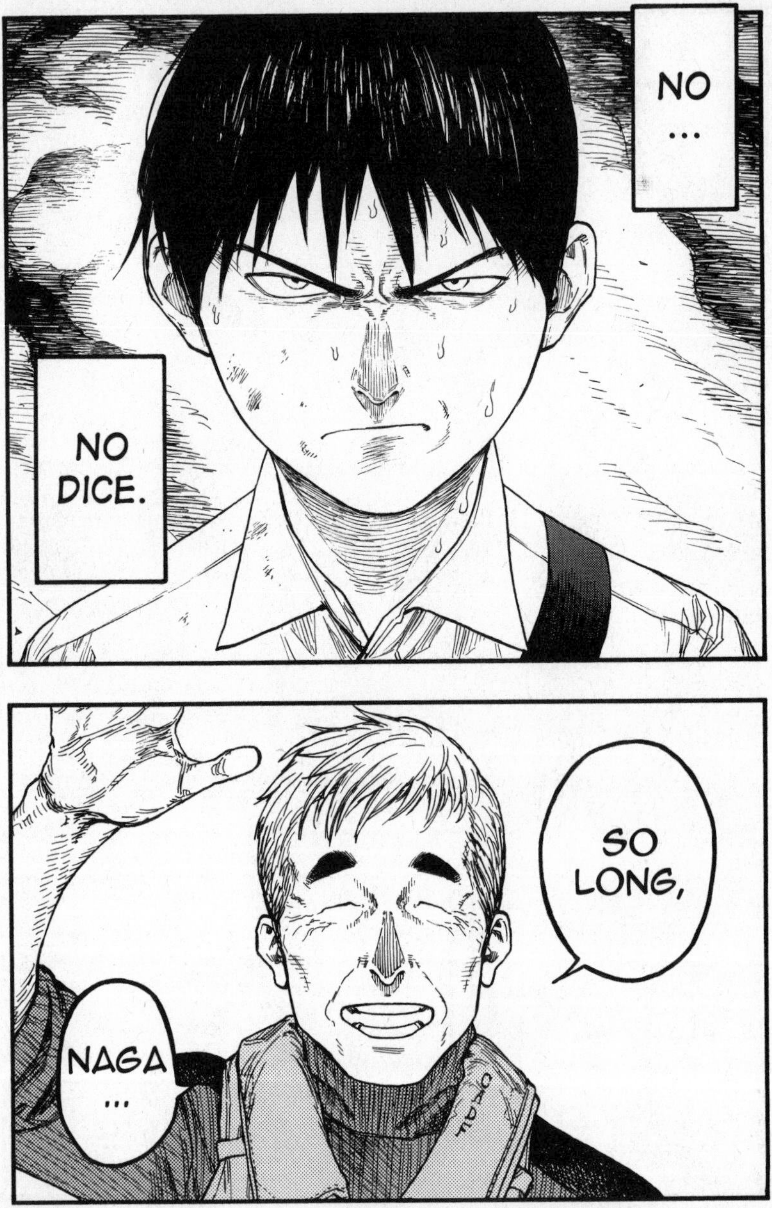
NO ...
NO DICE.
SO LONG,
NAGA ...

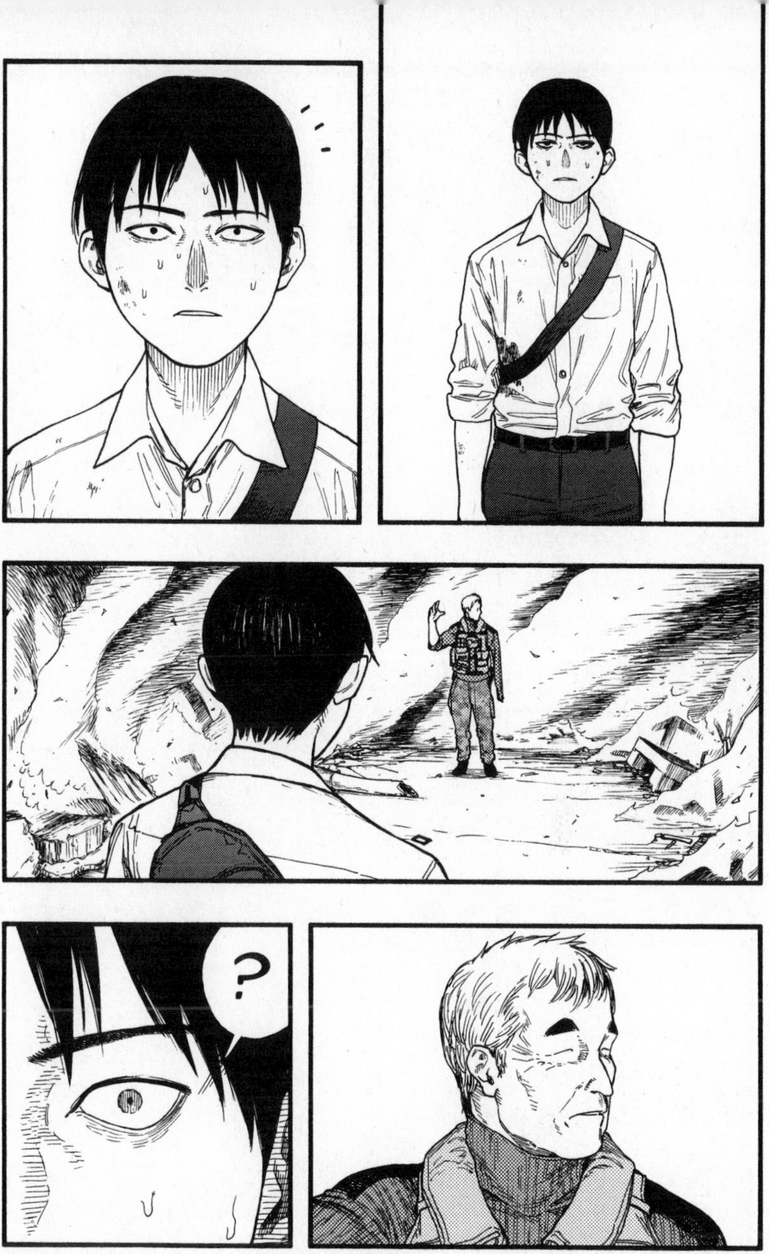
?

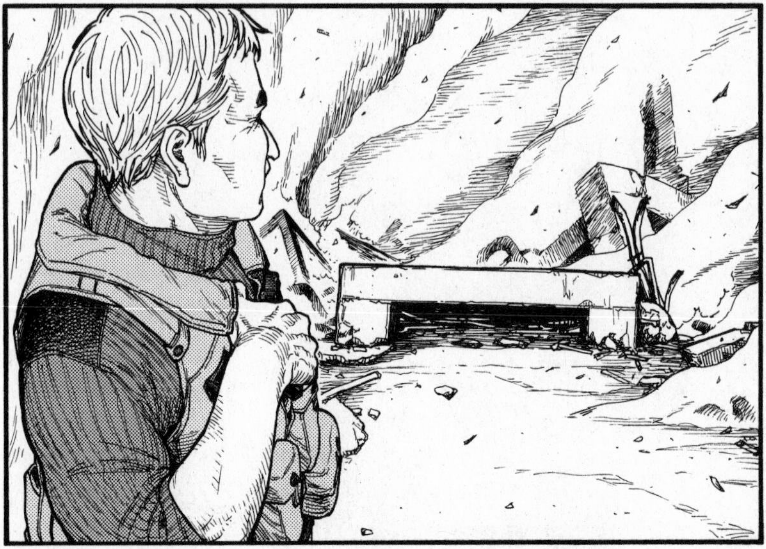

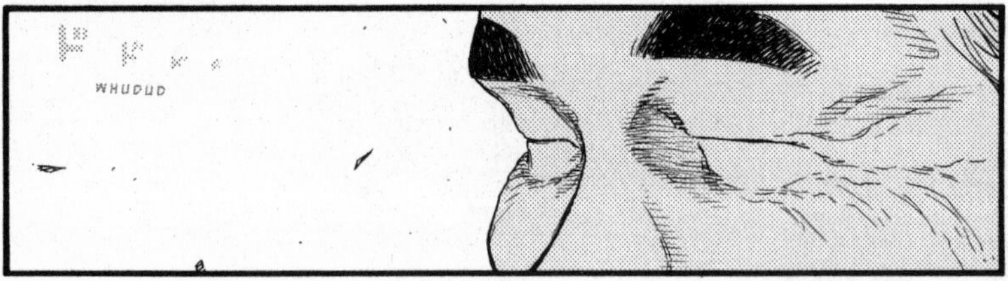
WHUDUD

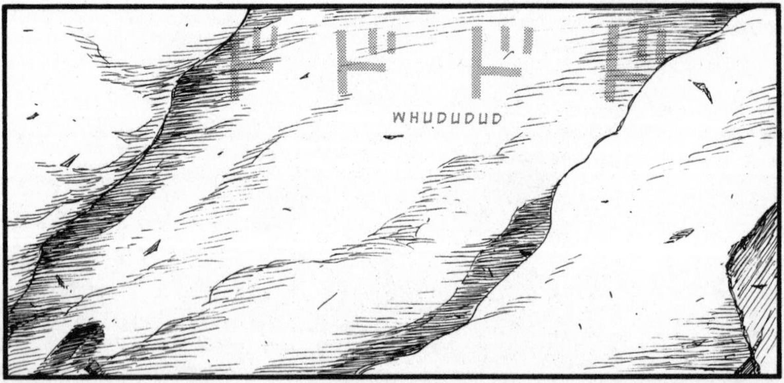
ドドドド
WHUDUDUD

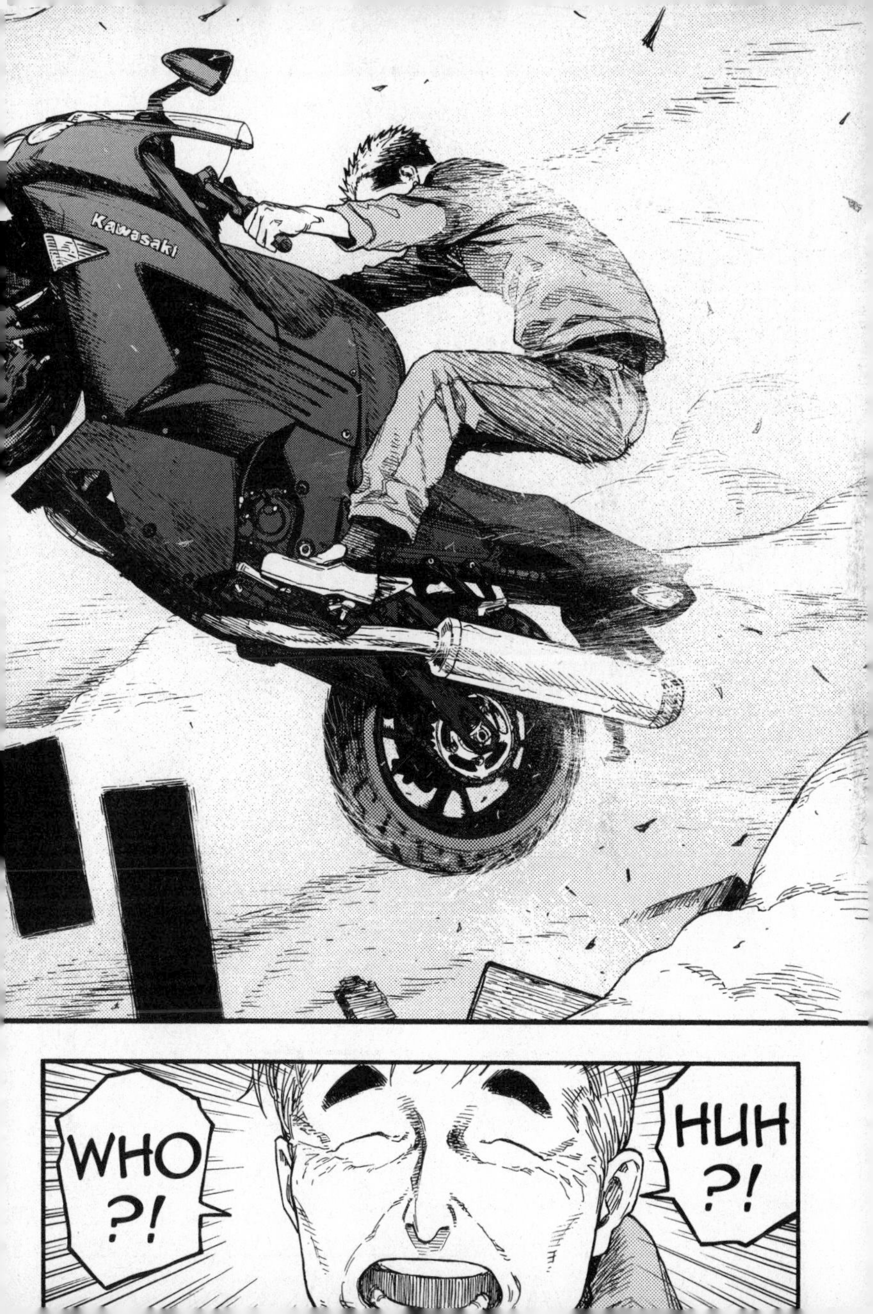
Kawasaki
HUH ?!
WHO ?!

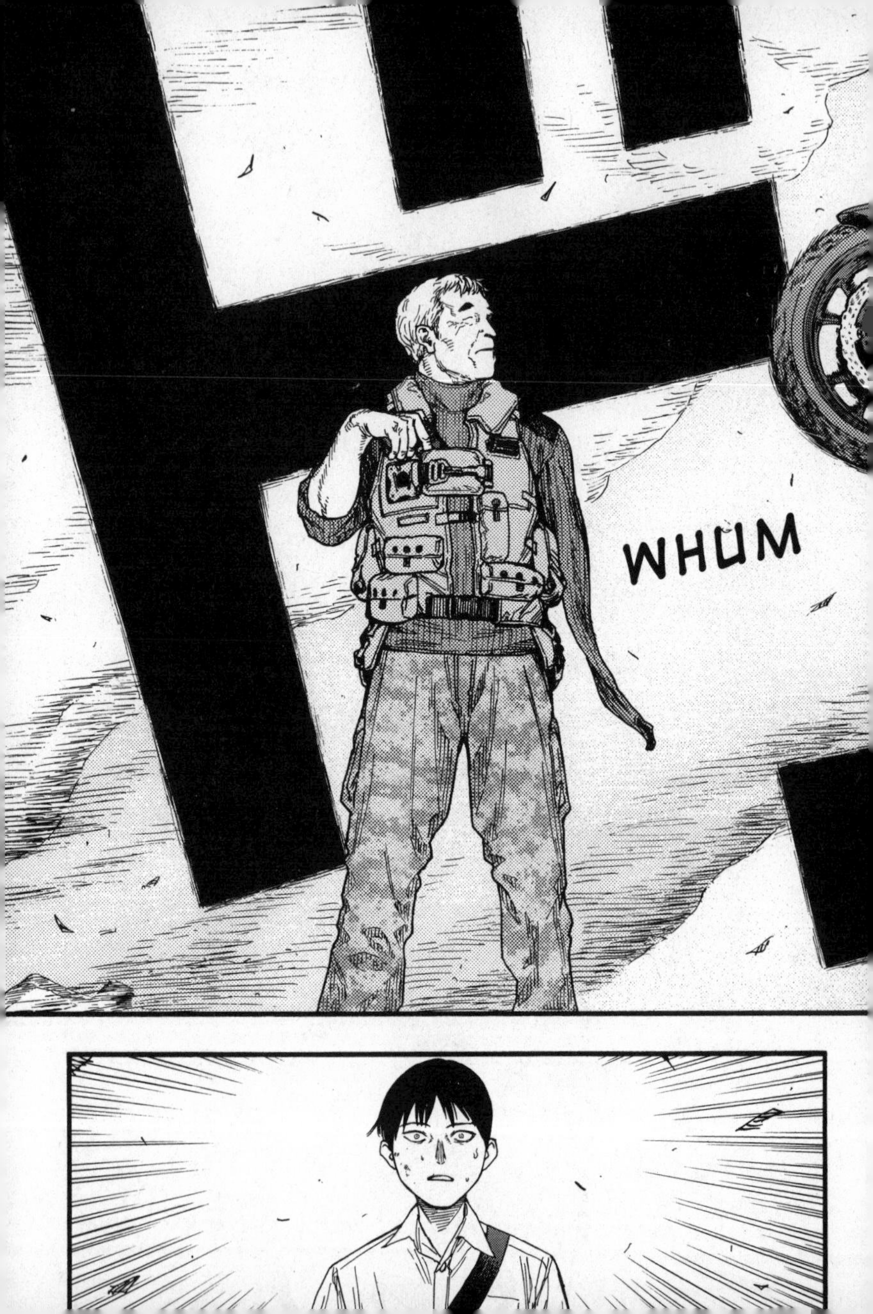
WHUM

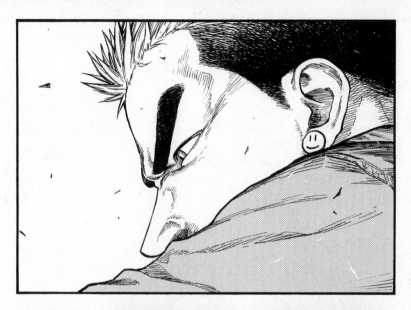

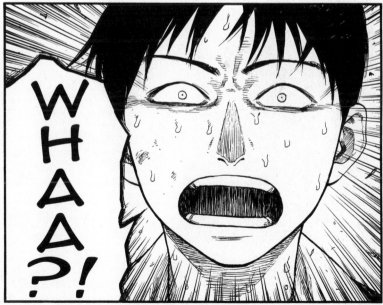

WHAA?!

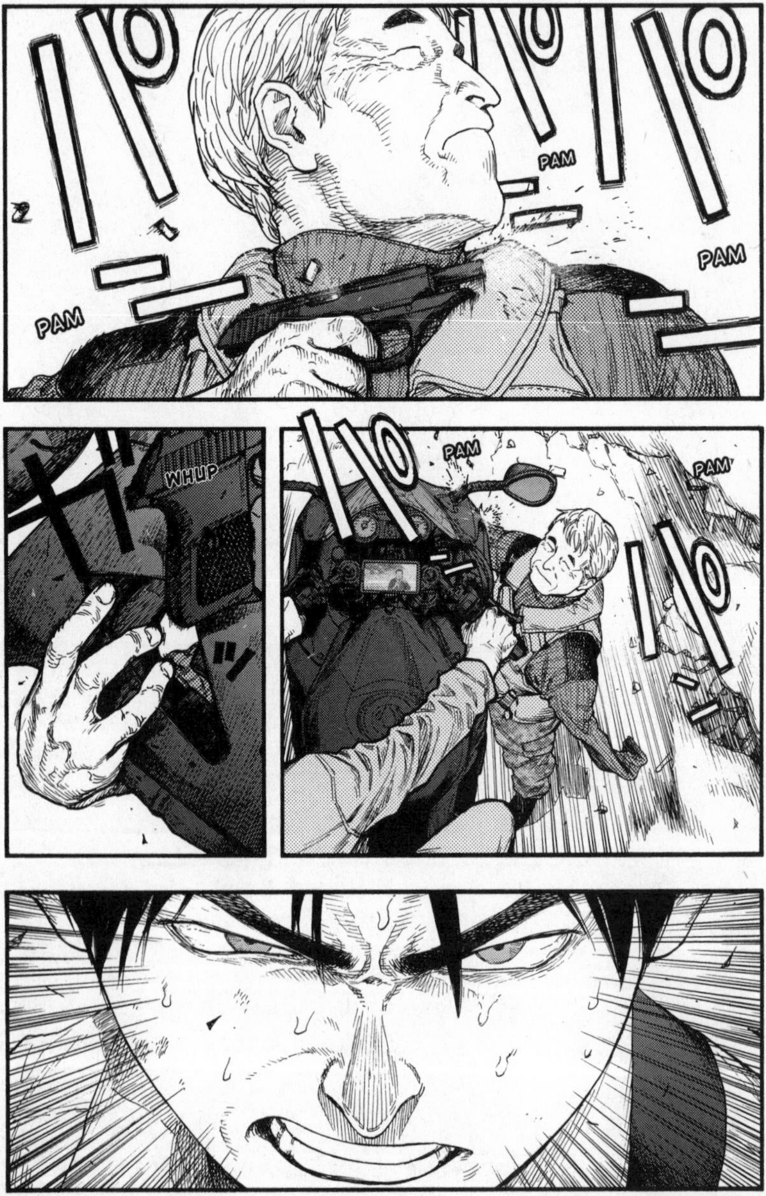
PAM
PAM
PAM
PAM
PAM
WHUP

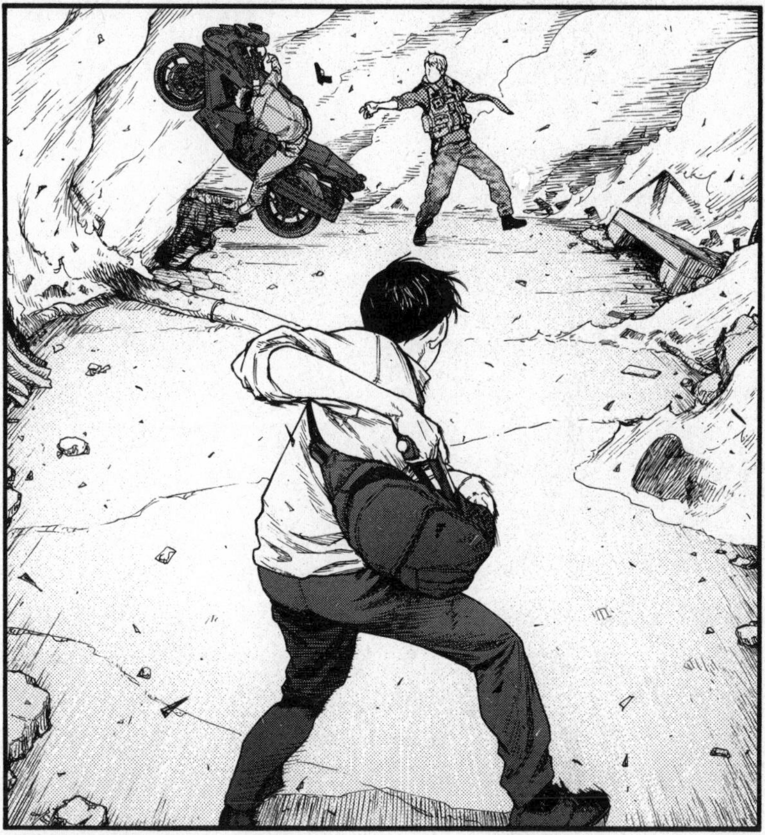

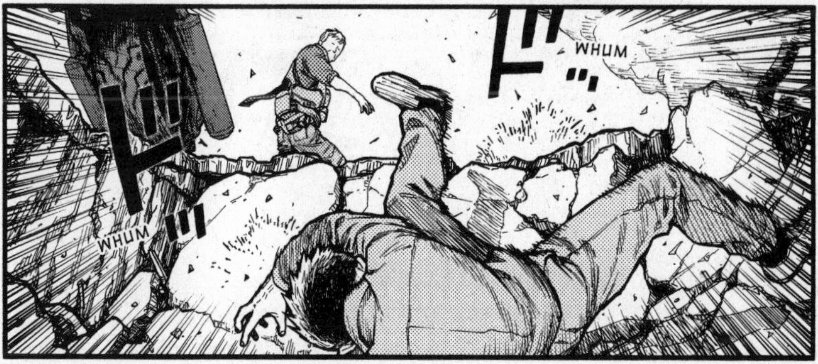
WHUM
WHUM

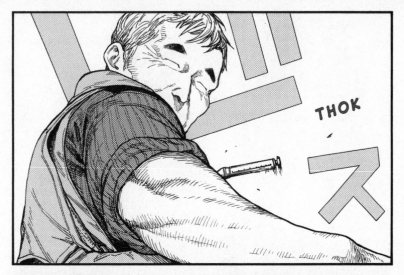

THOK

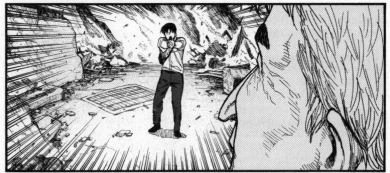

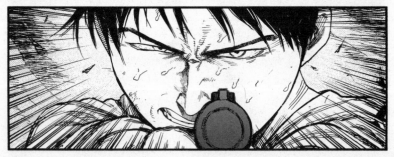

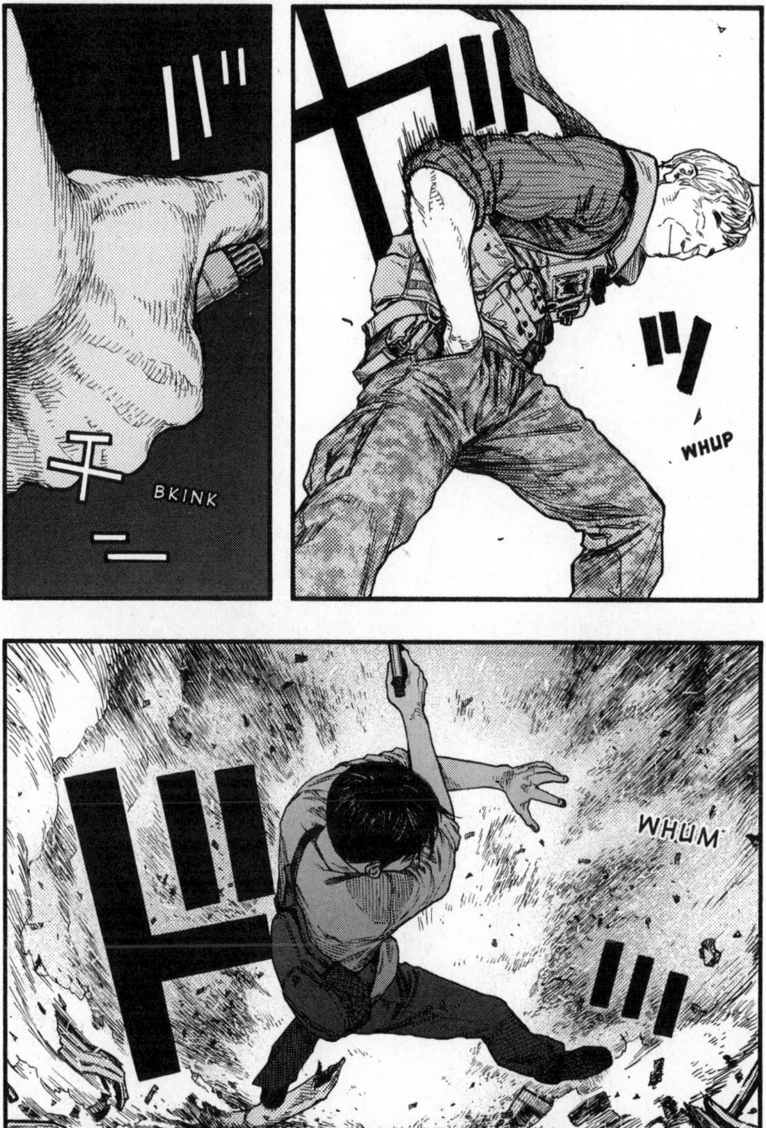
WHUP
BKINK
WHUM

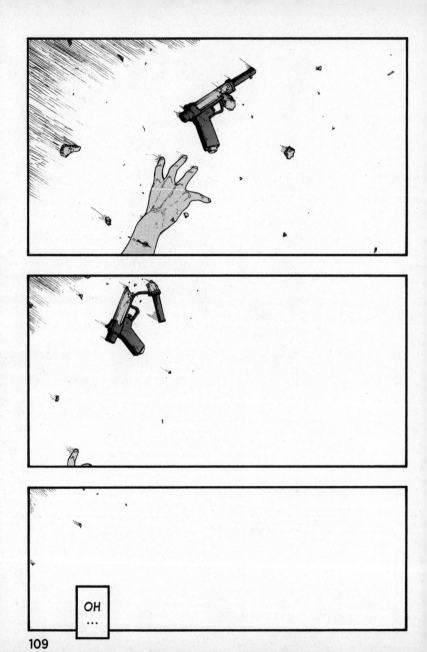

OH
...

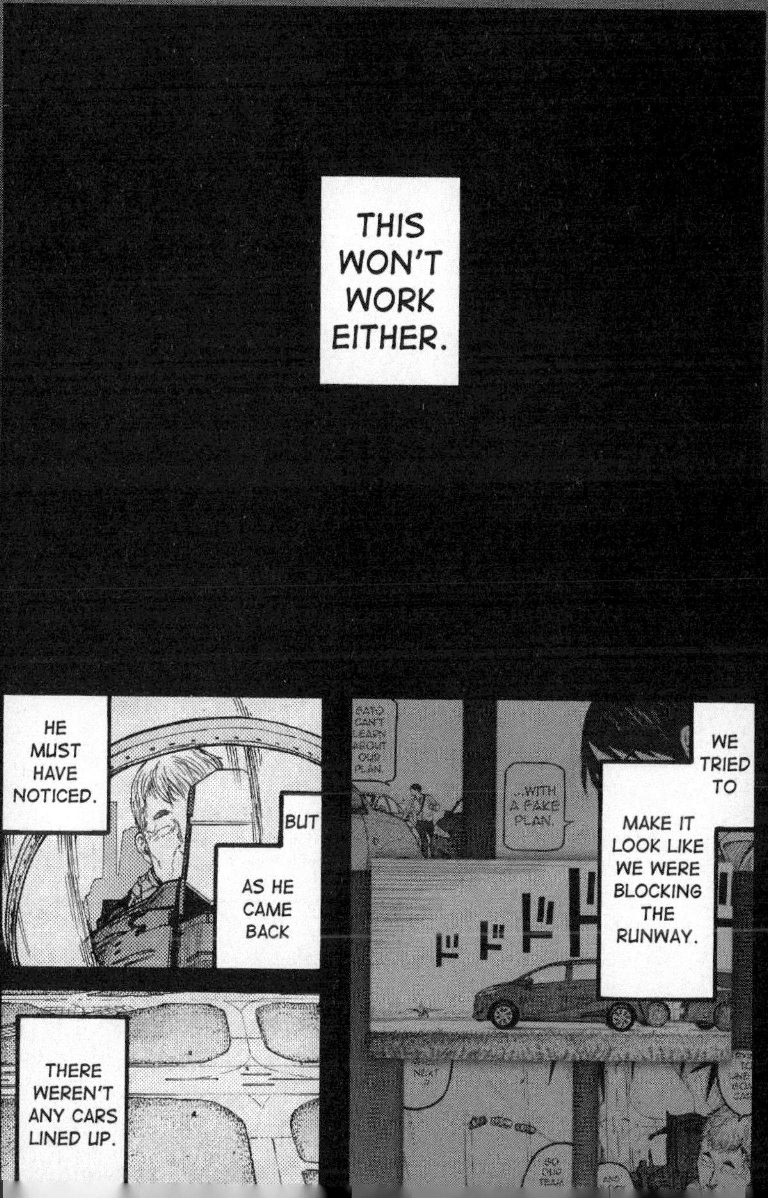
THIS WON'T WORK EITHER.
WE TRIED TO
MAKE IT LOOK LIKE WE WERE BLOCKING THE RUNWAY.
...WITH A FAKE PLAN.
SATO CAN'T LEARN ABOUT OUR PLAN.
ドドドド
HE MUST HAVE NOTICED.
BUT
AS HE CAME BACK
THERE WEREN'T ANY CARS LINED UP.

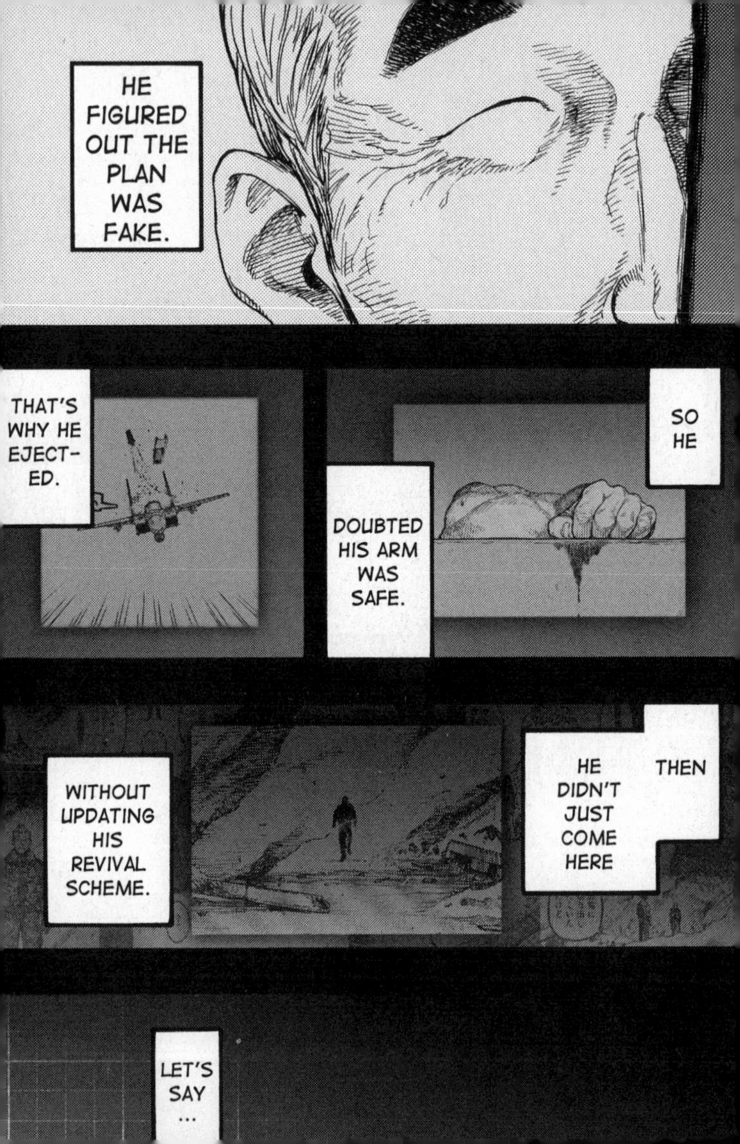
HE FIGURED OUT THE PLAN WAS FAKE.
SO HE
DOUBTED HIS ARM WAS SAFE.
THAT'S WHY HE EJECT-ED.
THEN
HE DIDN'T JUST COME HERE
WITHOUT UPDATING HIS REVIVAL SCHEME.
LET'S SAY ...

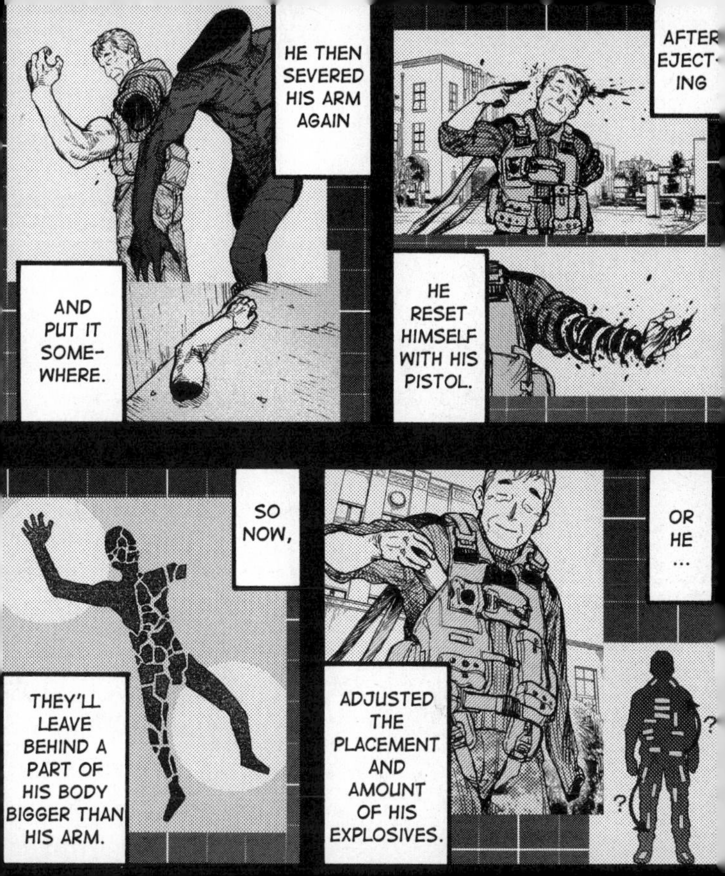
AFTER EJECT-ING
HE RESET HIMSELF WITH HIS PISTOL.
HE THEN SEVERED HIS ARM AGAIN
AND PUT IT SOME-WHERE.
OR HE ...
?
?
ADJUSTED THE PLACEMENT AND AMOUNT OF HIS EXPLOSIVES.
SO NOW,
THEY'LL LEAVE BEHIND A PART OF HIS BODY BIGGER THAN HIS ARM.

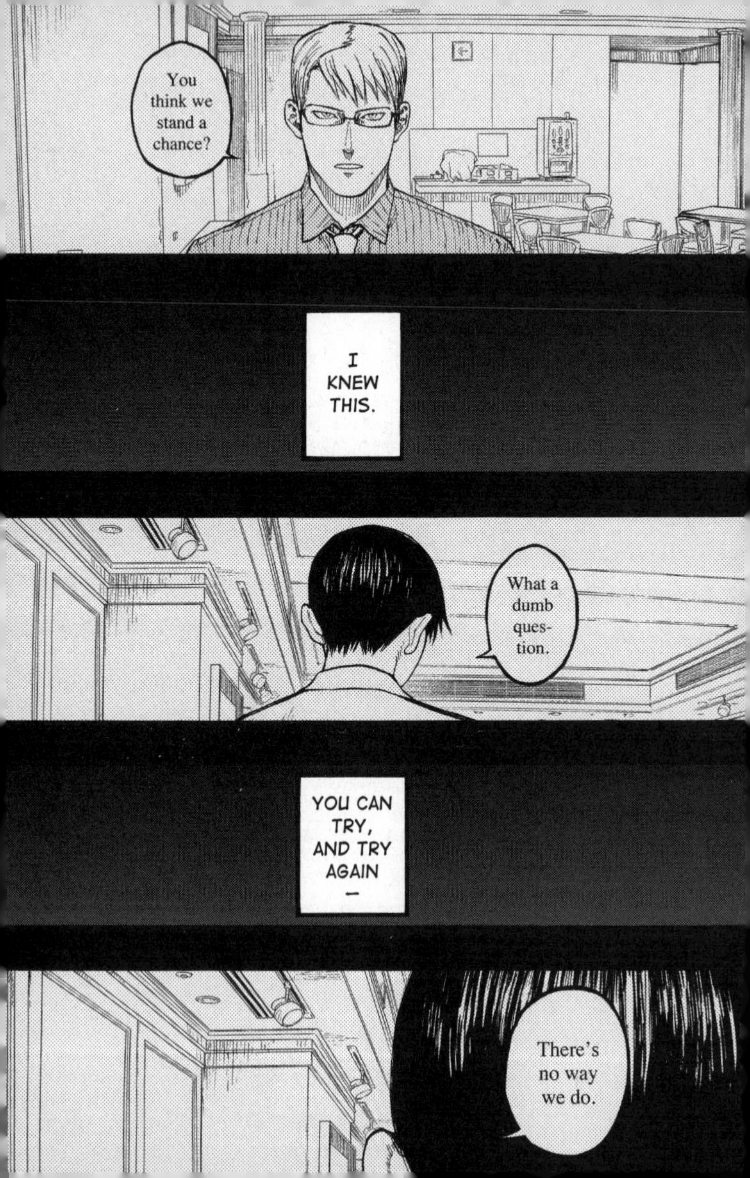
You think we stand a chance?
I KNEW THIS.
What a dumb ques-tion.
YOU CAN TRY, AND TRY AGAIN –
There's no way we do.

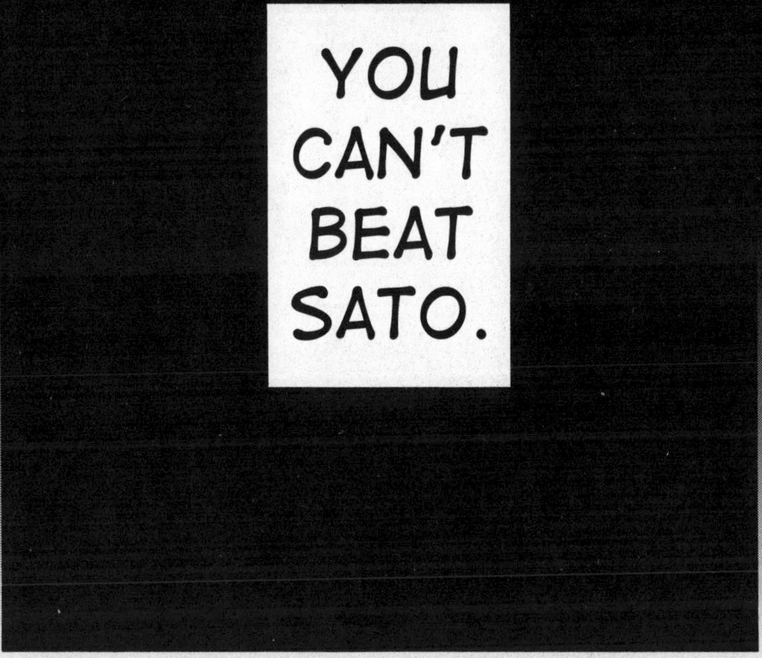
YOU CAN'T BEAT SATO.
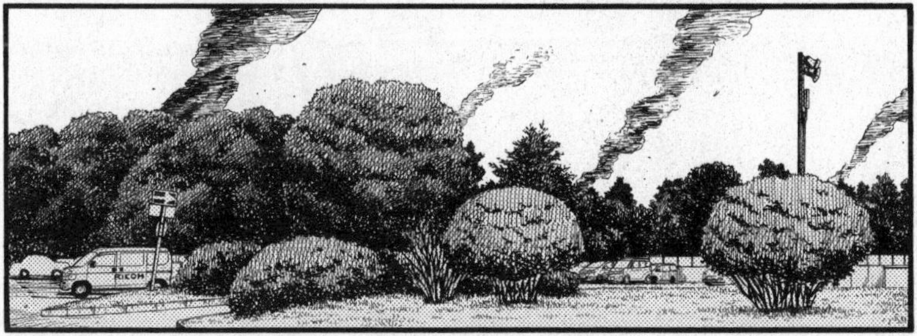

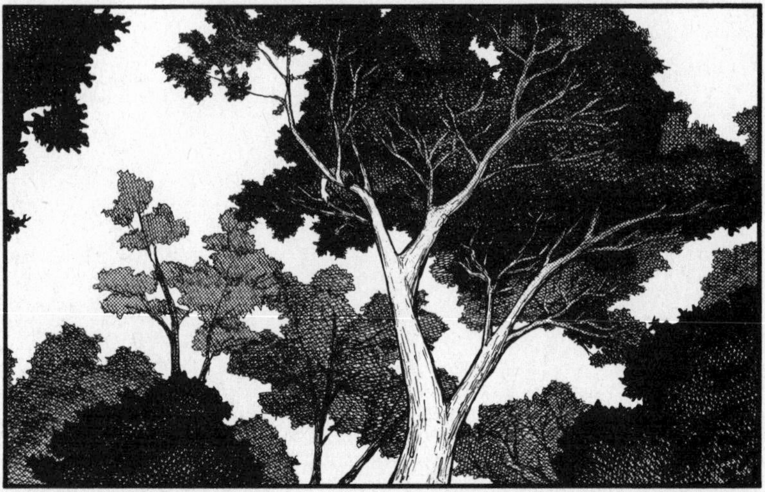

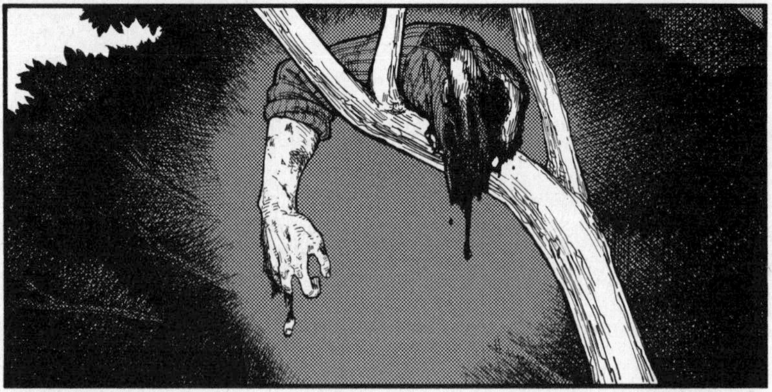

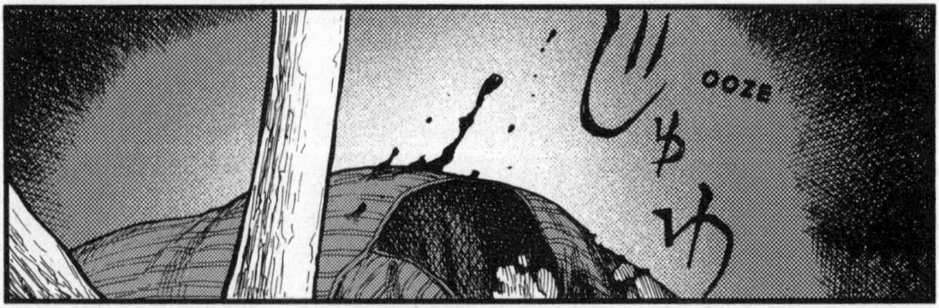
OOZE

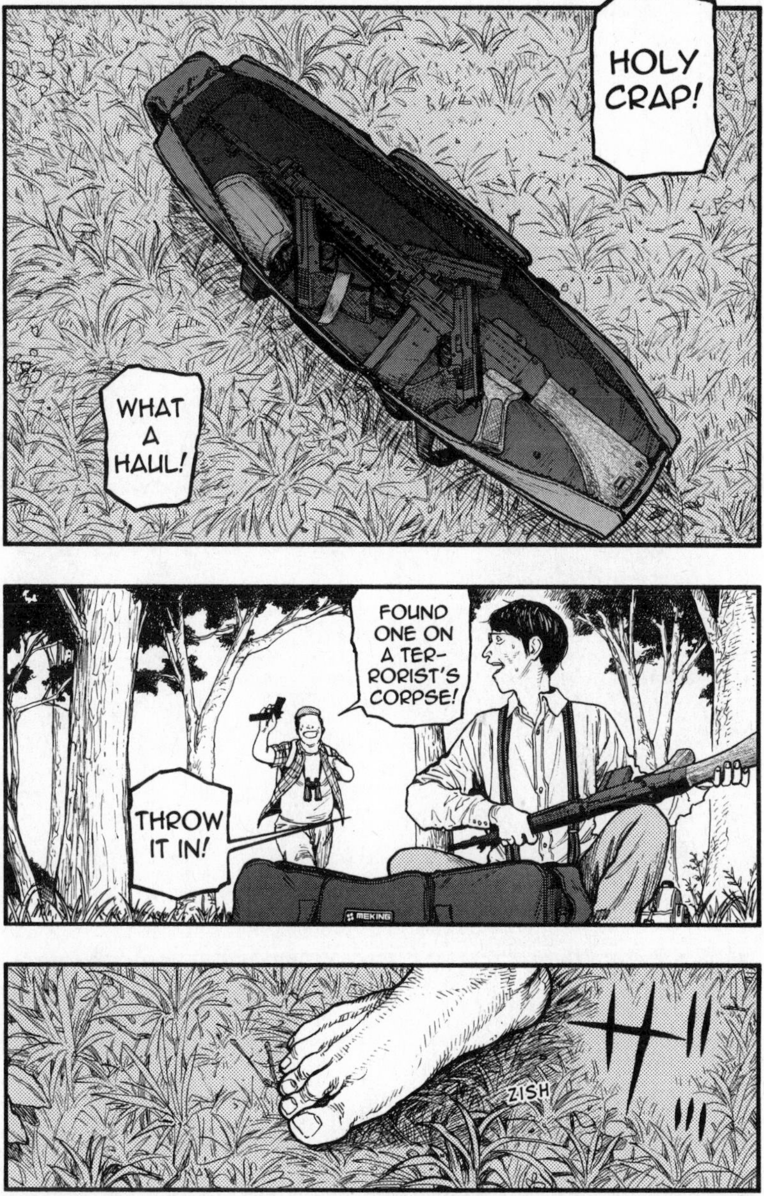
HOLY CRAP!
WHAT A HAUL!
FOUND ONE ON A TER-RORIST'S CORPSE!
THROW IT IN!
MEKING
ZISH

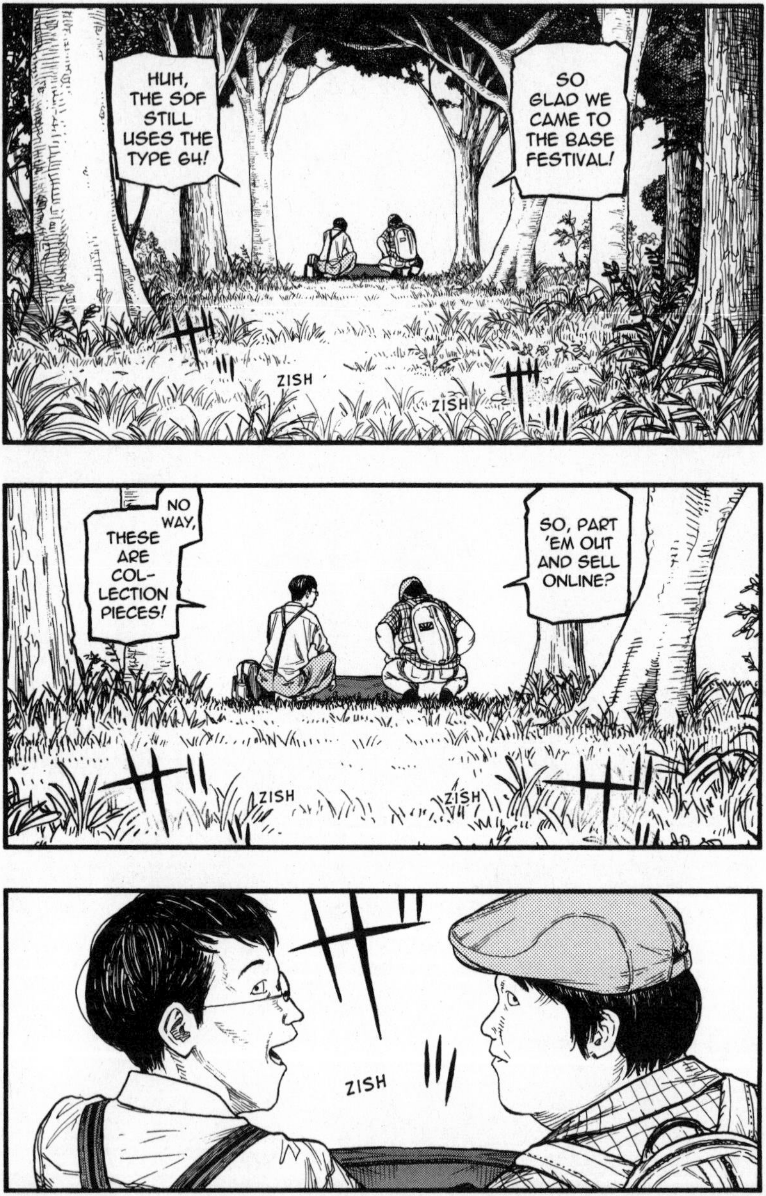
SO GLAD WE CAME TO THE BASE FESTIVAL!
HUH, THE SDF STILL USES THE TYPE 64!
ZISH
ZISH
SO, PART 'EM OUT AND SELL ONLINE?
NO WAY, THESE ARE COL-LECTION PIECES!
ZISH
ZISH
ZISH

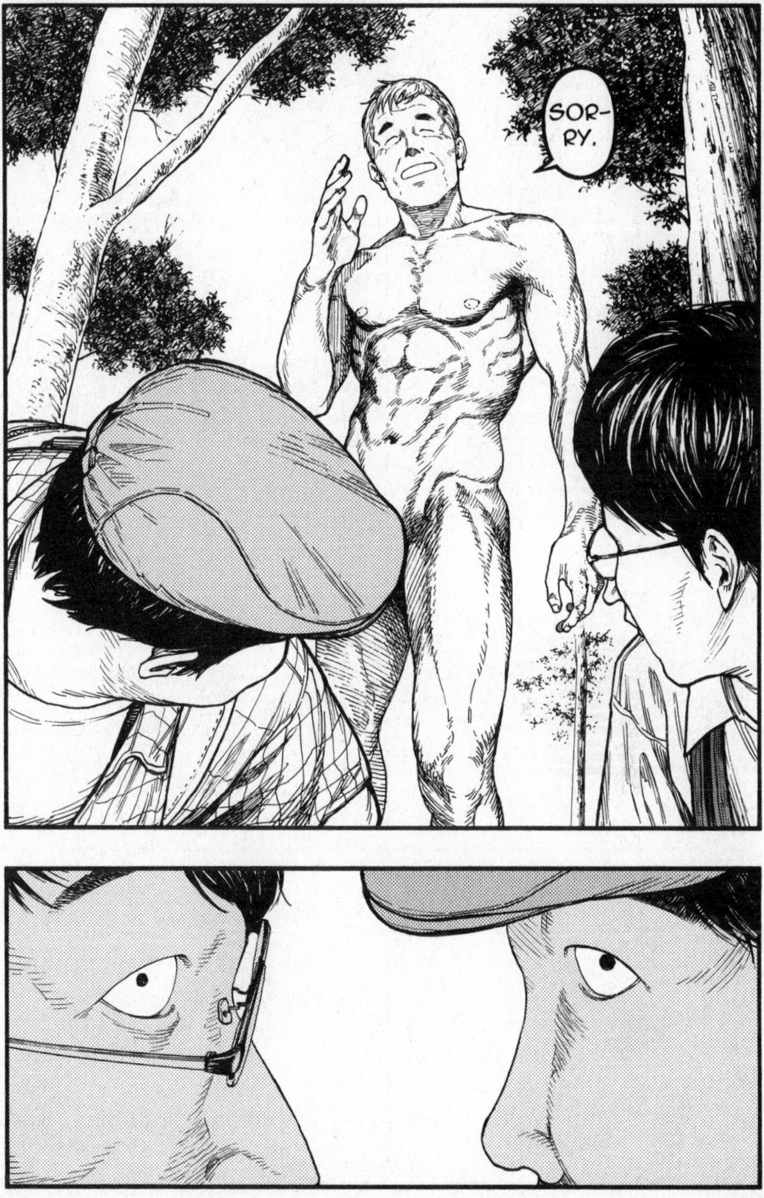
SOR-
RY.

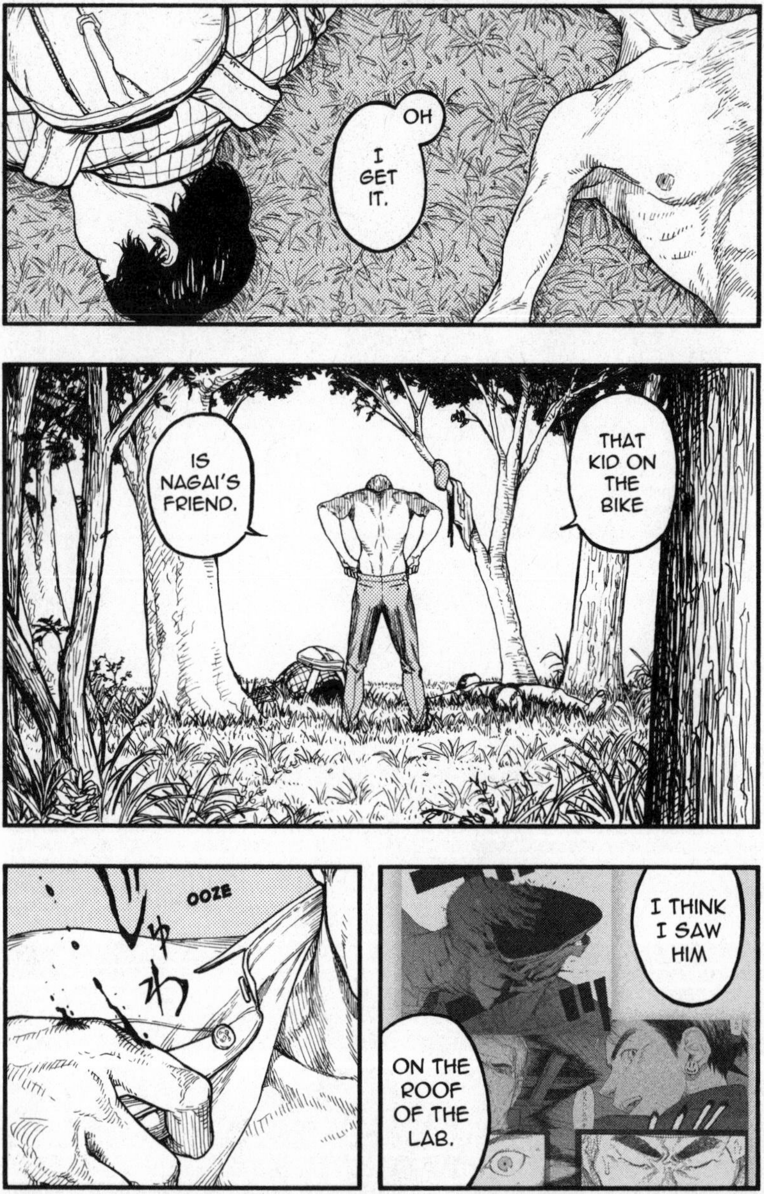
OH
I GET IT.
THAT KID ON THE BIKE
IS NAGAI'S FRIEND.
I THINK I SAW HIM
ON THE ROOF OF THE LAB.
OOZE

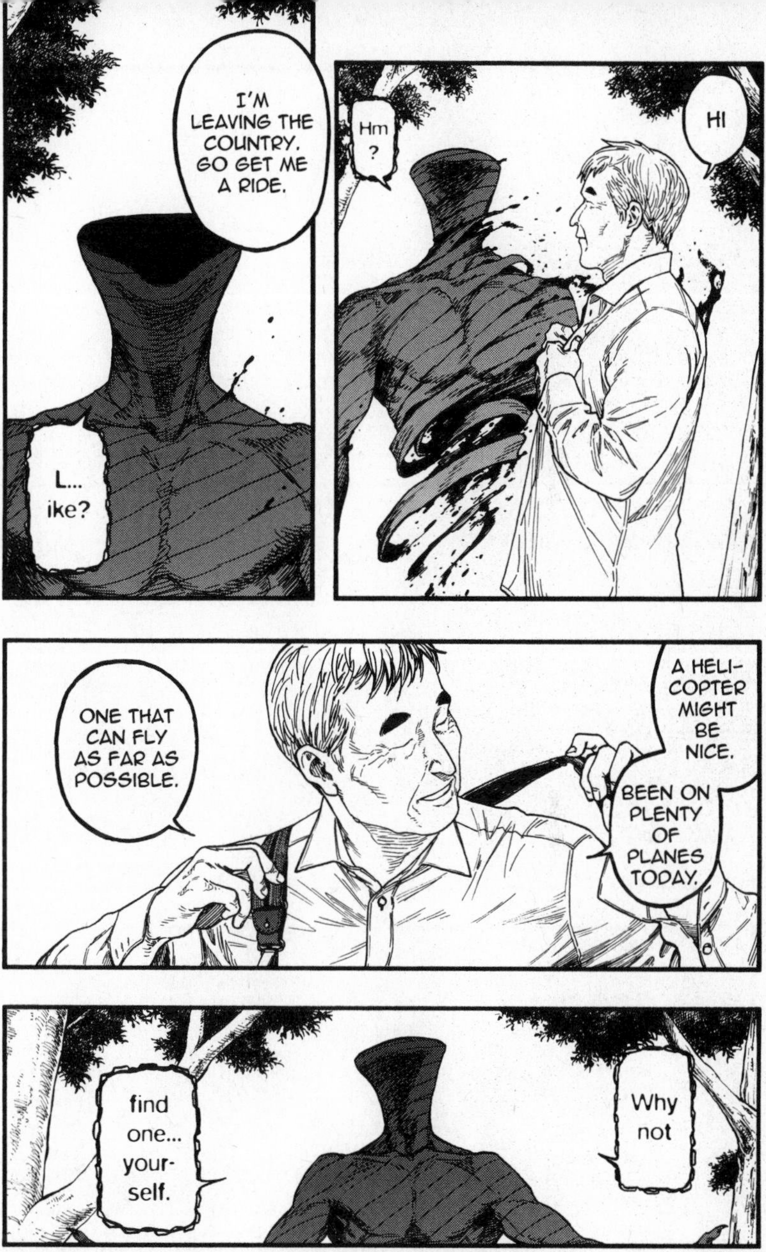
HI
Hm ?
I'M LEAVING THE COUNTRY. GO GET ME A RIDE.
L... ike?
A HELI-COPTER MIGHT BE NICE.
BEEN ON PLENTY OF PLANES TODAY.
ONE THAT CAN FLY AS FAR AS POSSIBLE.
Why not
find one... your-self.

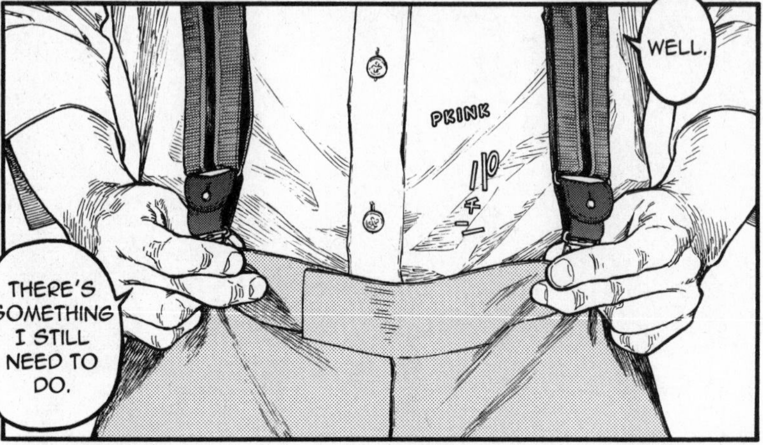
WELL.
PKINK
THERE'S SOMETHING I STILL NEED TO DO.

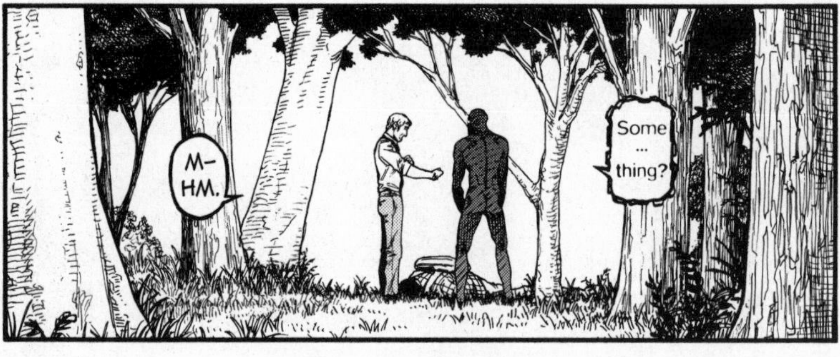
Some ... thing?
M-HM.

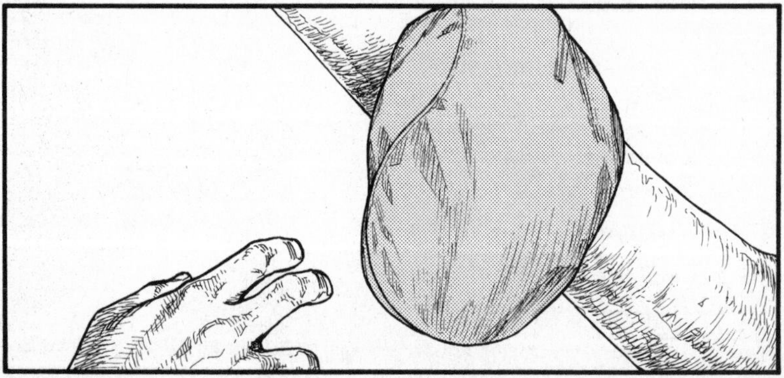

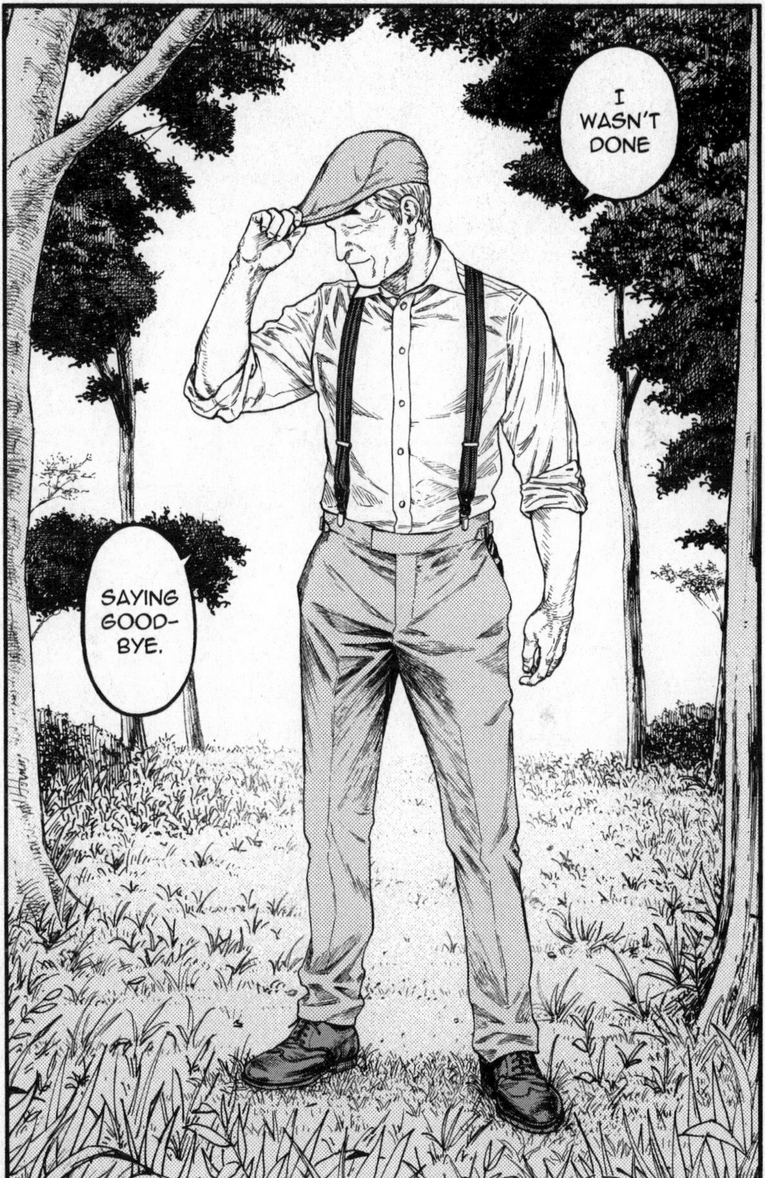
I WASN'T DONE
SAYING GOOD-BYE.

File:71 End

File 72: Limit

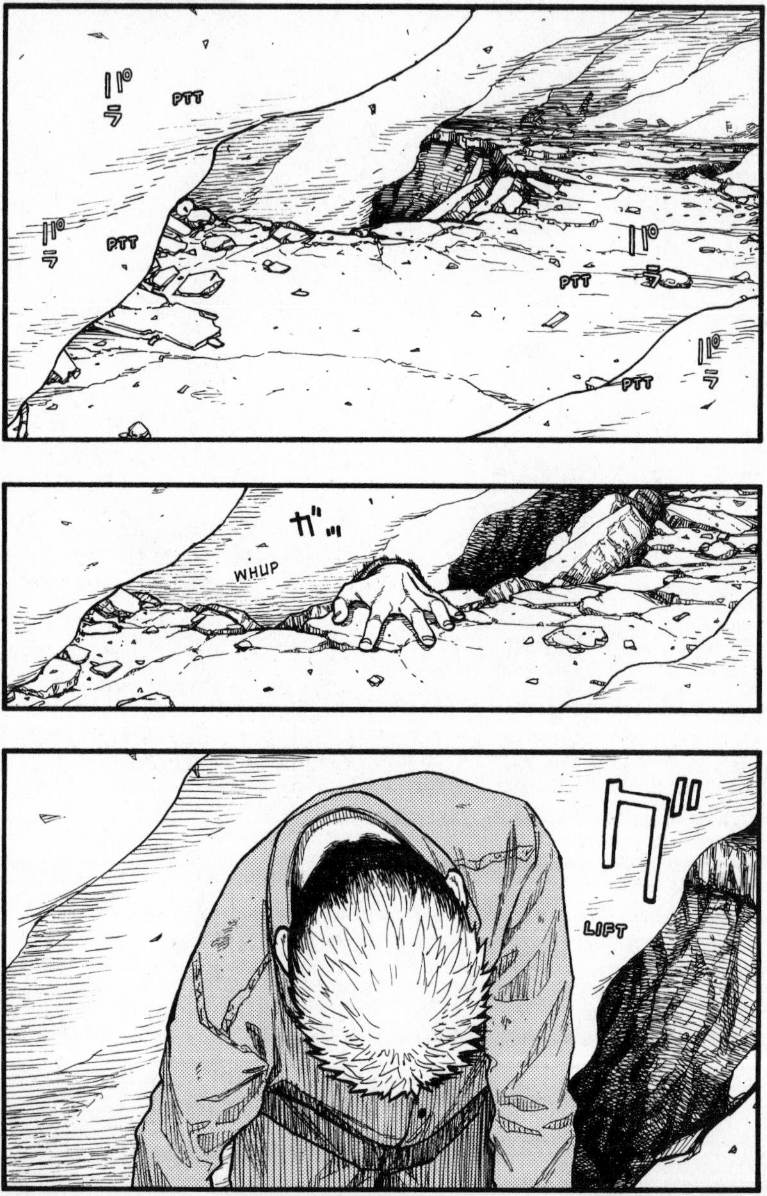
パラ
PTT
パラ
PTT
パラ
PTT
パラ
PTT
ガッ
WHUP
グッ
LIFT

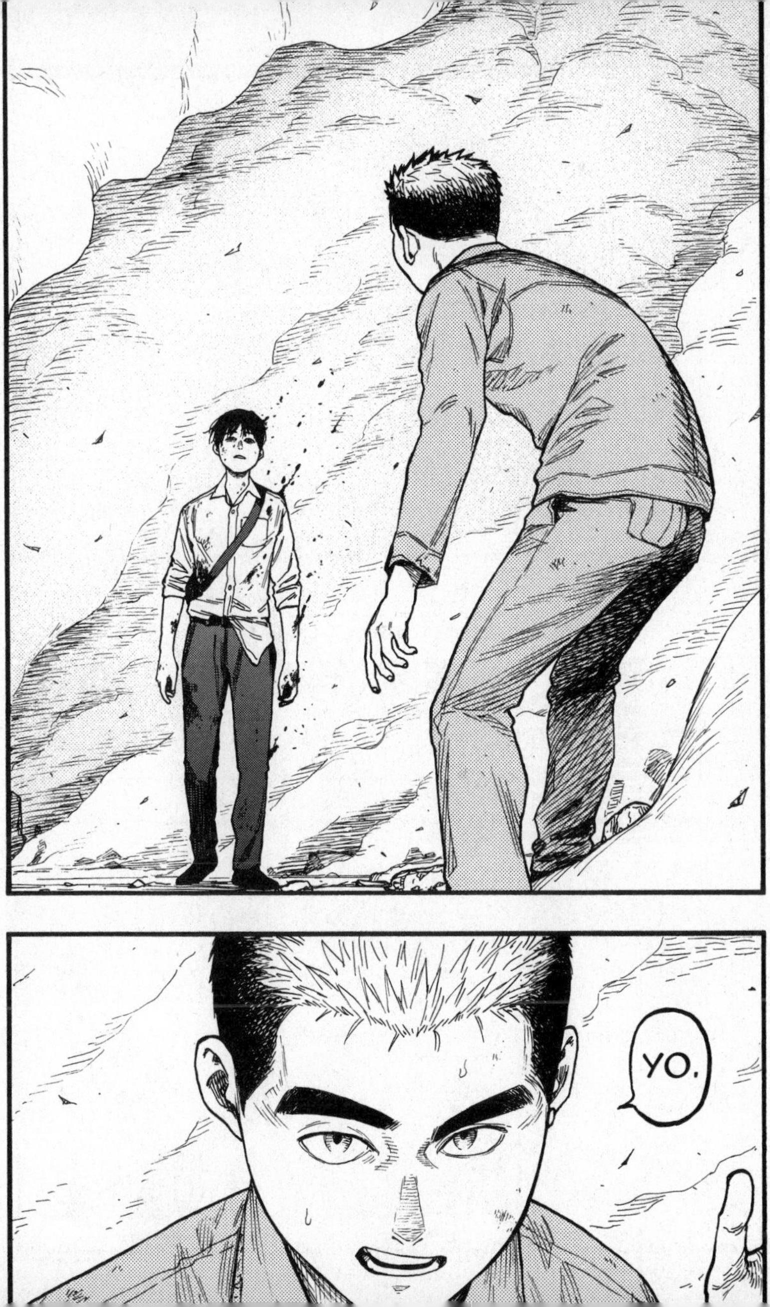
YO.

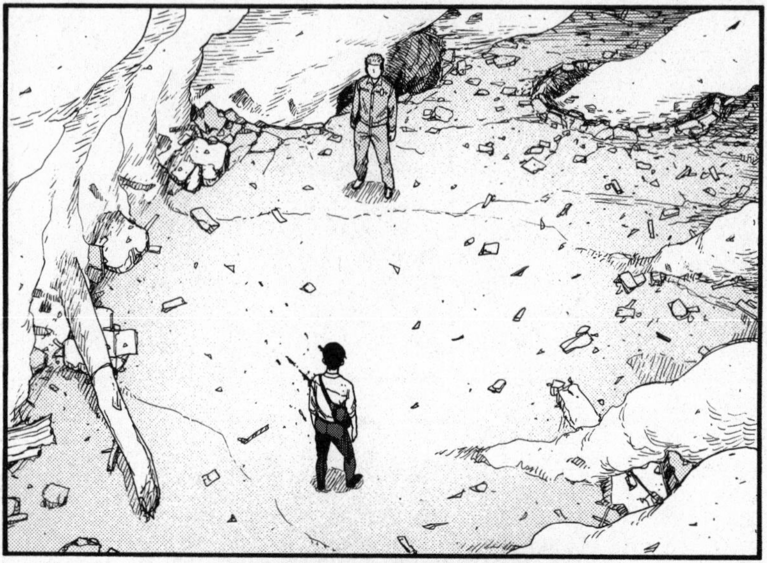

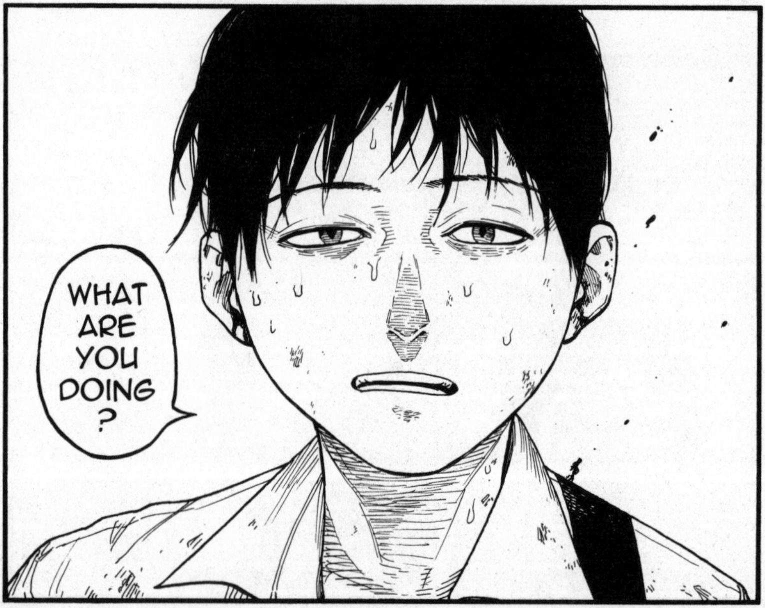
WHAT ARE YOU DOING?

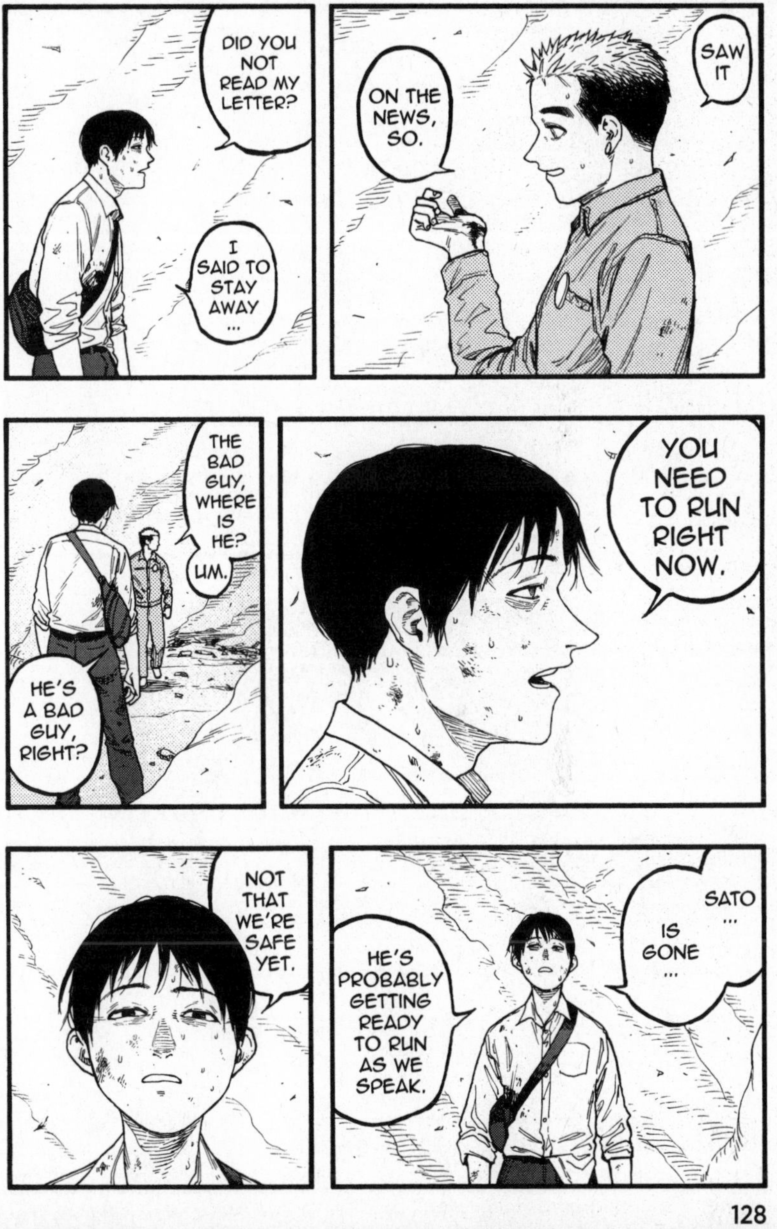
SAW IT
ON THE NEWS, SO.
DID YOU NOT READ MY LETTER?
I SAID TO STAY AWAY ...
YOU NEED TO RUN RIGHT NOW.
THE BAD GUY, WHERE IS HE?
UM.
HE'S A BAD GUY, RIGHT?
SATO ...
IS GONE ...
HE'S PROBABLY GETTING READY TO RUN AS WE SPEAK.
NOT THAT WE'RE SAFE YET.

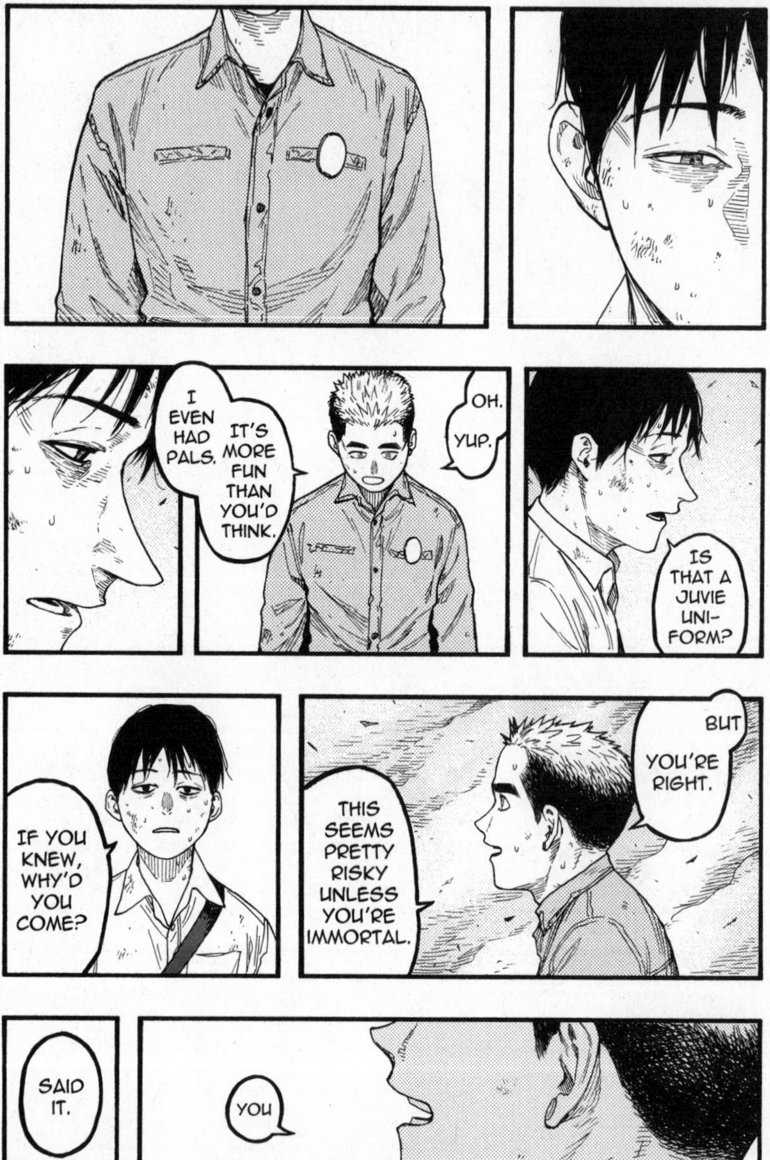
IS THAT A JUVIE UNIFORM?
OH.
YUP.
IT'S MORE FUN THAN YOU'D THINK.
I EVEN HAD PALS.
BUT
YOU'RE RIGHT.
THIS SEEMS PRETTY RISKY UNLESS YOU'RE IMMORTAL.
IF YOU KNEW, WHY'D YOU COME?
YOU
SAID IT.

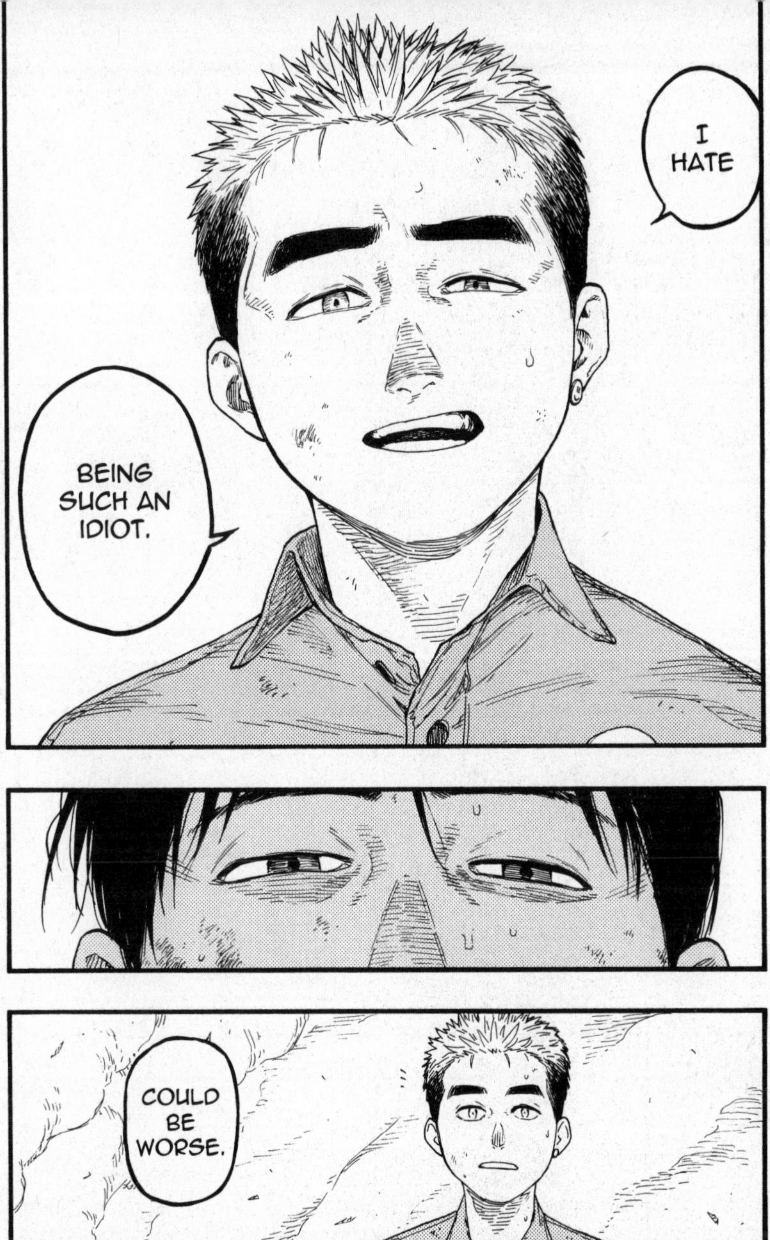
I HATE
BEING SUCH AN IDIOT.
COULD BE WORSE.

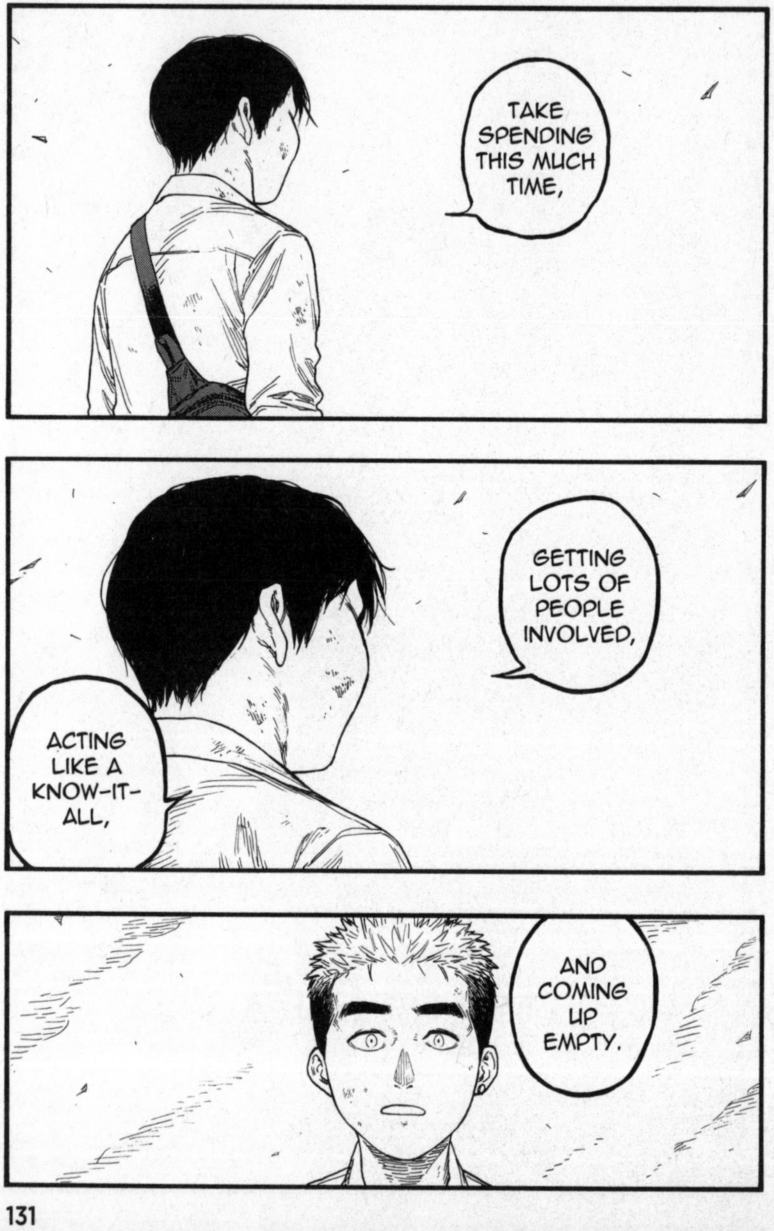
TAKE SPENDING THIS MUCH TIME,
GETTING LOTS OF PEOPLE INVOLVED,
ACTING LIKE A KNOW-IT-ALL,
AND COMING UP EMPTY.

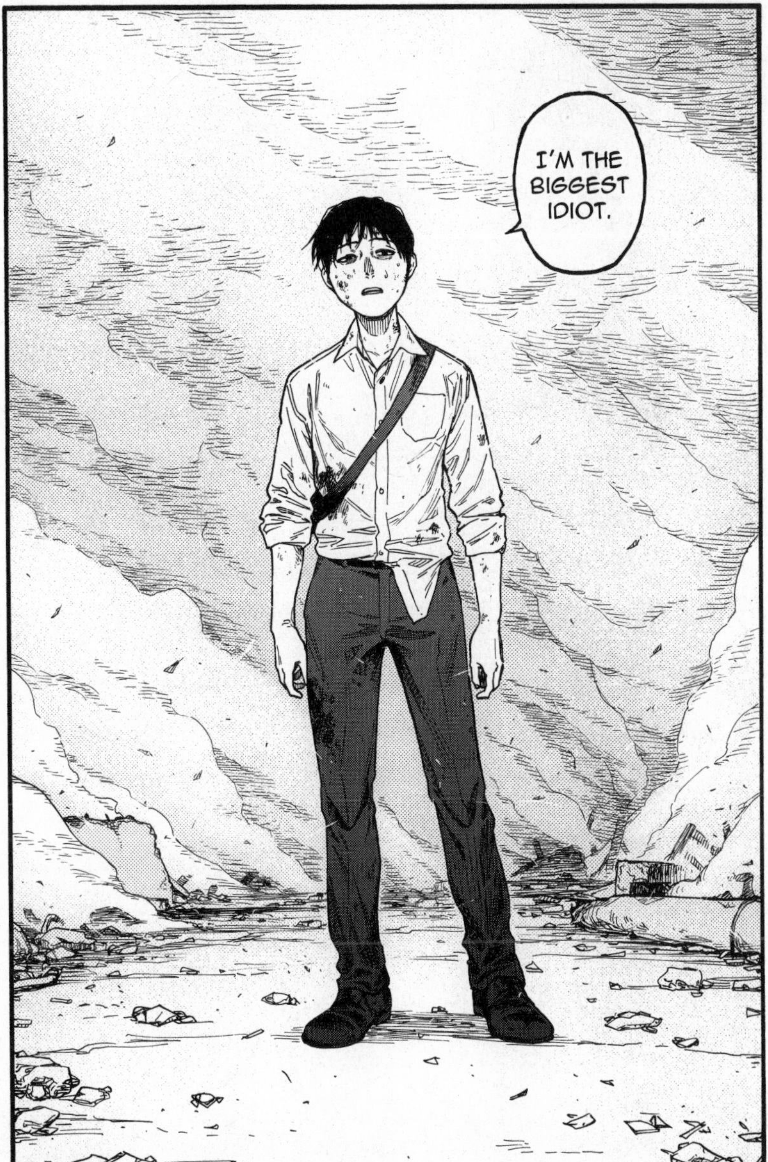
I'M THE BIGGEST IDIOT.

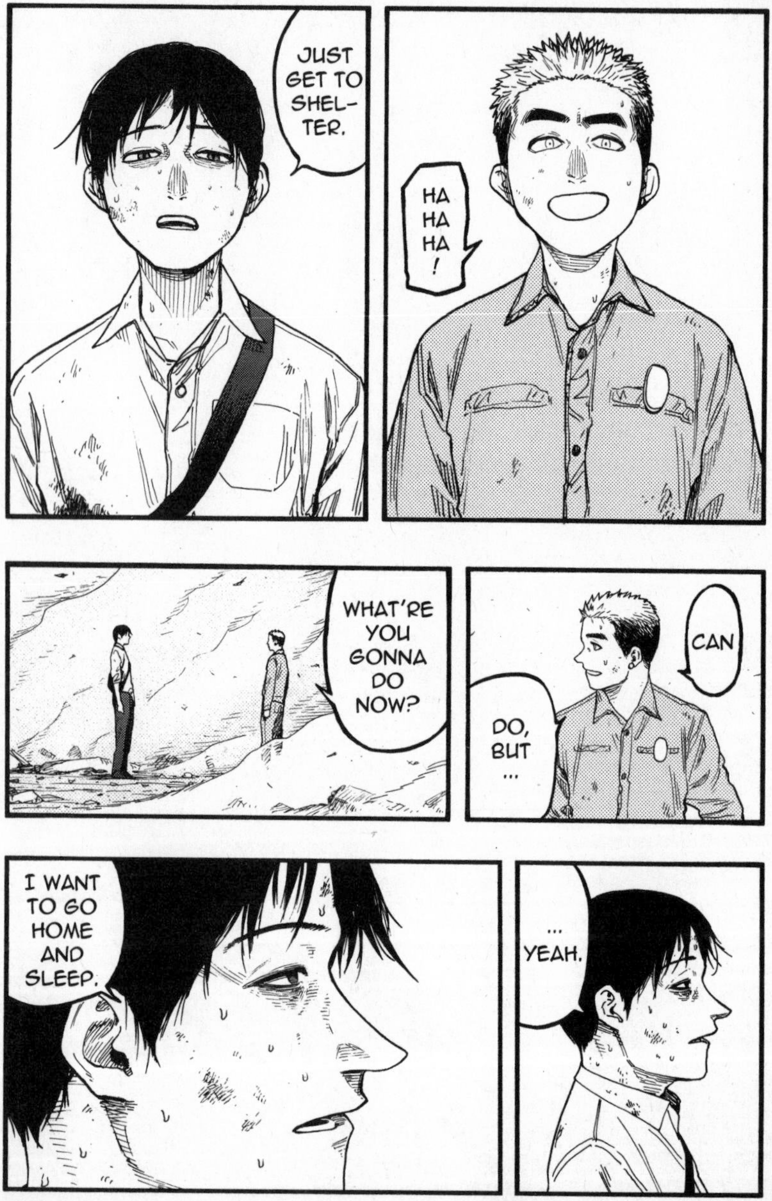
HA HA HA!
JUST GET TO SHEL- TER.
CAN
DO, BUT ...
WHAT'RE YOU GONNA DO NOW?
... YEAH.
I WANT TO GO HOME AND SLEEP.

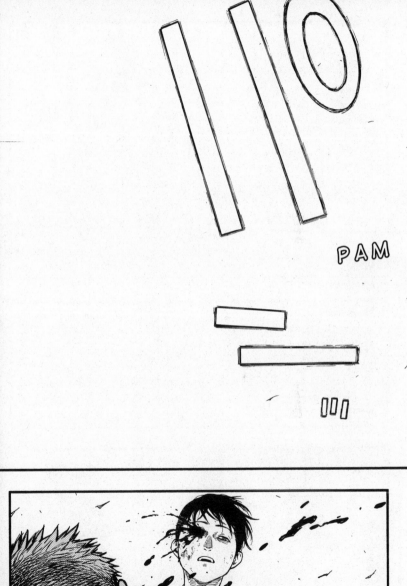

PAM

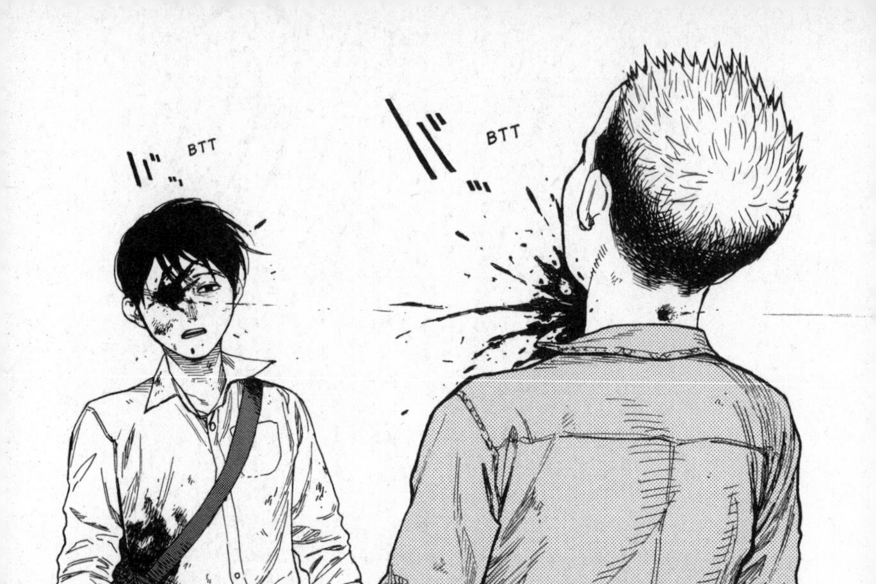
BTT
BTT

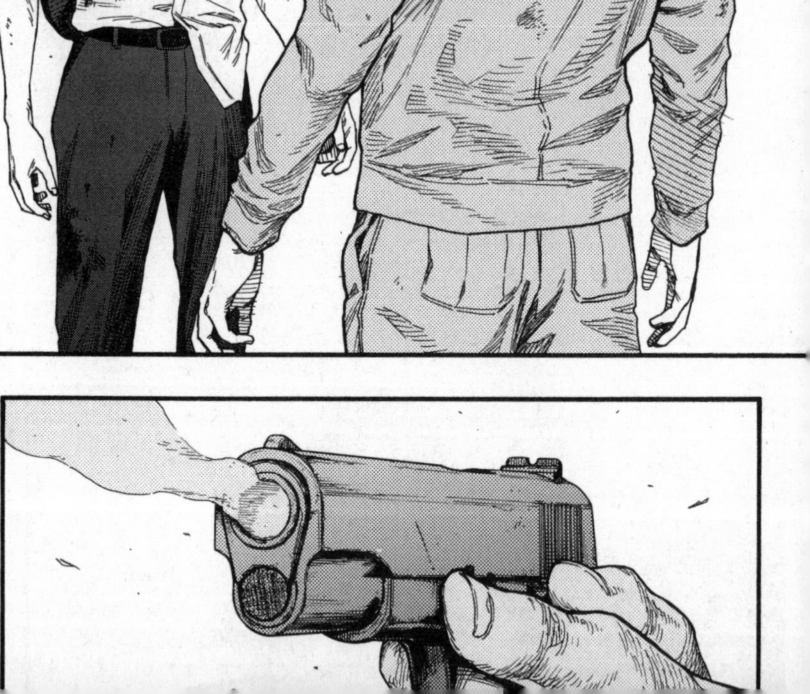

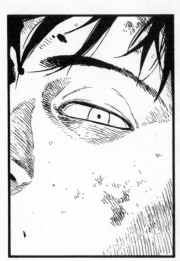

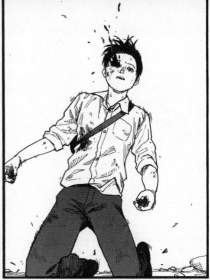

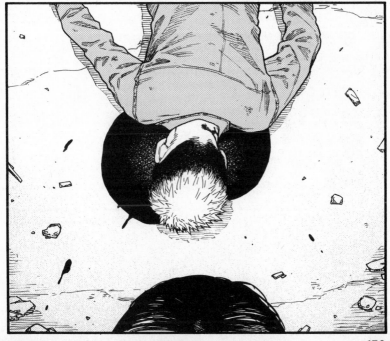

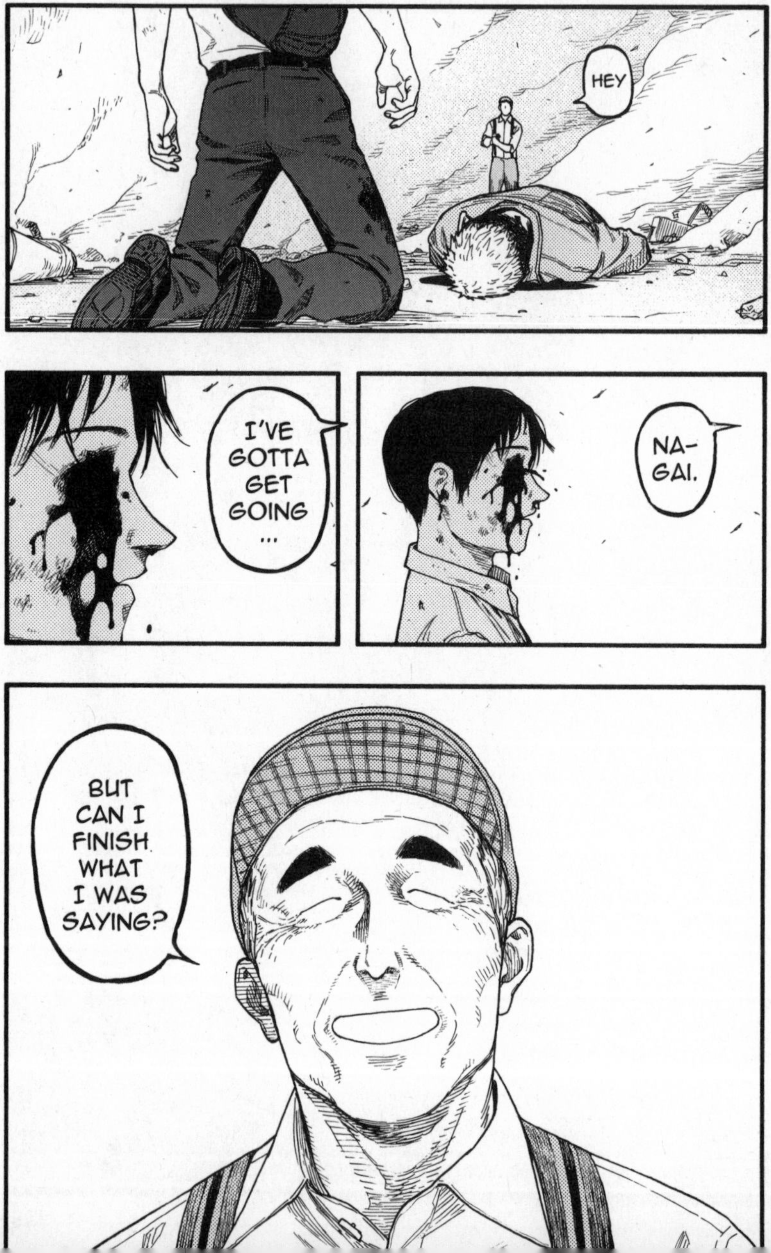
HEY
NA-GAI.
I'VE GOTTA GET GOING ...
BUT CAN I FINISH WHAT I WAS SAYING?

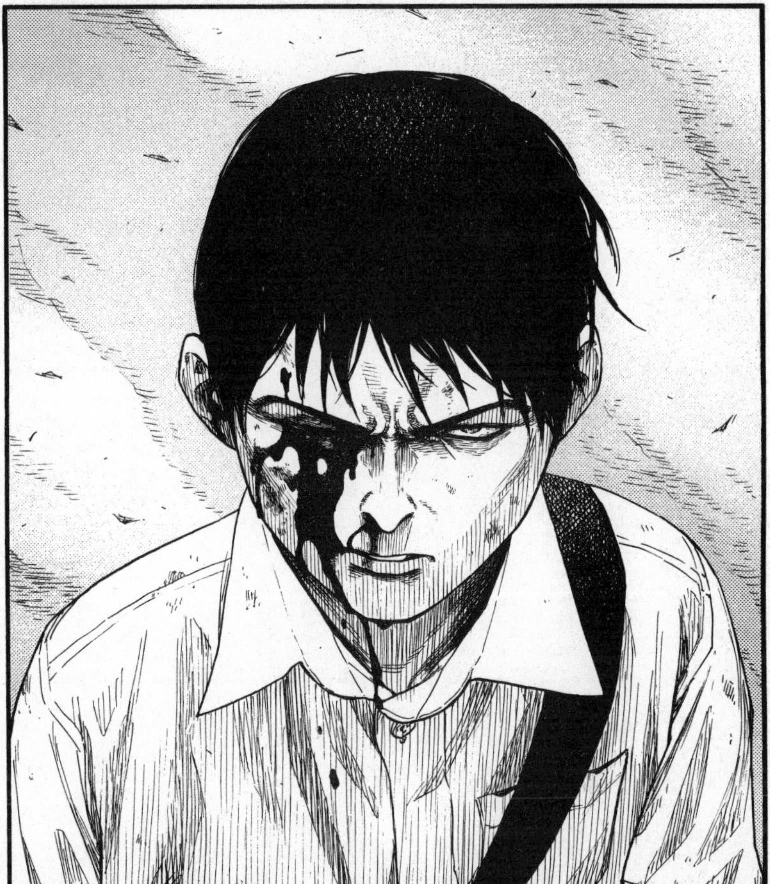

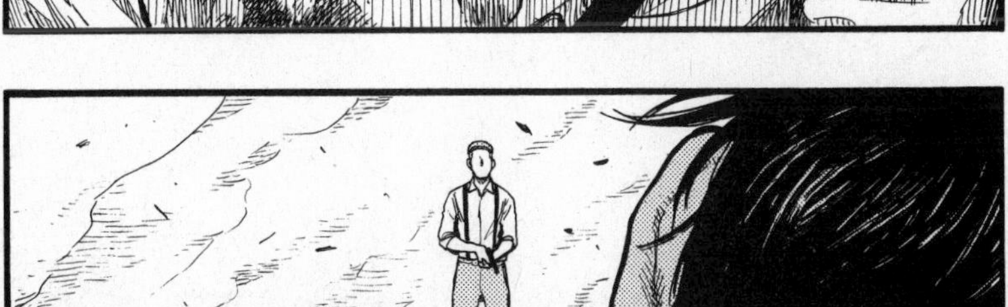

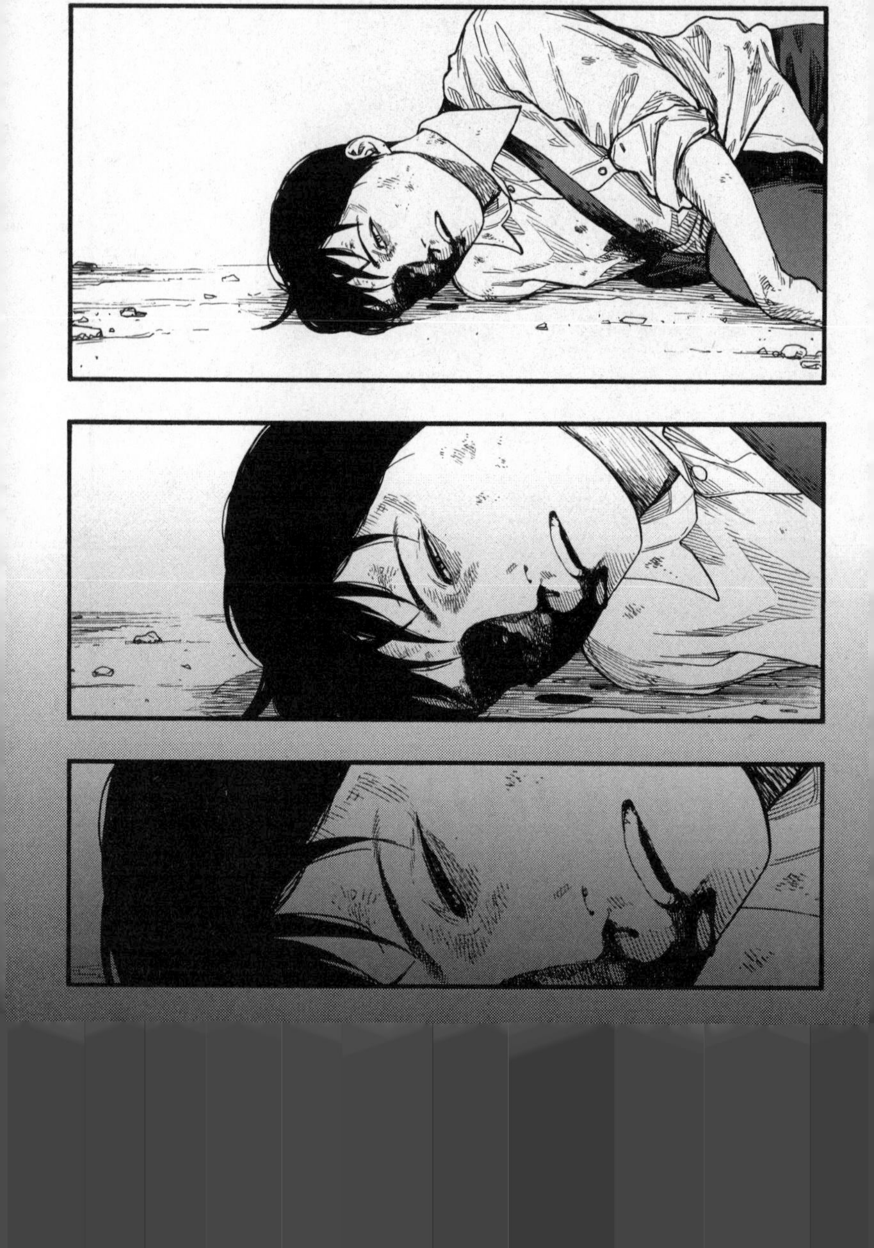

BADUM
ドクン

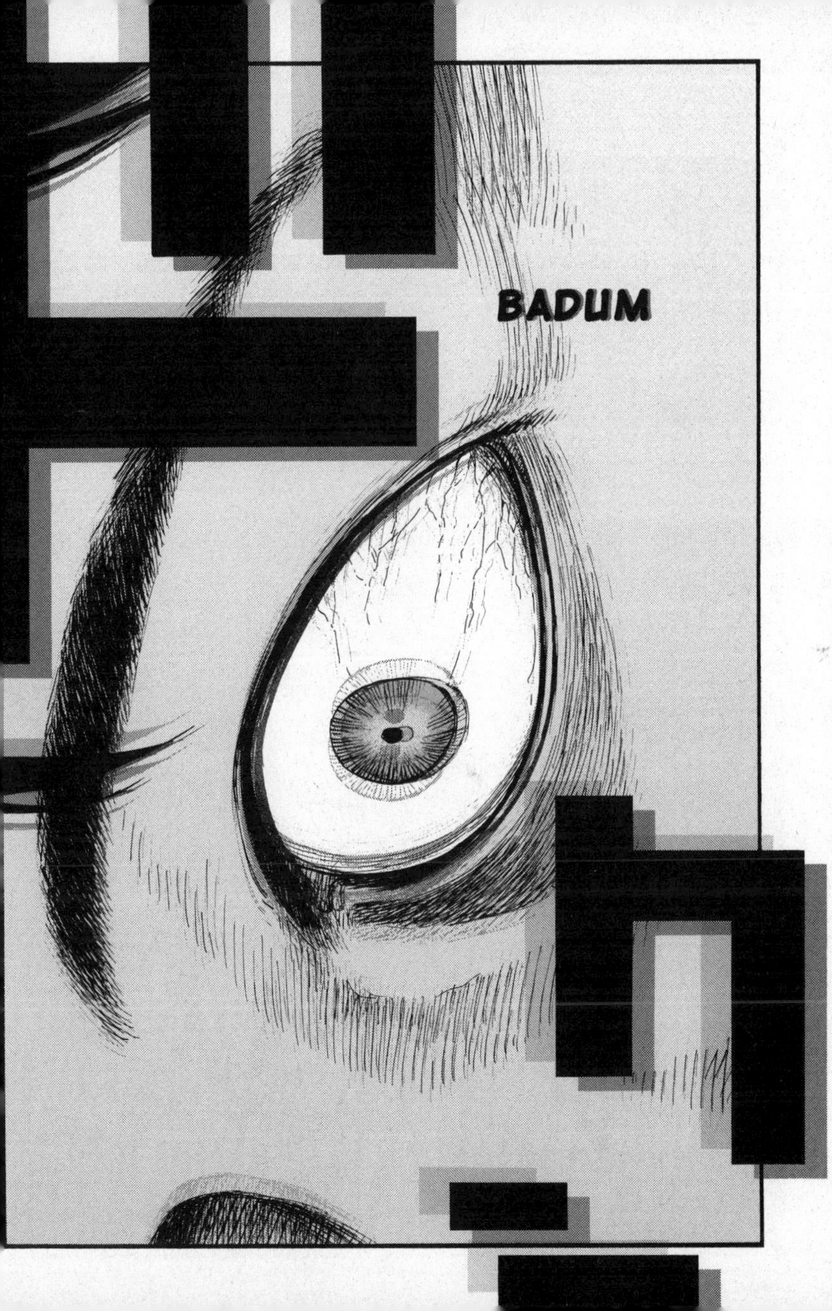
BADUM

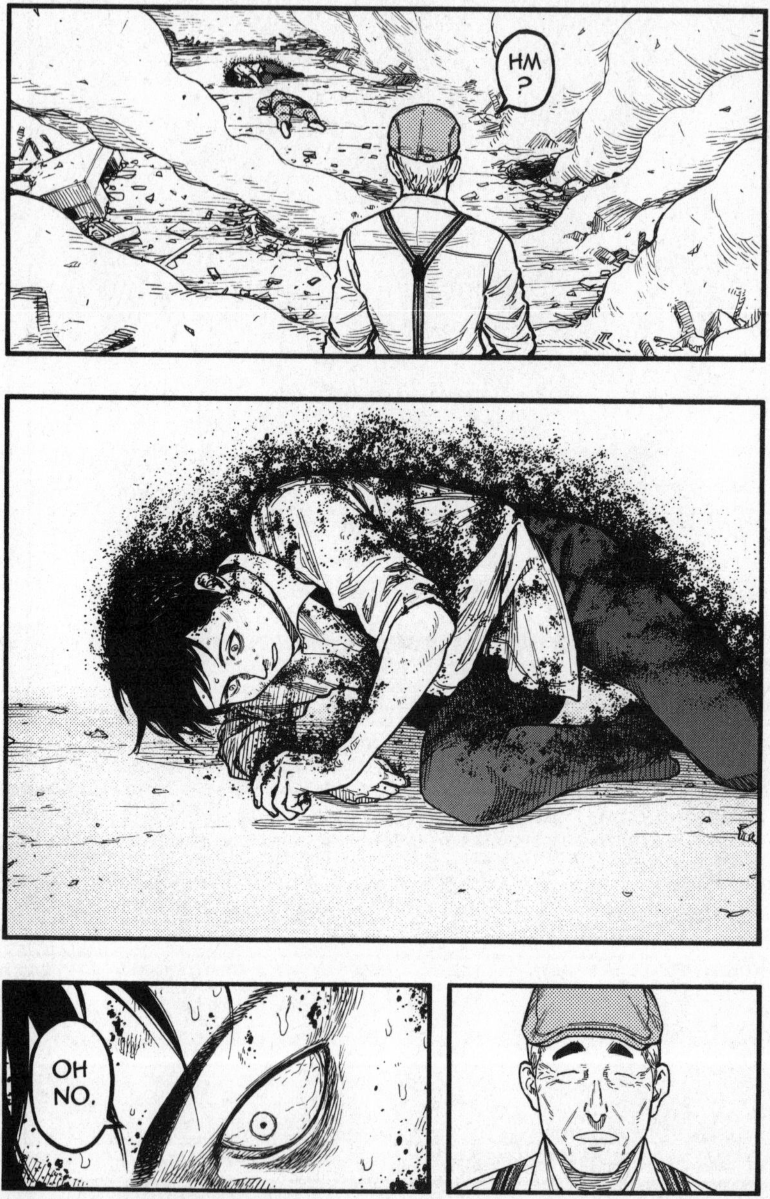
HM?
OH NO.

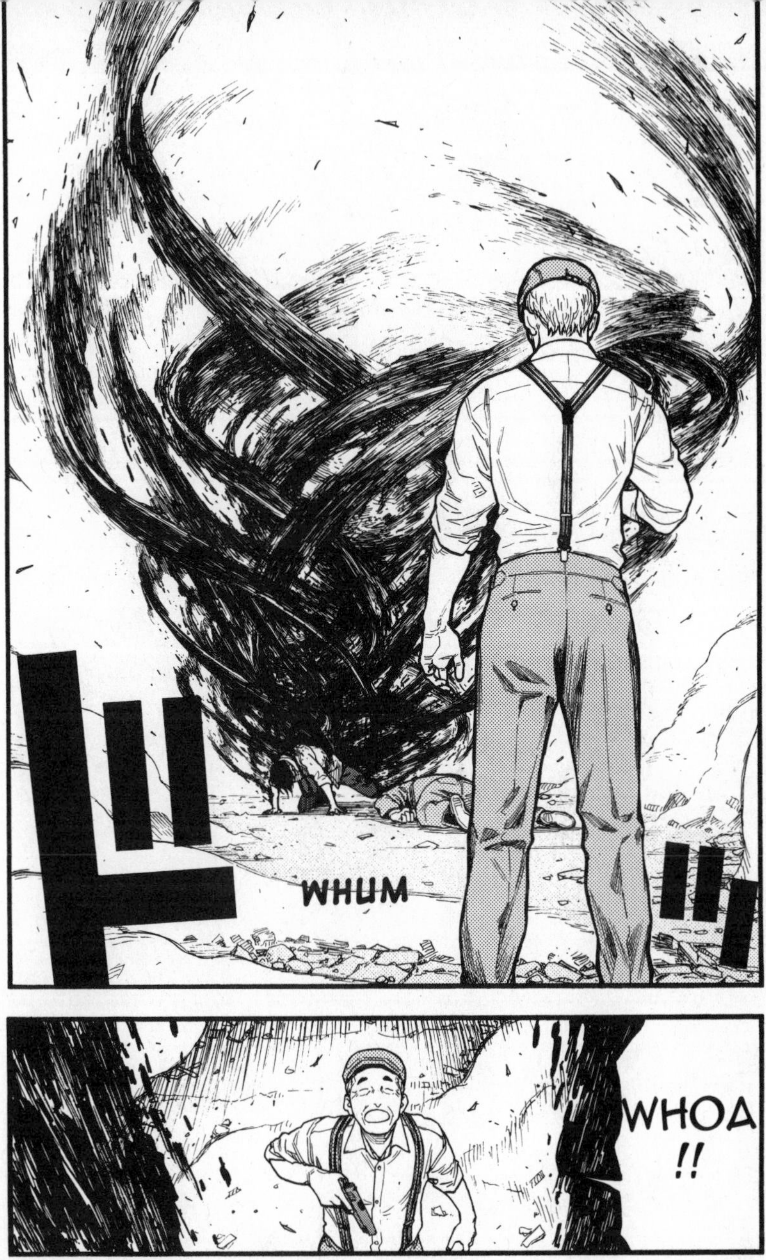
WHUM
WHOA !!

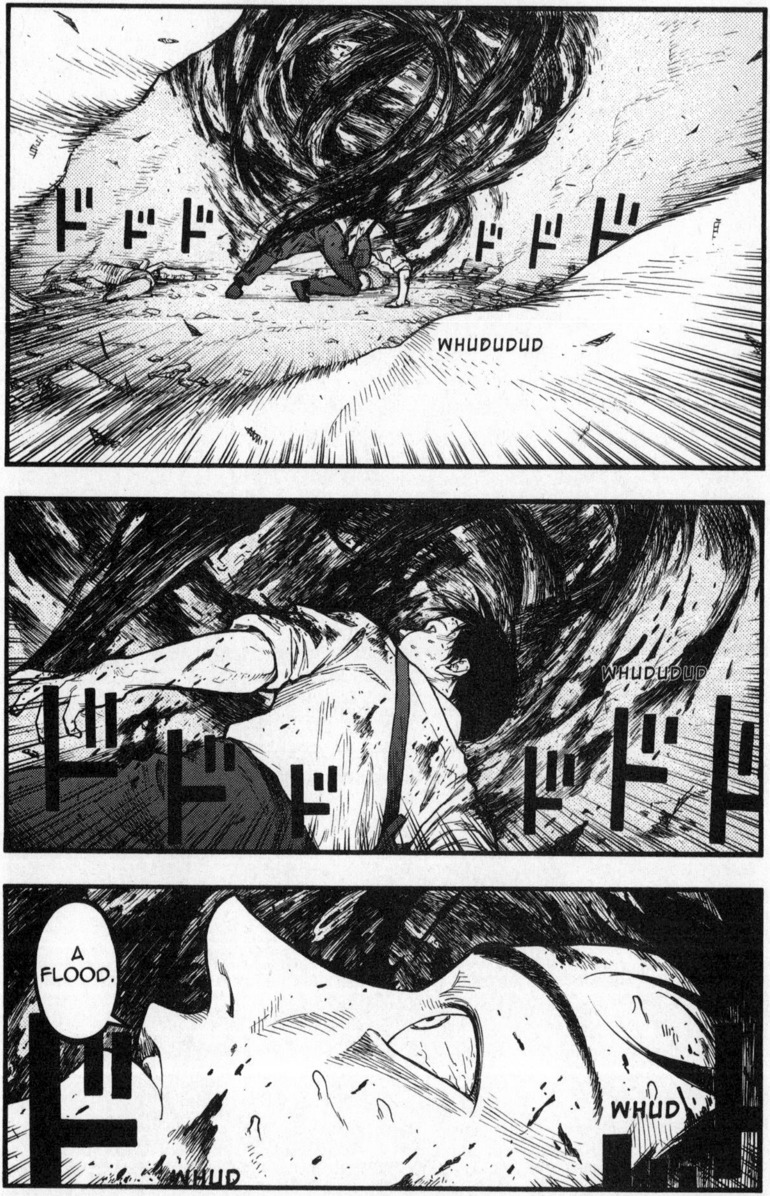
ドドド
ドドド
WHUDUDUD
ドドド
ドドド
WHUDUDUD
A FLOOD.
WHUD
ド
ド
WHUD

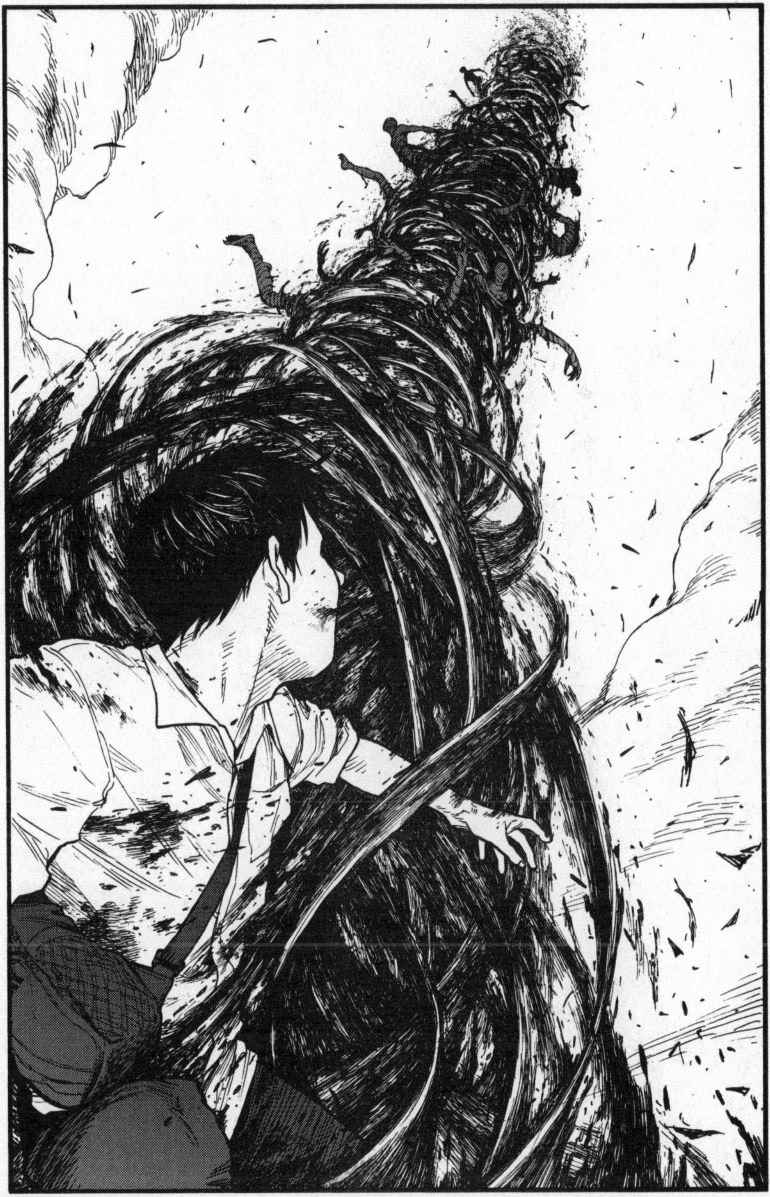

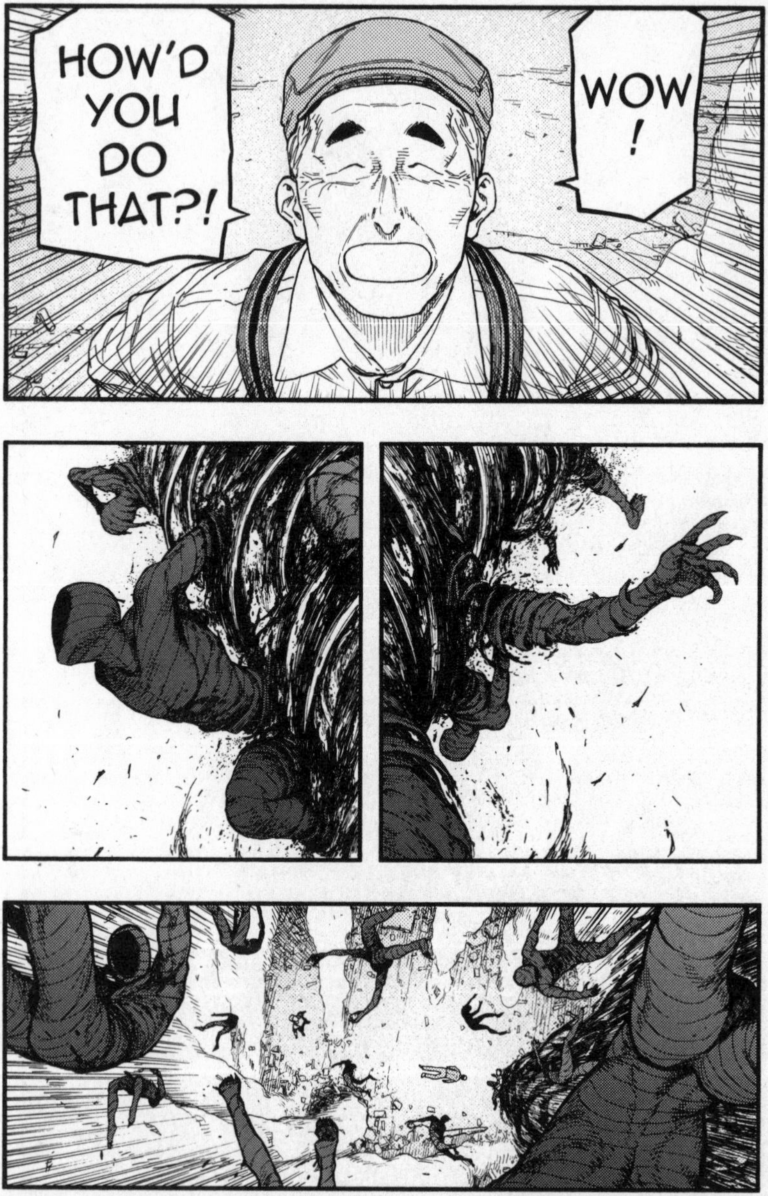
WOW!
HOW'D YOU DO THAT?!

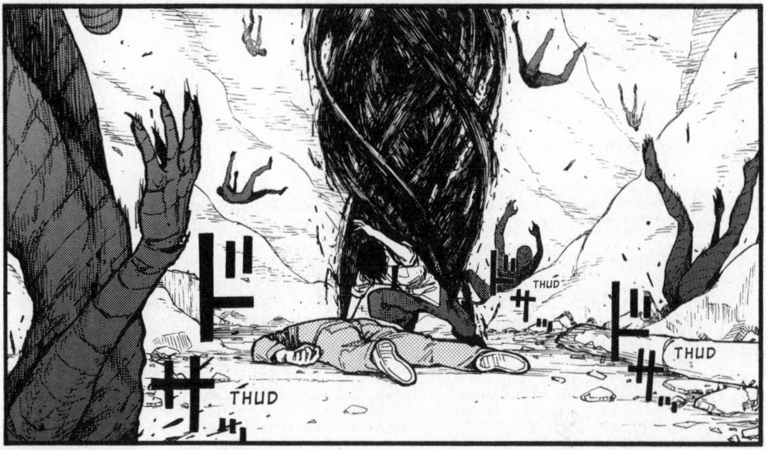
ドサッ
THUD
ドサッ
THUD
ドサッ
THUD
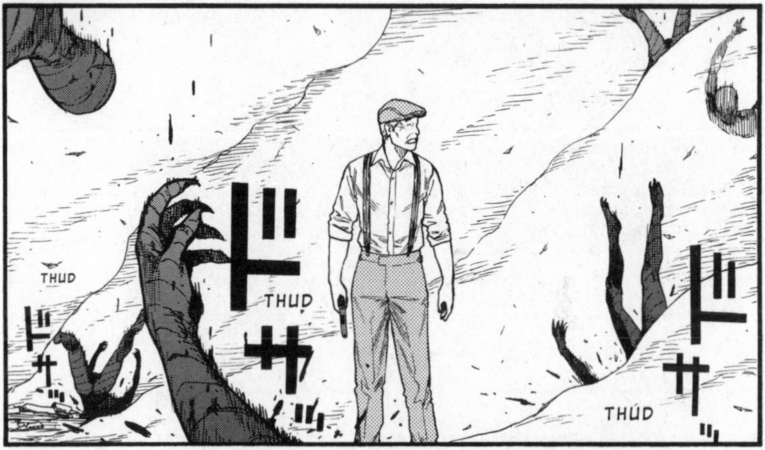
ドサッ
THUD
ドサッ
THUD
ドサッ
THUD
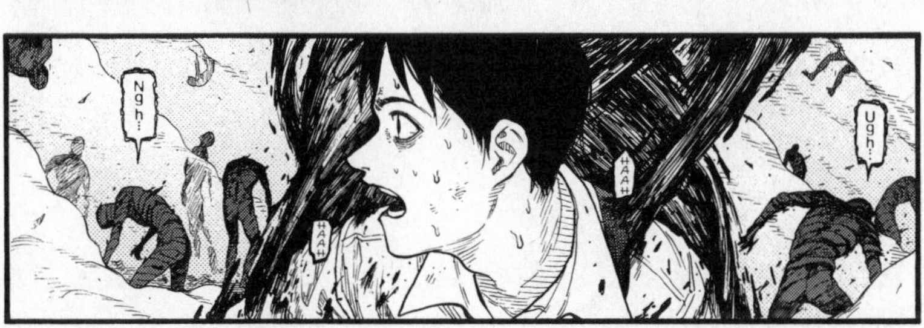
Ugh...
HAAH
HAAH
Ngh...

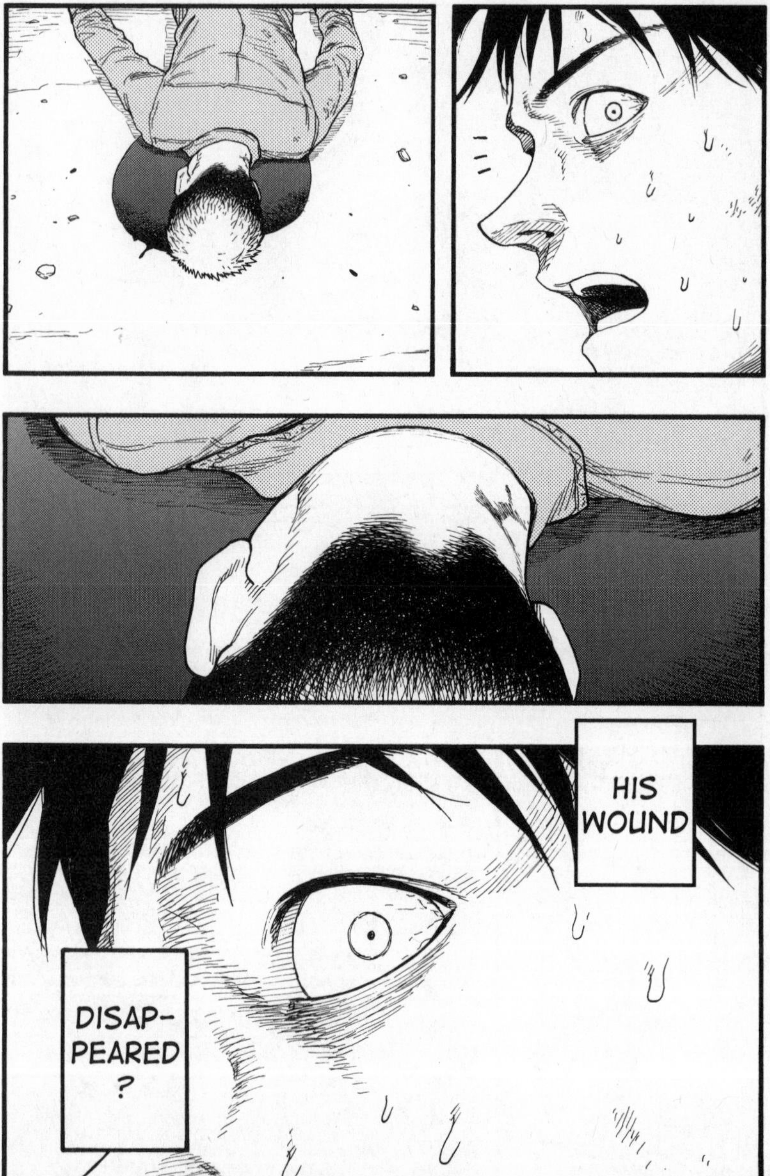
HIS WOUND
DISAP-PEARED?

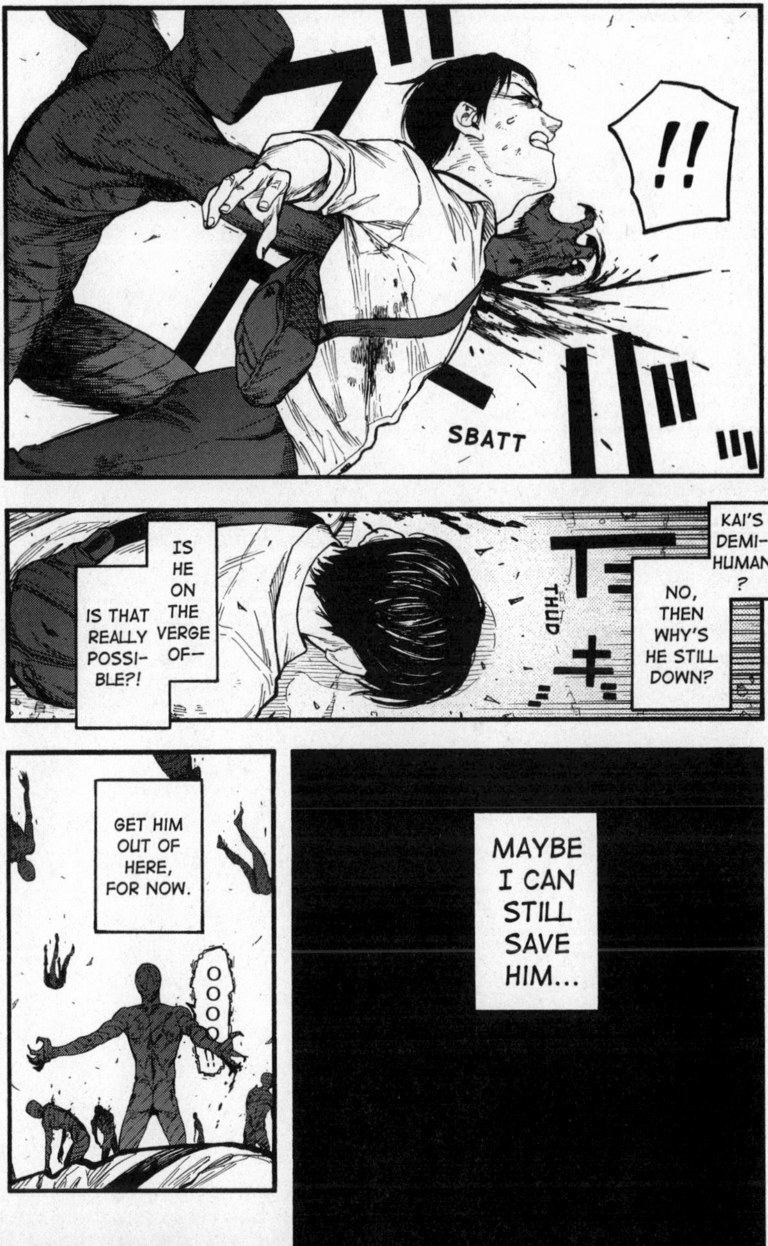
!!
SBATT
KAI'S DEMI-HUMAN?
NO, THEN WHY'S HE STILL DOWN?
THUD
IS HE ON THE VERGE OF—
IS THAT REALLY POSSI-BLE?!
MAYBE I CAN STILL SAVE HIM...
GET HIM OUT OF HERE, FOR NOW.
OOOO

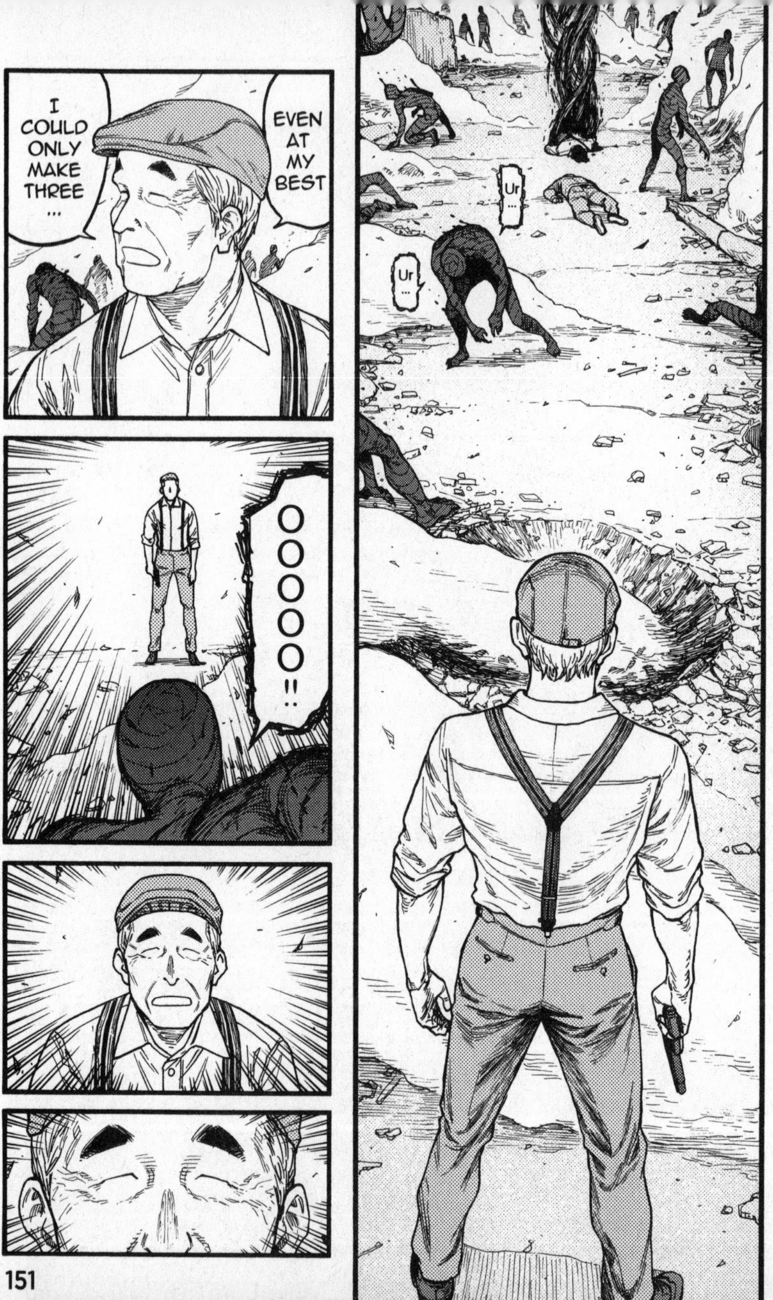
Ur...
Ur...
EVEN AT MY BEST
I COULD ONLY MAKE THREE...
OOOOO!!

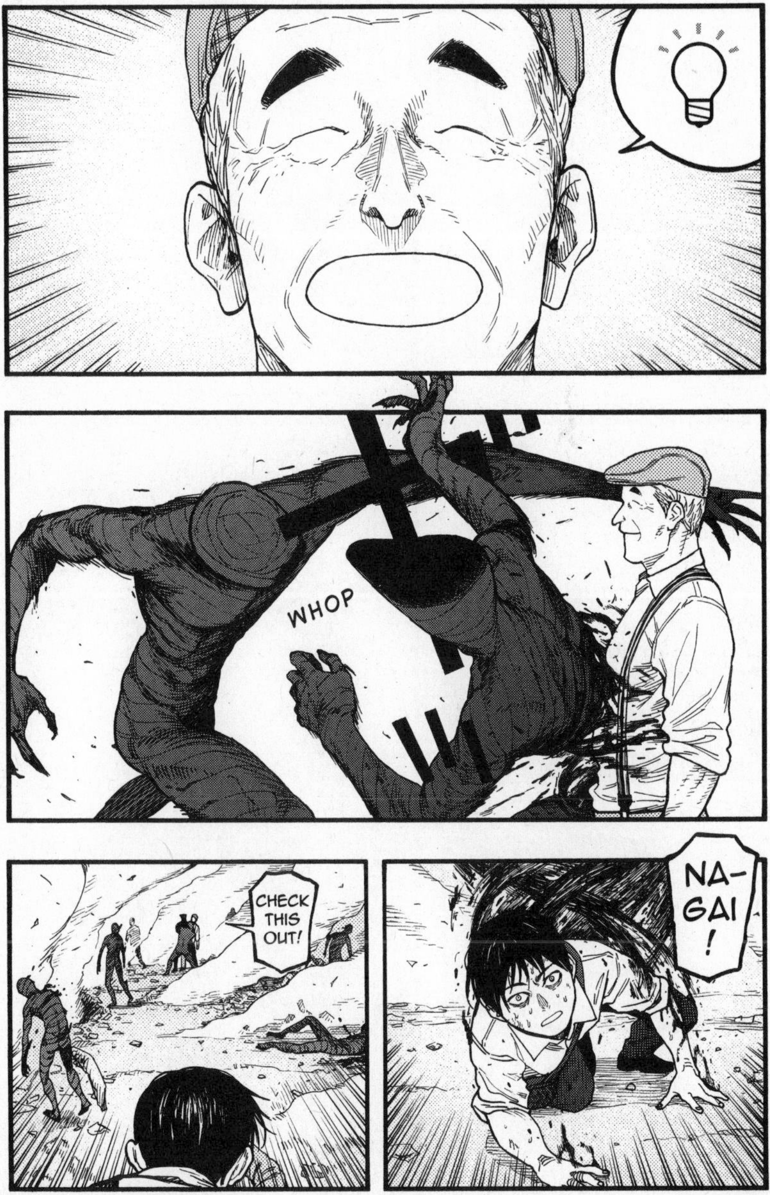
WHOP
NA-GAI!
CHECK THIS OUT!

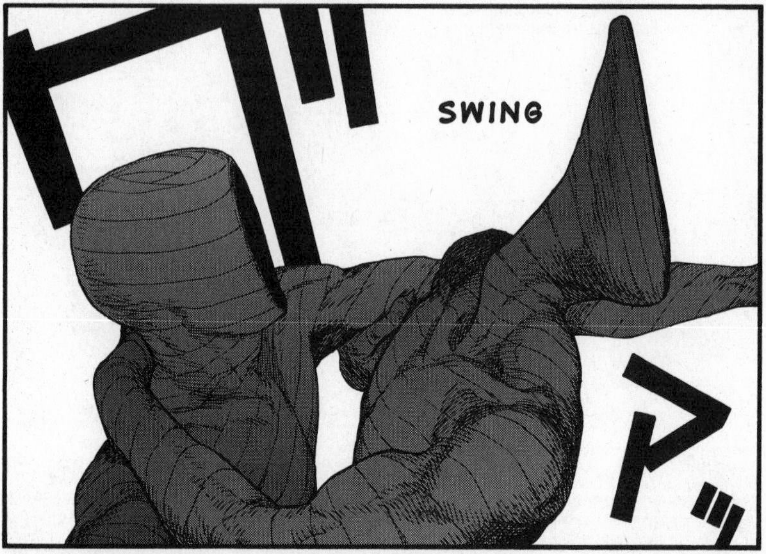
SWING
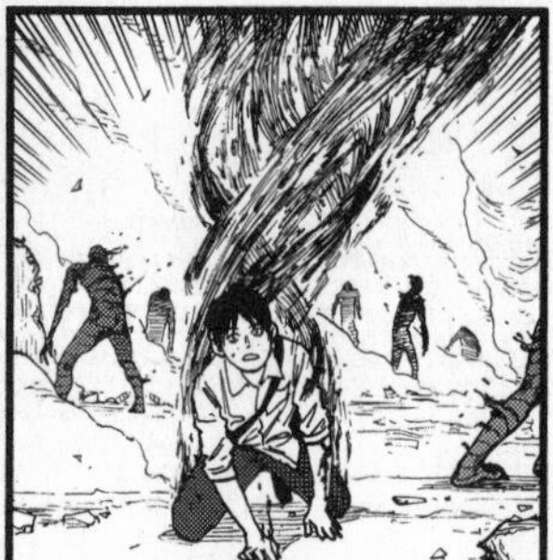
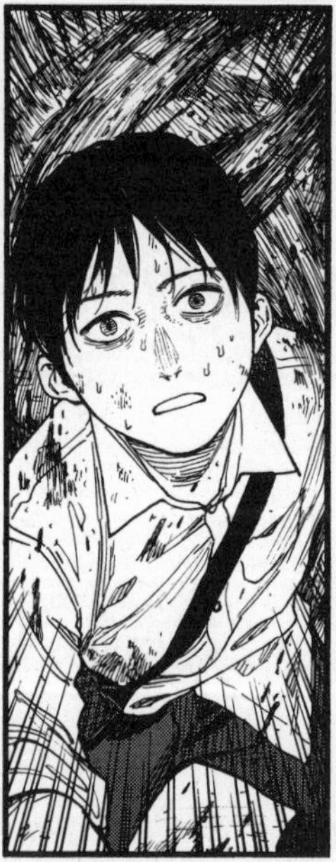
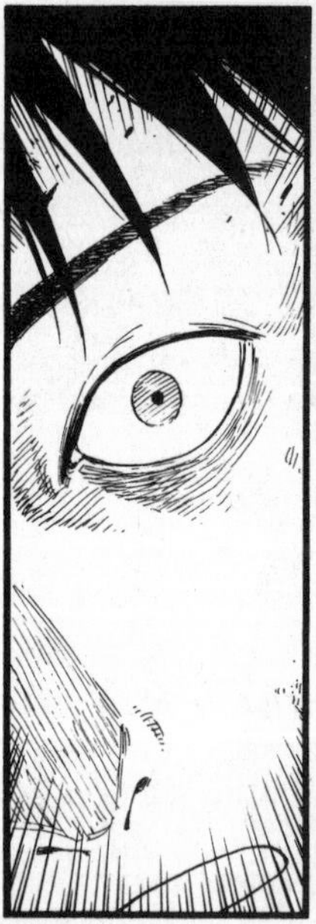

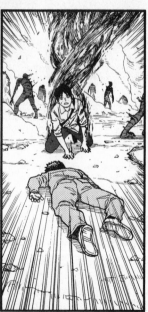

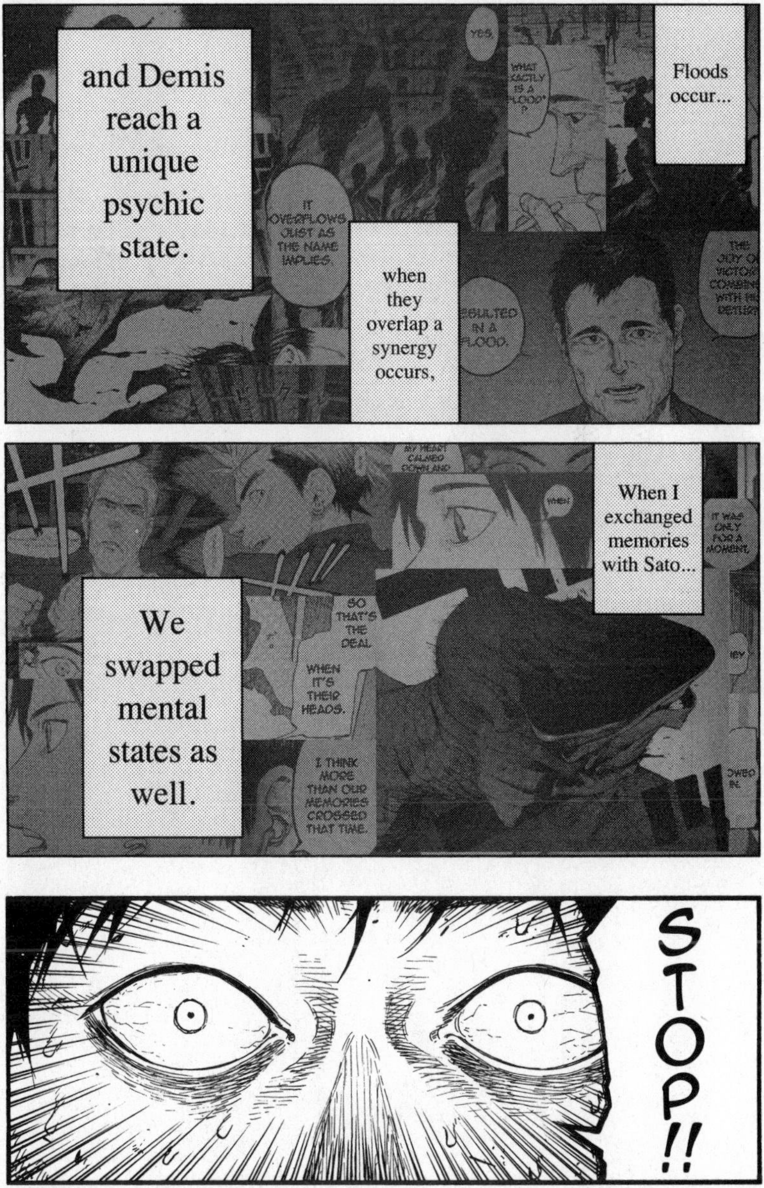
Floods occur...
YES,
WHAT EXACTLY IS A "FLOOD"?
RESULTED IN A FLOOD.
when they overlap a synergy occurs,
IT OVERFLOWS JUST AS THE NAME IMPLIES.
and Demis reach a unique psychic state.
When I exchanged memories with Sato...
IT WAS ONLY FOR A MOMENT.
SO THAT'S THE DEAL
WHEN IT'S THEIR HEADS.
I THINK MORE THAN OUR MEMORIES CROSSED THAT TIME.
We swapped mental states as well.
STOP!!

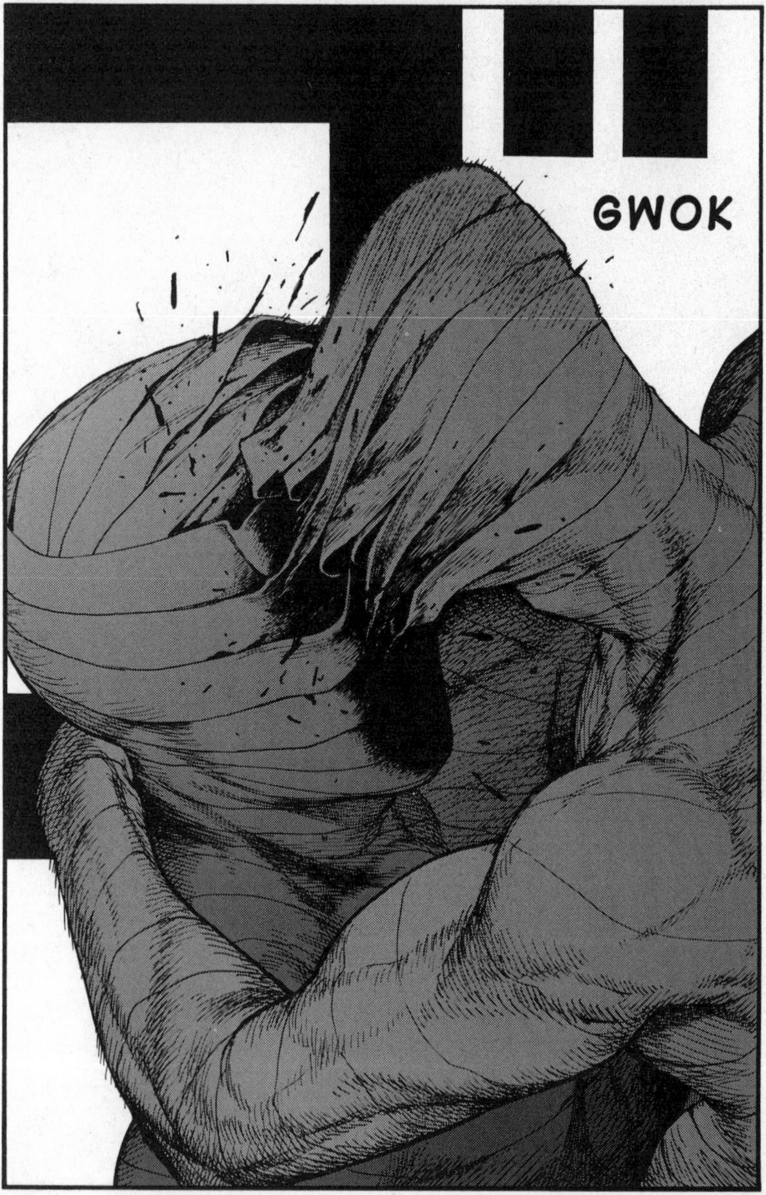
GWOK

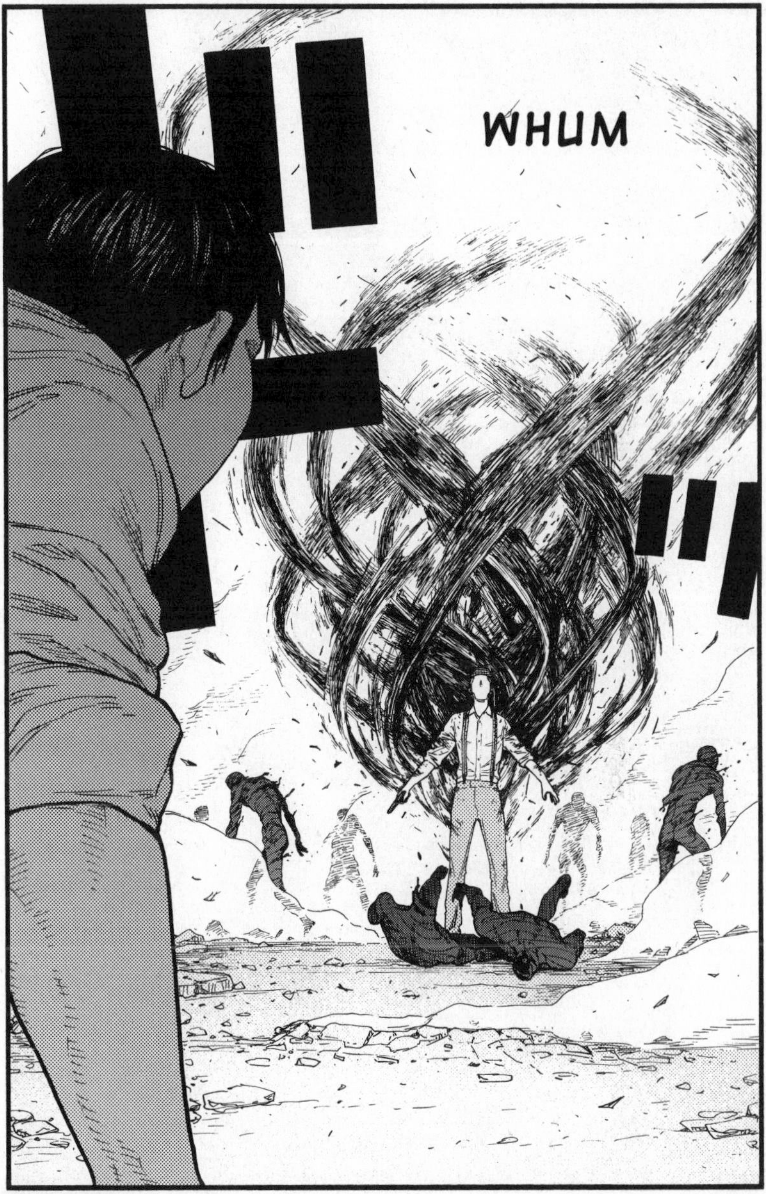
WHUM

File: 73

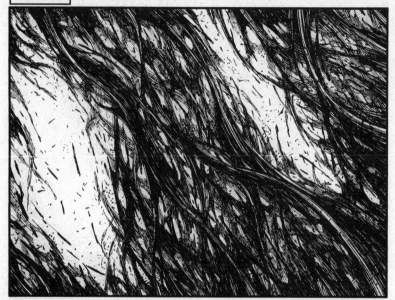

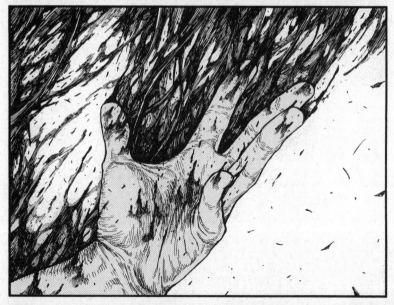

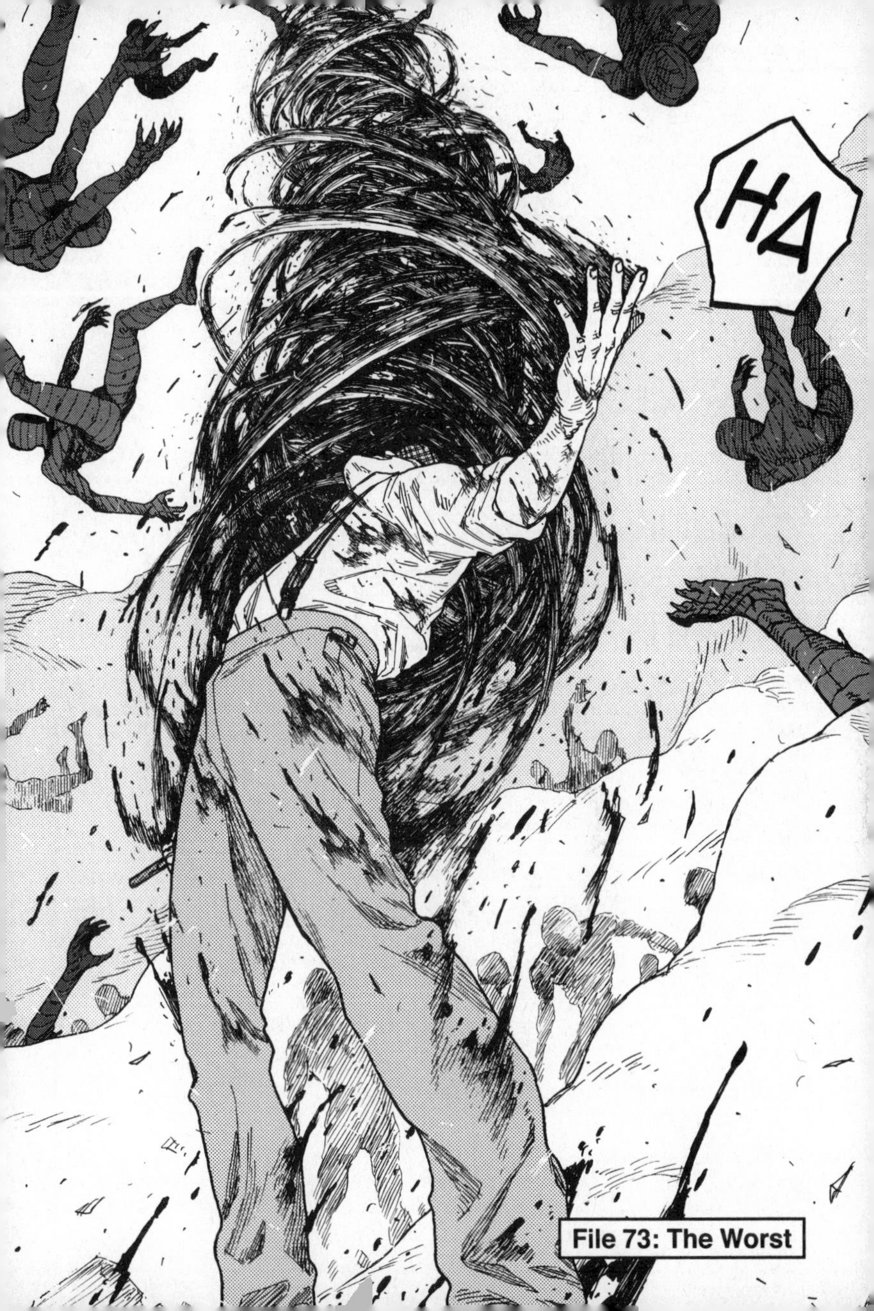
HA
File 73: The Worst

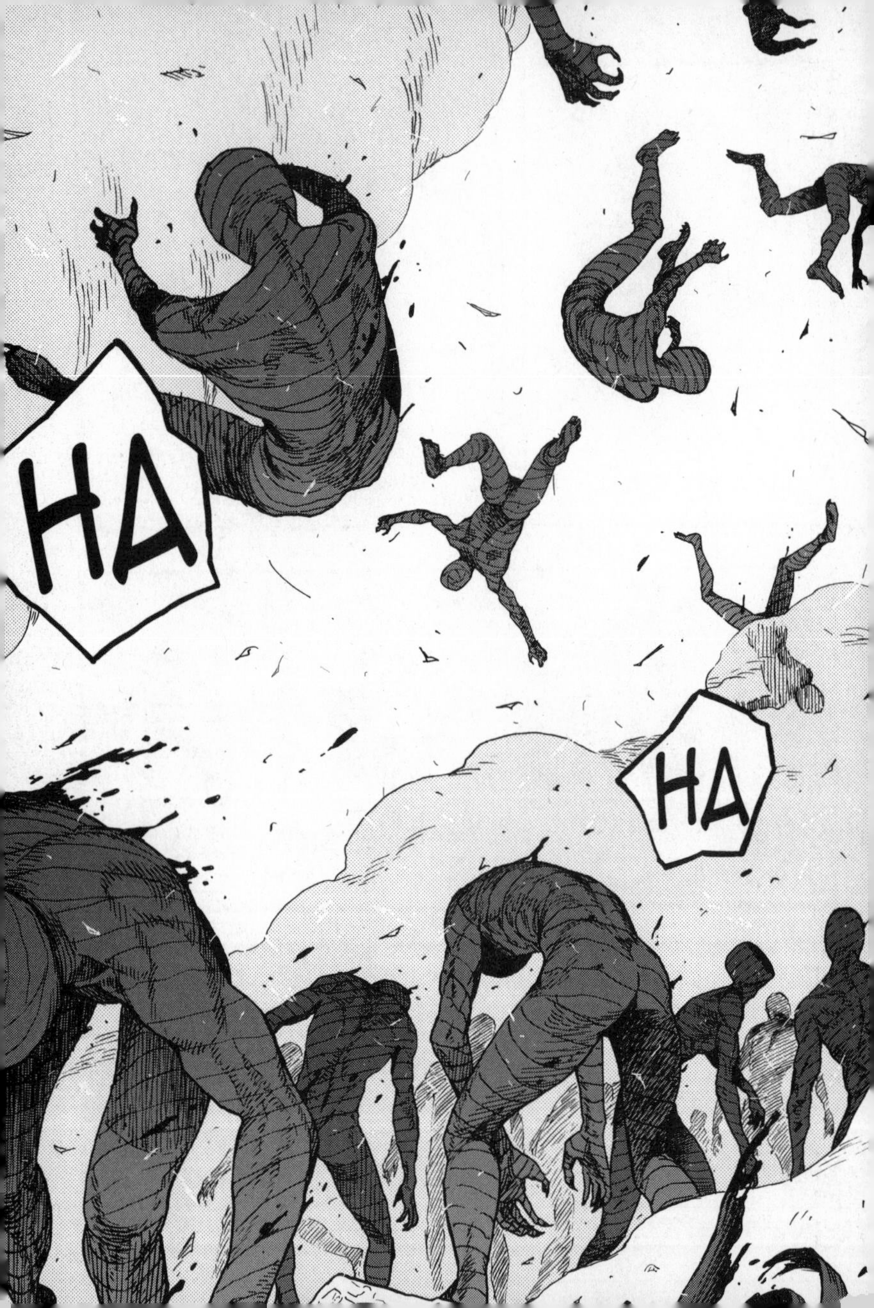
HA
HA

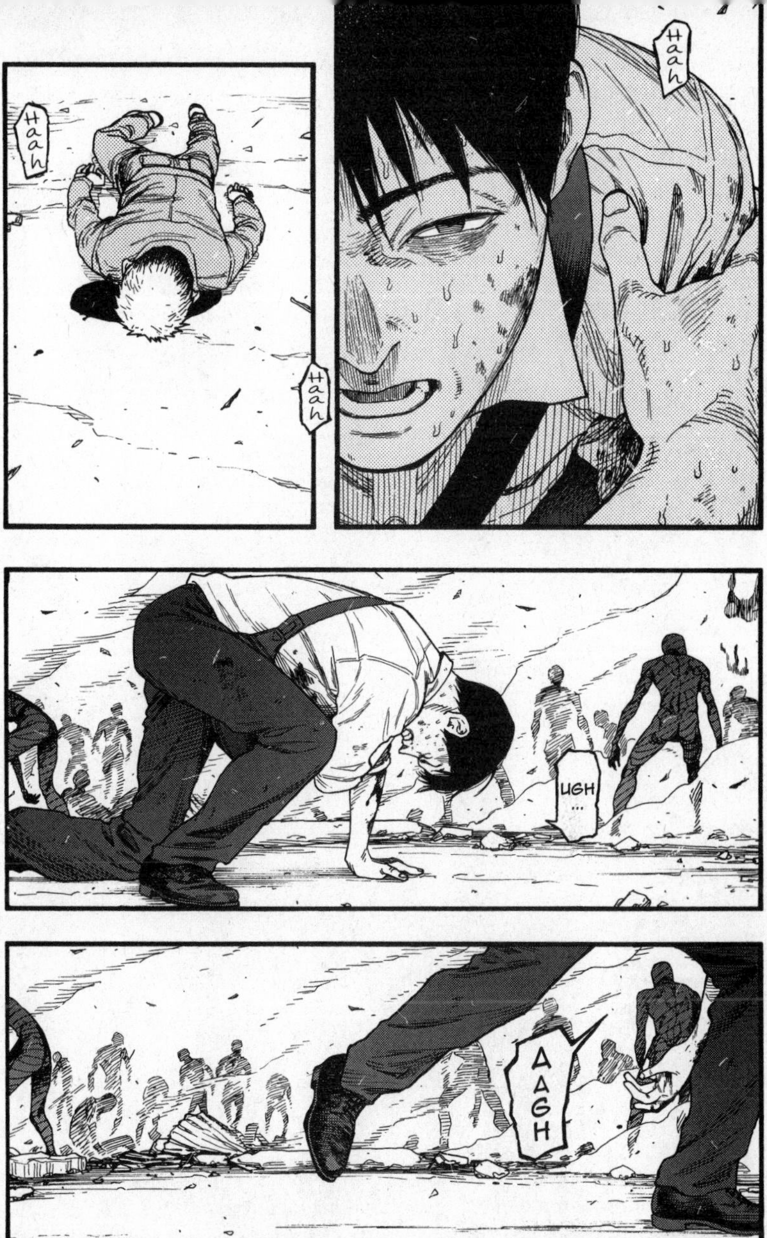
Haah
Haah
Haah
UGH...
AAGH

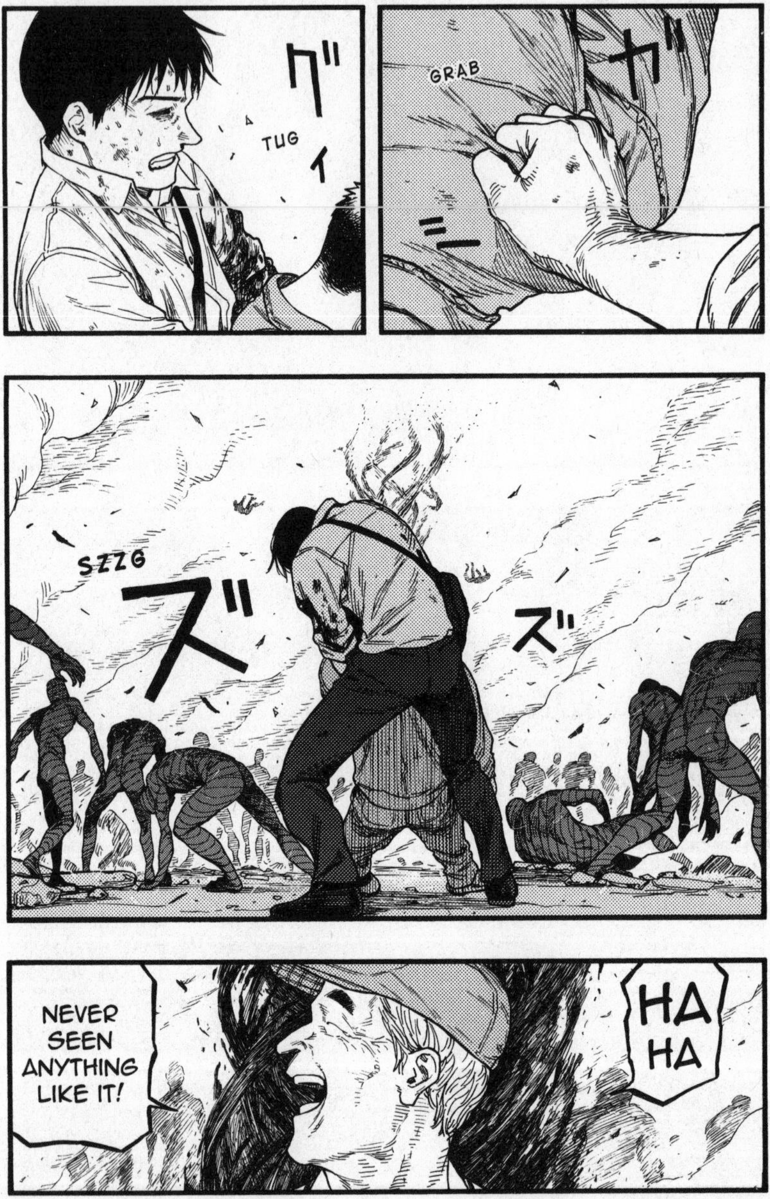
GRAB
TUG
グイ
SZZG
ズズ
HA
HA
NEVER SEEN ANYTHING LIKE IT!

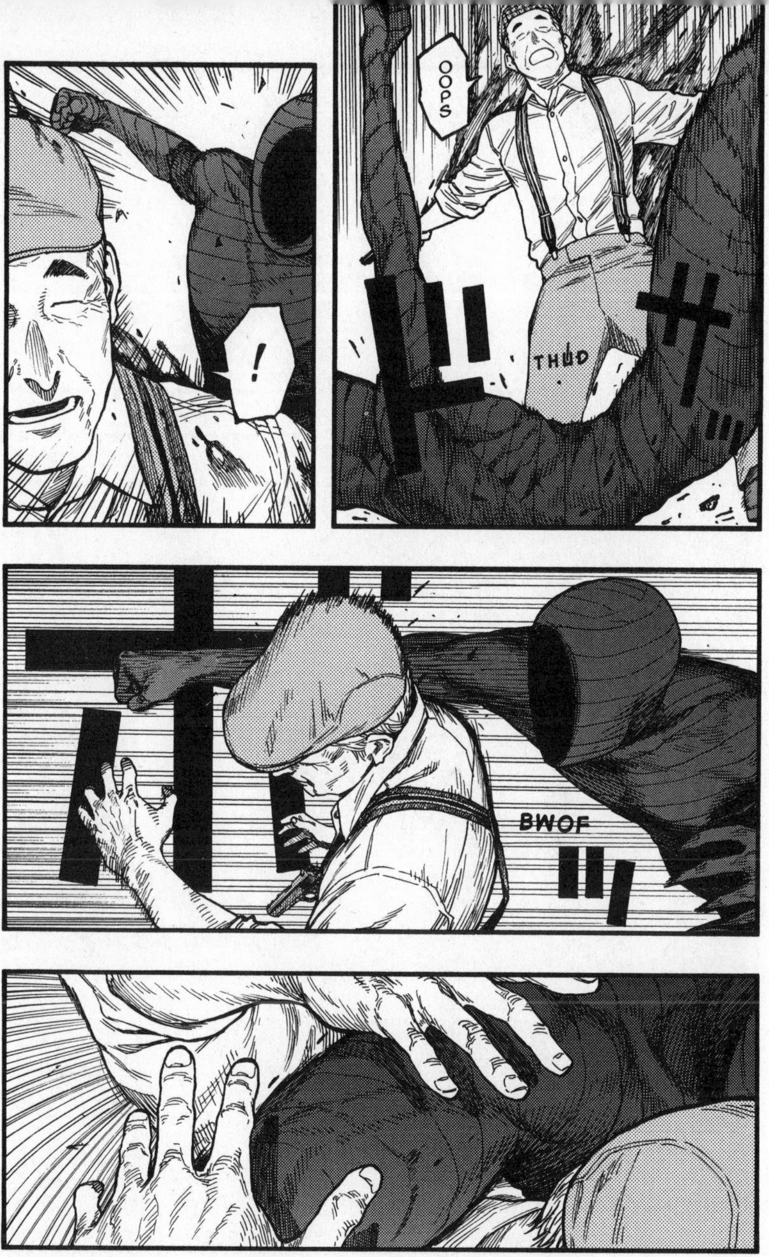
OOPS
THUD
!
BWOF

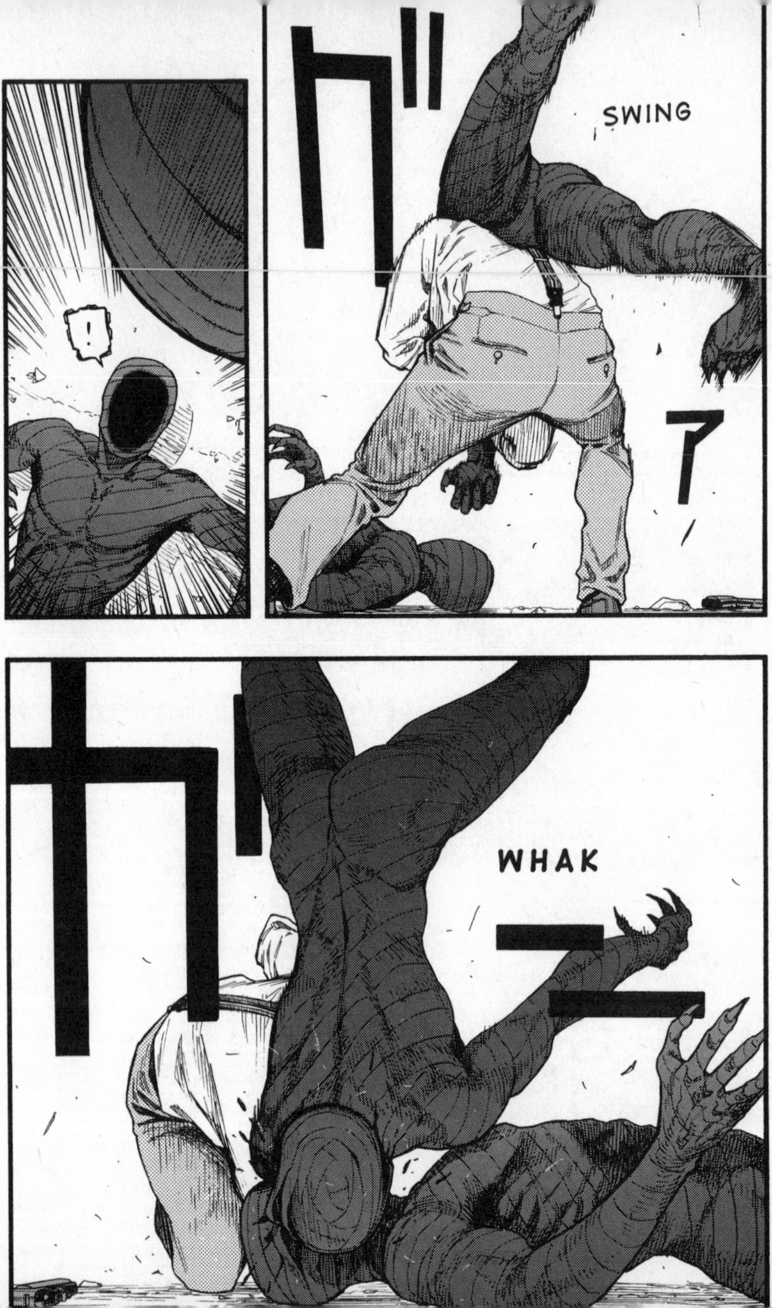

SWING
!
WHAK

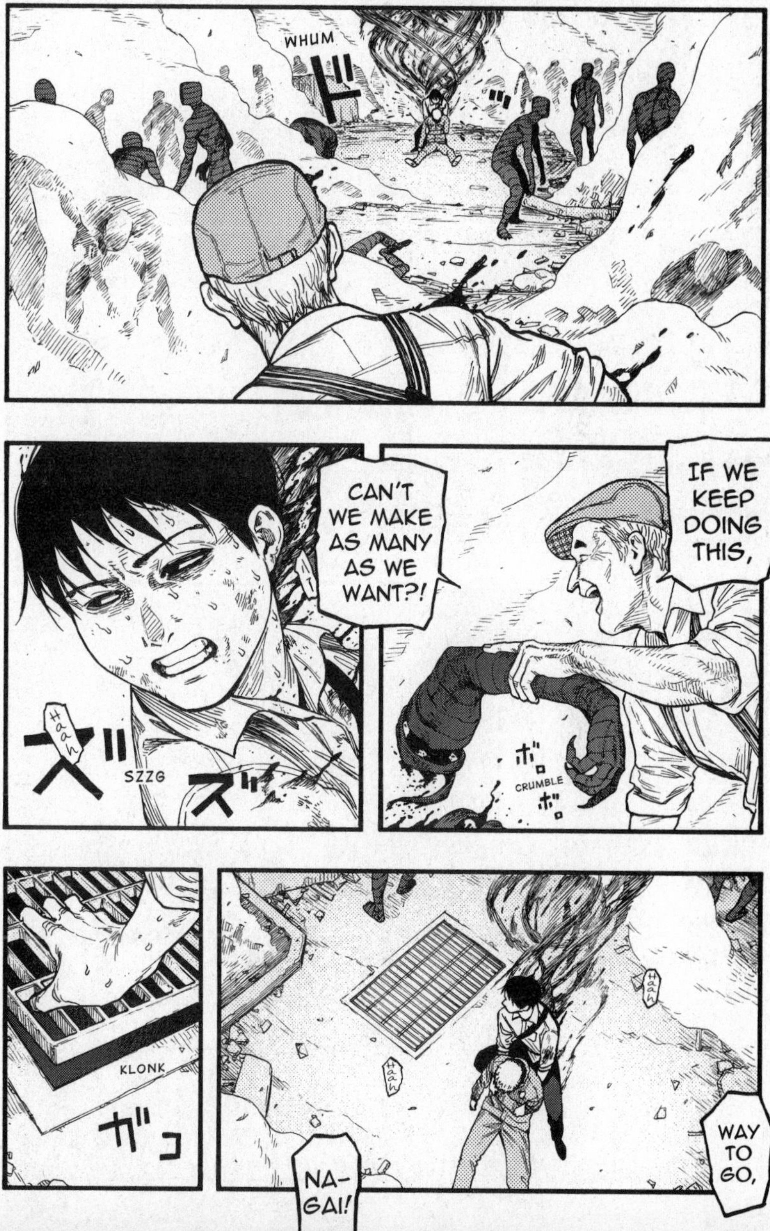
WHUM
ドドッ
IF WE KEEP DOING THIS,
ボロ
CRUMBLE
ボロ
CAN'T WE MAKE AS MANY AS WE WANT?!
Haah
ズズ
SZZG
Haah
Haah
WAY TO GO,
NA-GAI!
KLONK
ガコ

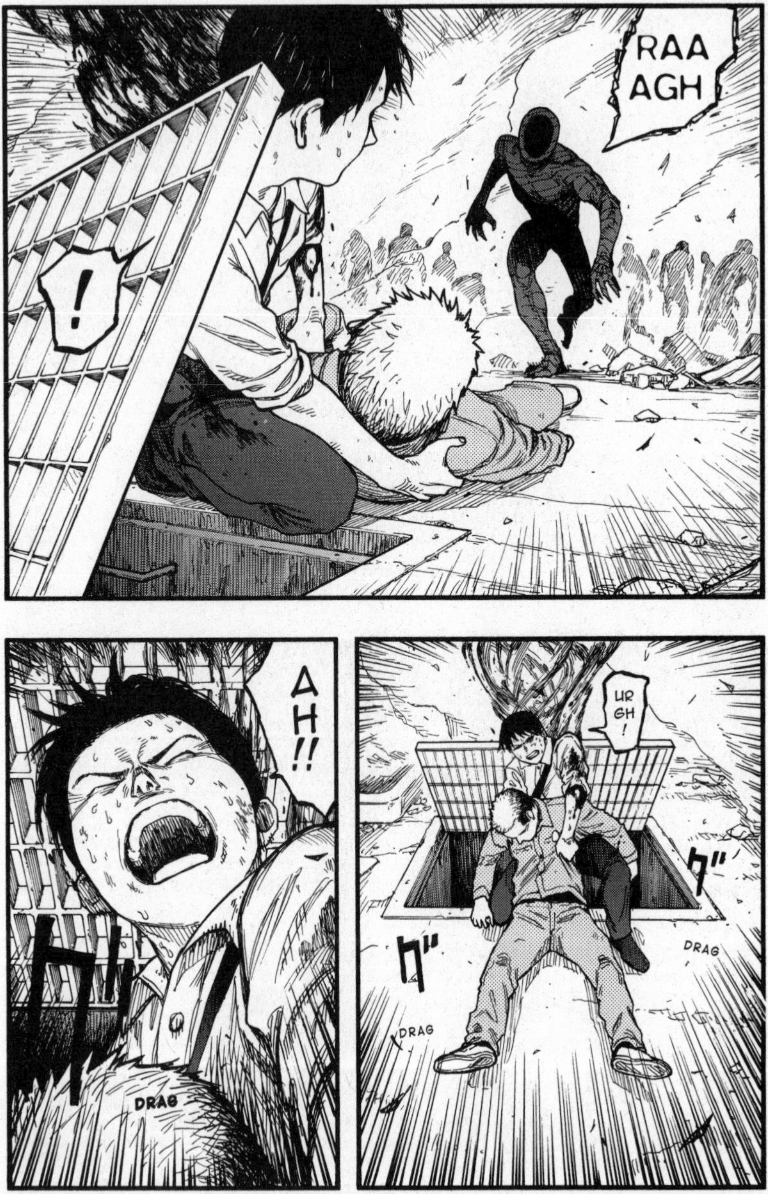
RAA AGH
!
URGH!
グ
DRAG
グ
DRAG
AH!!
グッ
DRAG

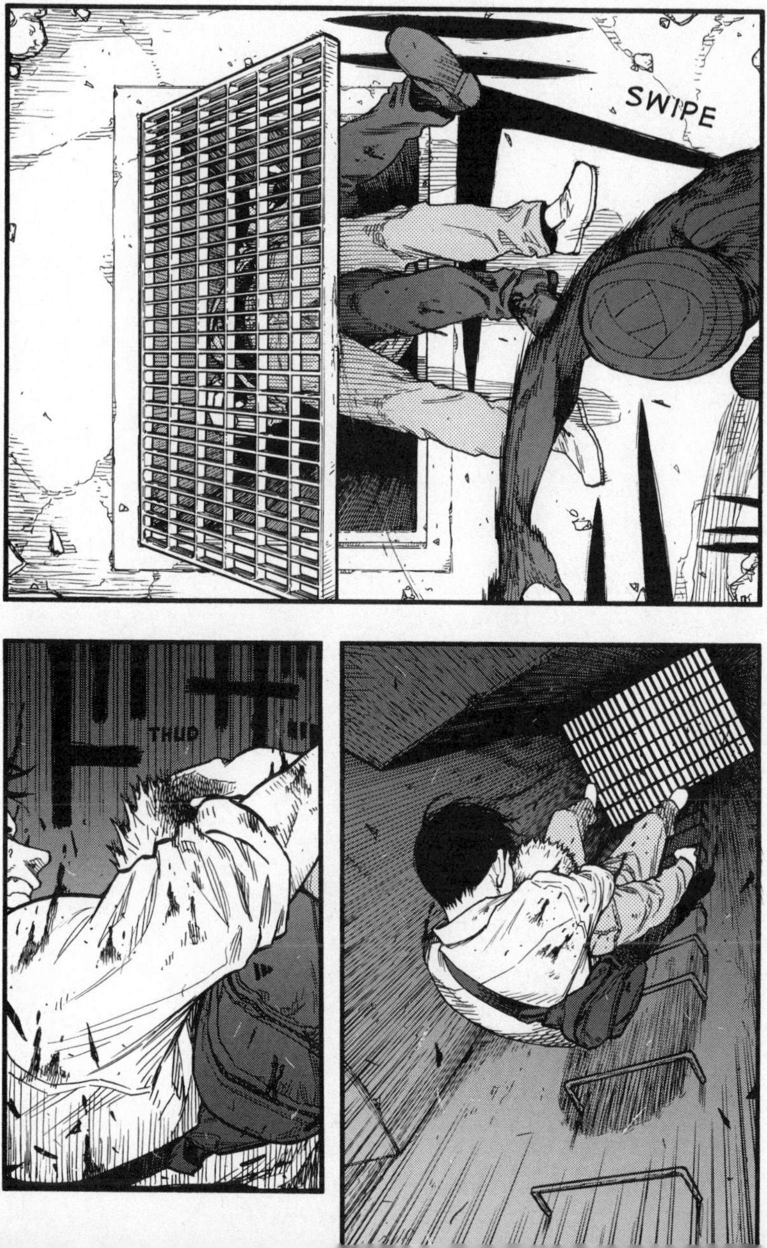
SWIPE
THUD

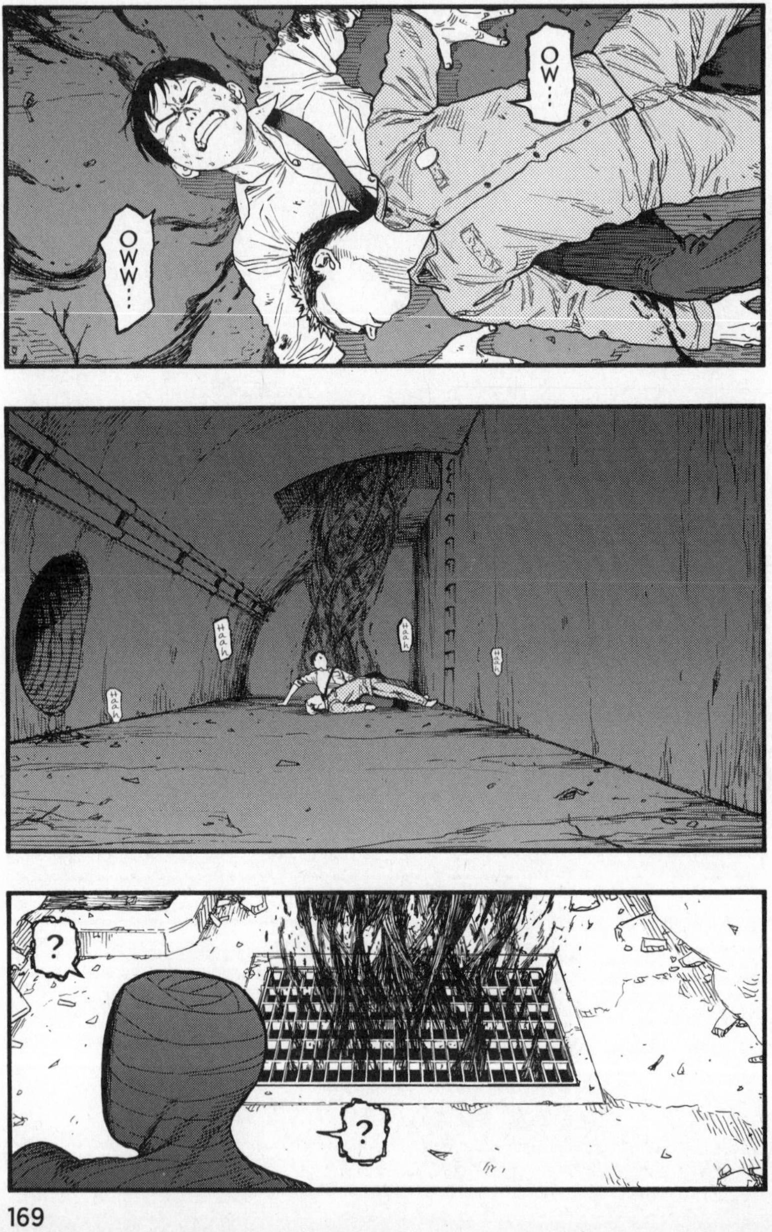
OW...
OWW...
Haah
Haah
Haah
Haah
?
?

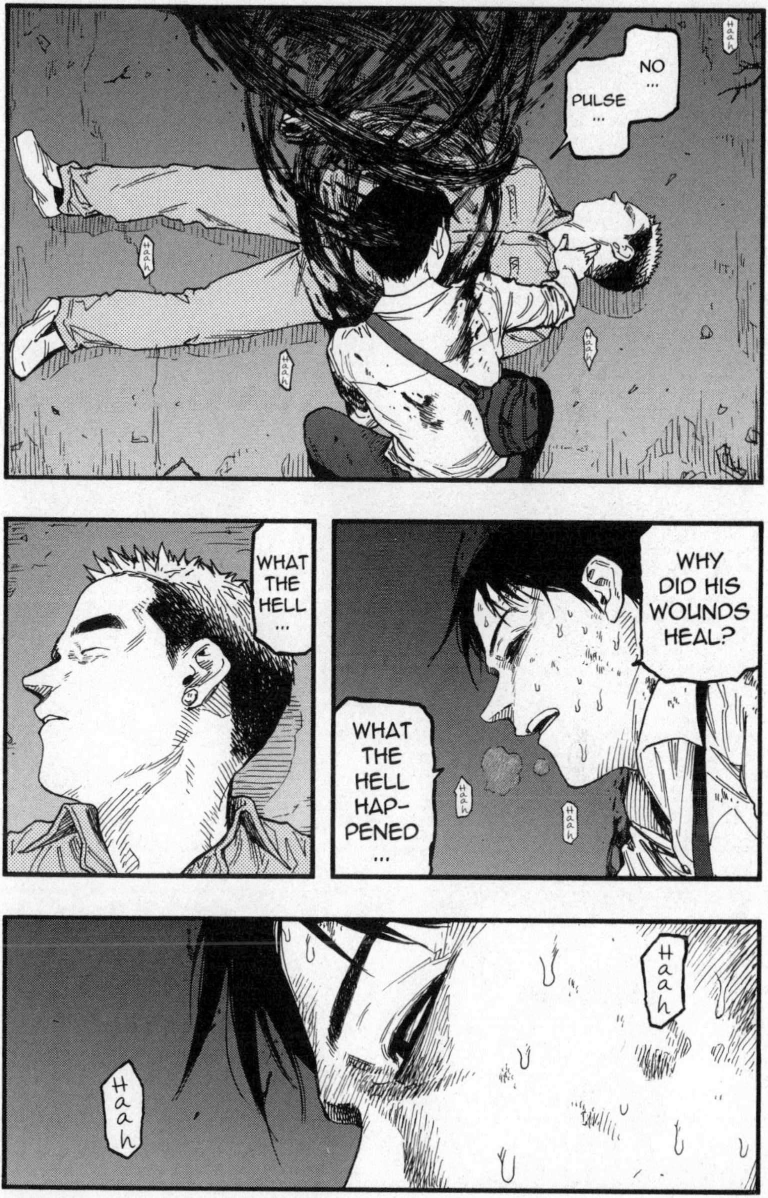

Haah
NO ... PULSE ...
Haah
Haah
Haah
WHY DID HIS WOUNDS HEAL?
WHAT THE HELL HAPPENED ...
Haah
Haah
WHAT THE HELL ...
Haah
Haah

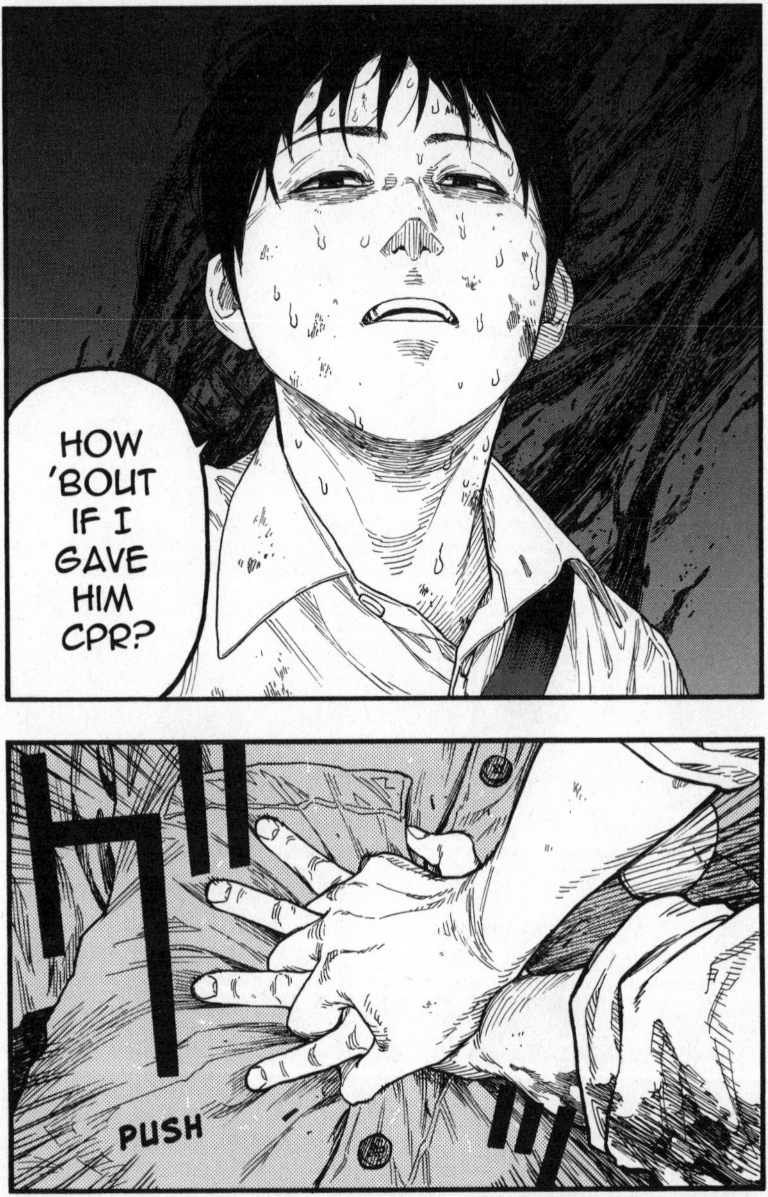
HOW 'BOUT IF I GAVE HIM CPR?
PUSH

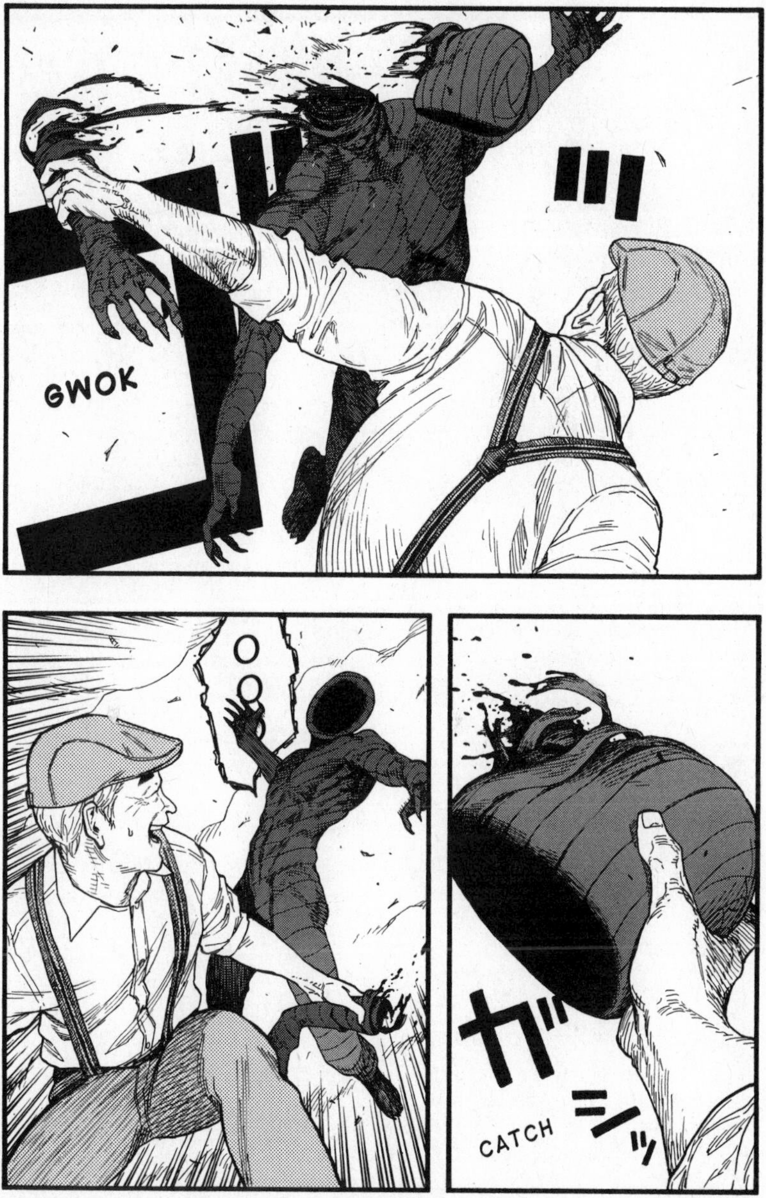
GWOK
ガシッ
CATCH

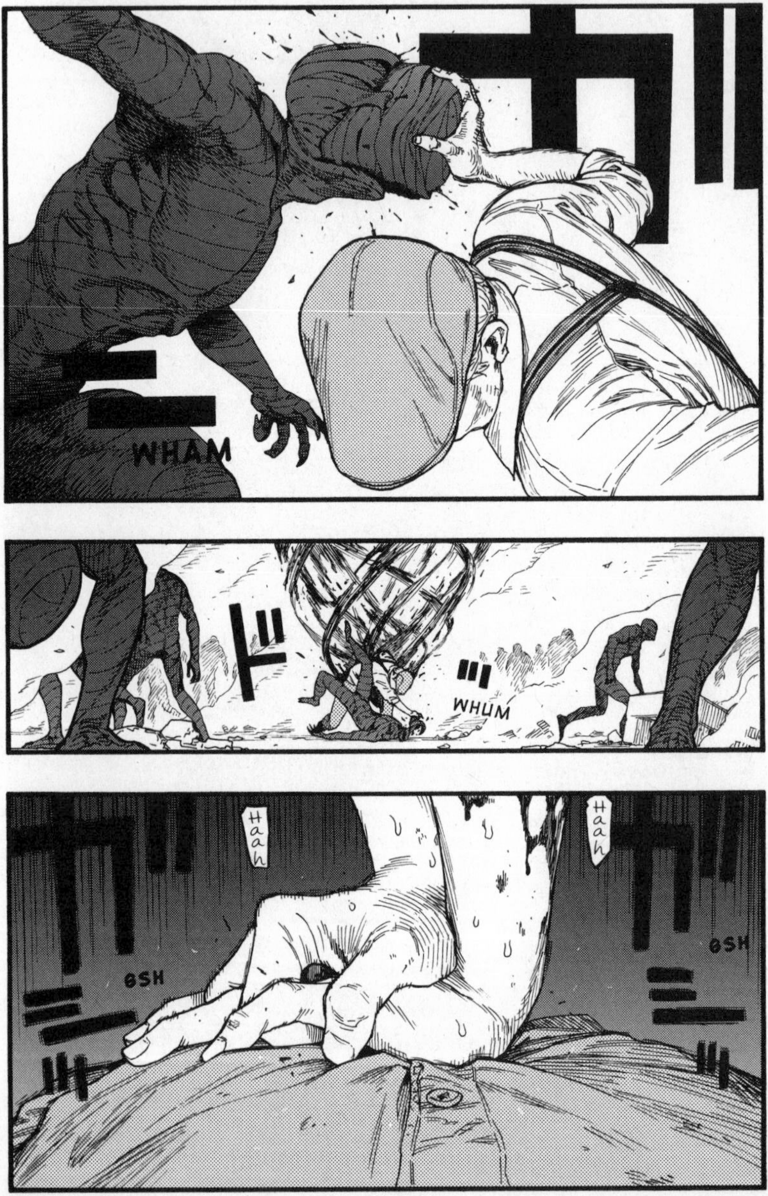
WHAM
WHUM
Haah
Haah
GSH
GSH

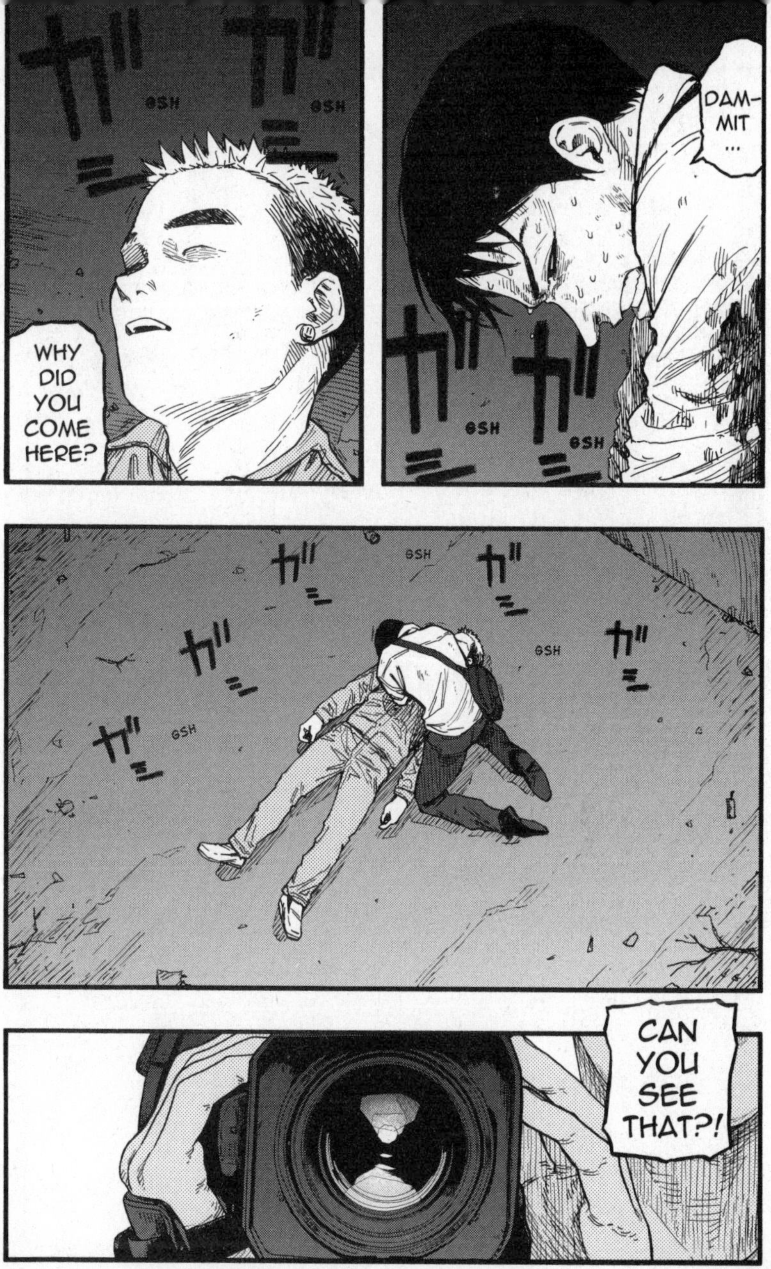
DAM-MIT ...
GSH
GSH
GSH
GSH
WHY DID YOU COME HERE?
GSH
GSH
GSH
CAN YOU SEE THAT?!

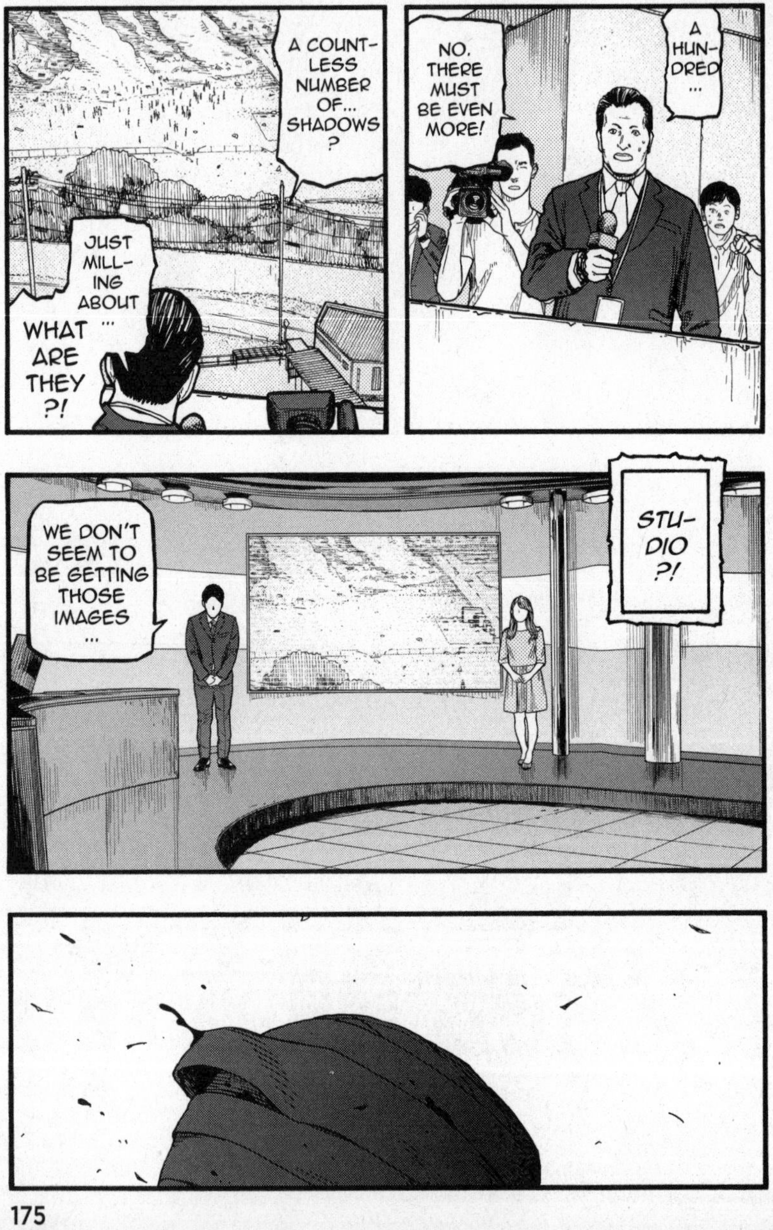
A HUN-DRED ...
NO. THERE MUST BE EVEN MORE!
A COUNT-LESS NUMBER OF... SHADOWS ?
JUST MILL-ING ABOUT ...
WHAT ARE THEY ?!
STU-DIO ?!
WE DON'T SEEM TO BE GETTING THOSE IMAGES ...

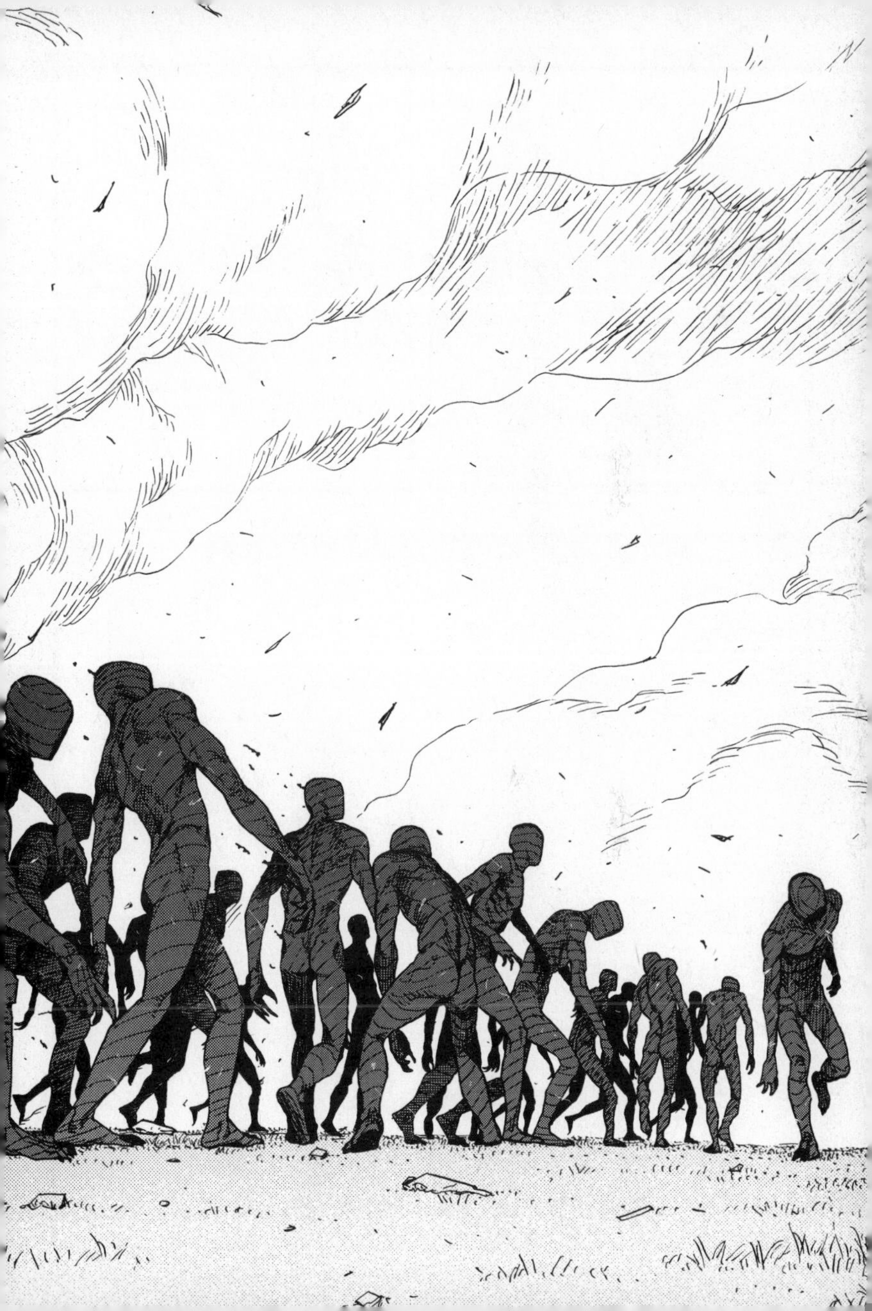

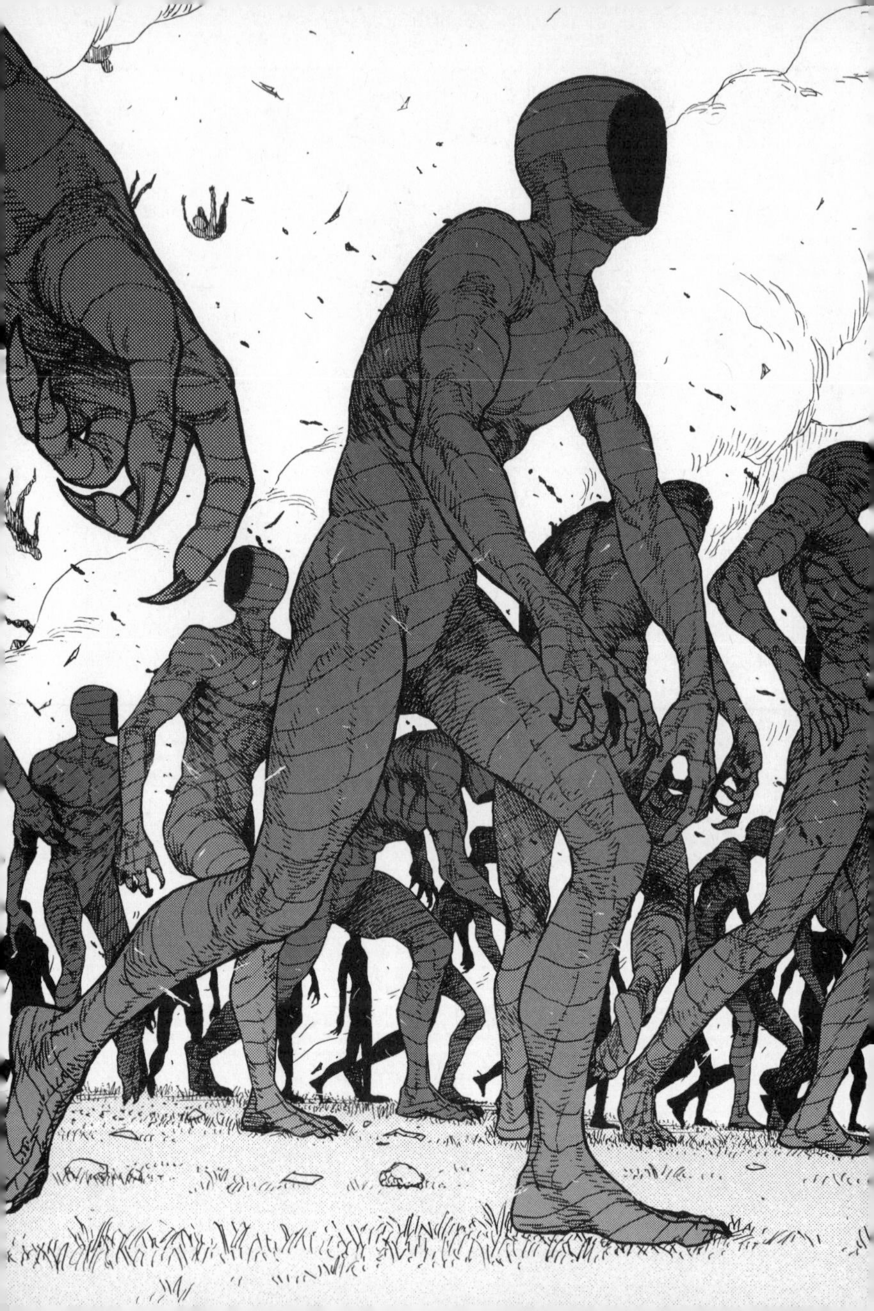

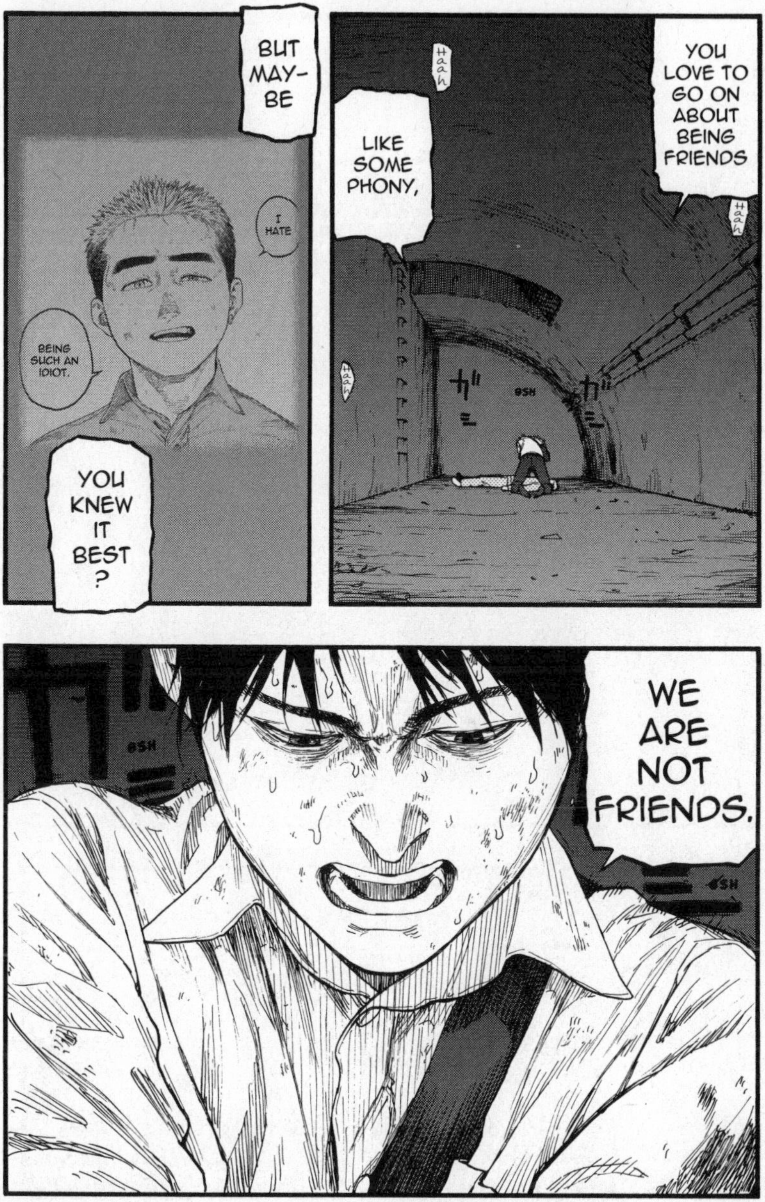

YOU LOVE TO GO ON ABOUT BEING FRIENDS
Haah
LIKE SOME PHONY,
Haah
Haah
ガ
GSH
ガ
BUT MAY-BE
I HATE
BEING SUCH AN IDIOT.
YOU KNEW IT BEST?
WE ARE NOT FRIENDS.
GSH
GSH

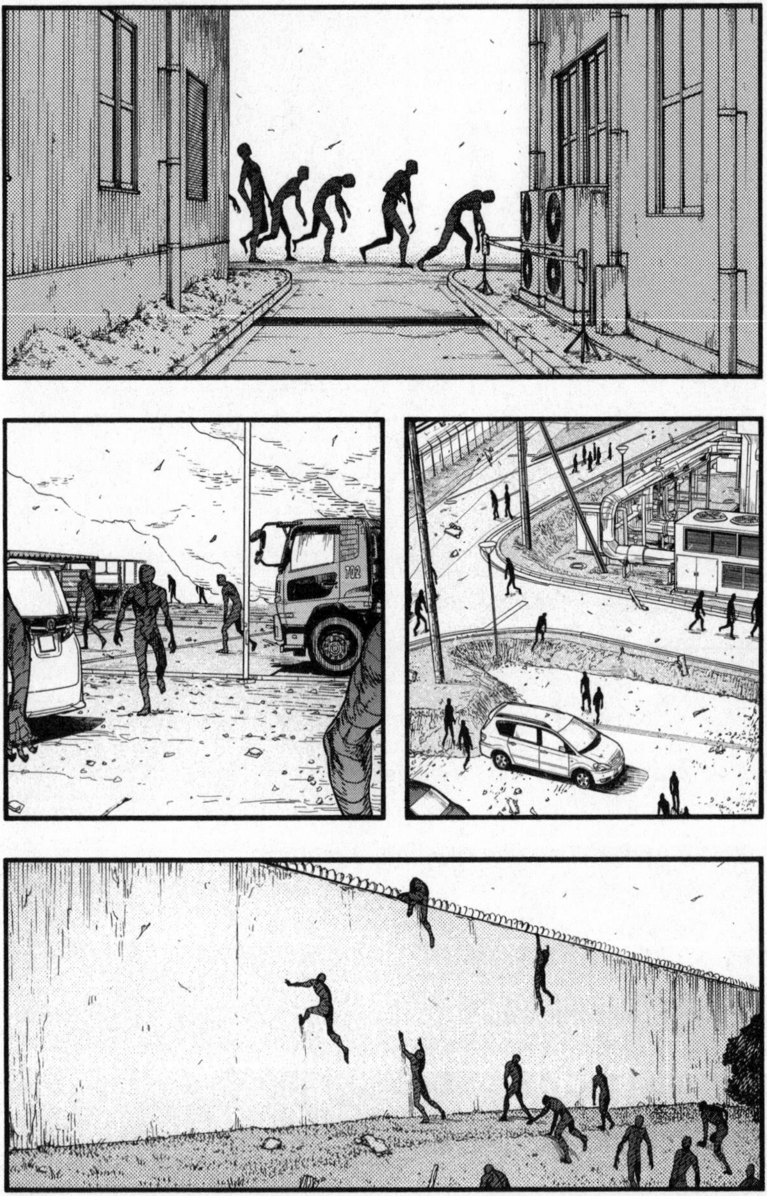
702

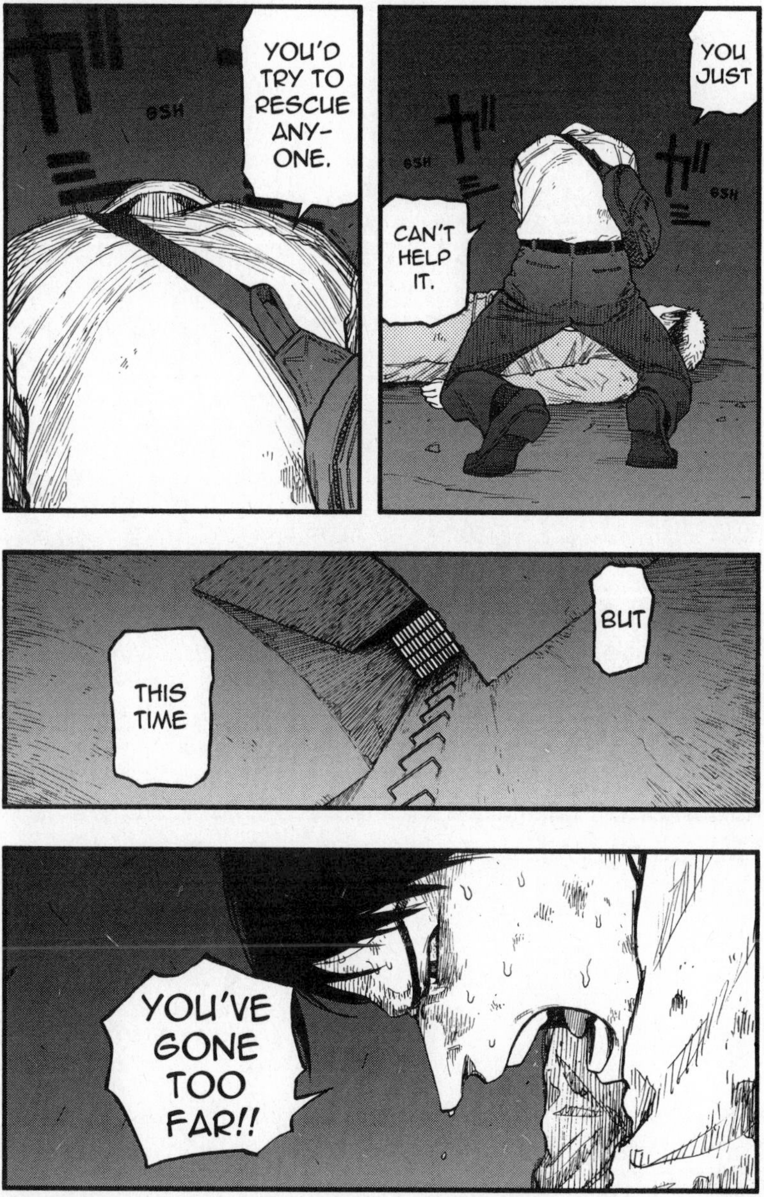
YOU JUST
CAN'T HELP IT.
YOU'D TRY TO RESCUE ANY-ONE.
BUT
THIS TIME
YOU'VE GONE TOO FAR!!

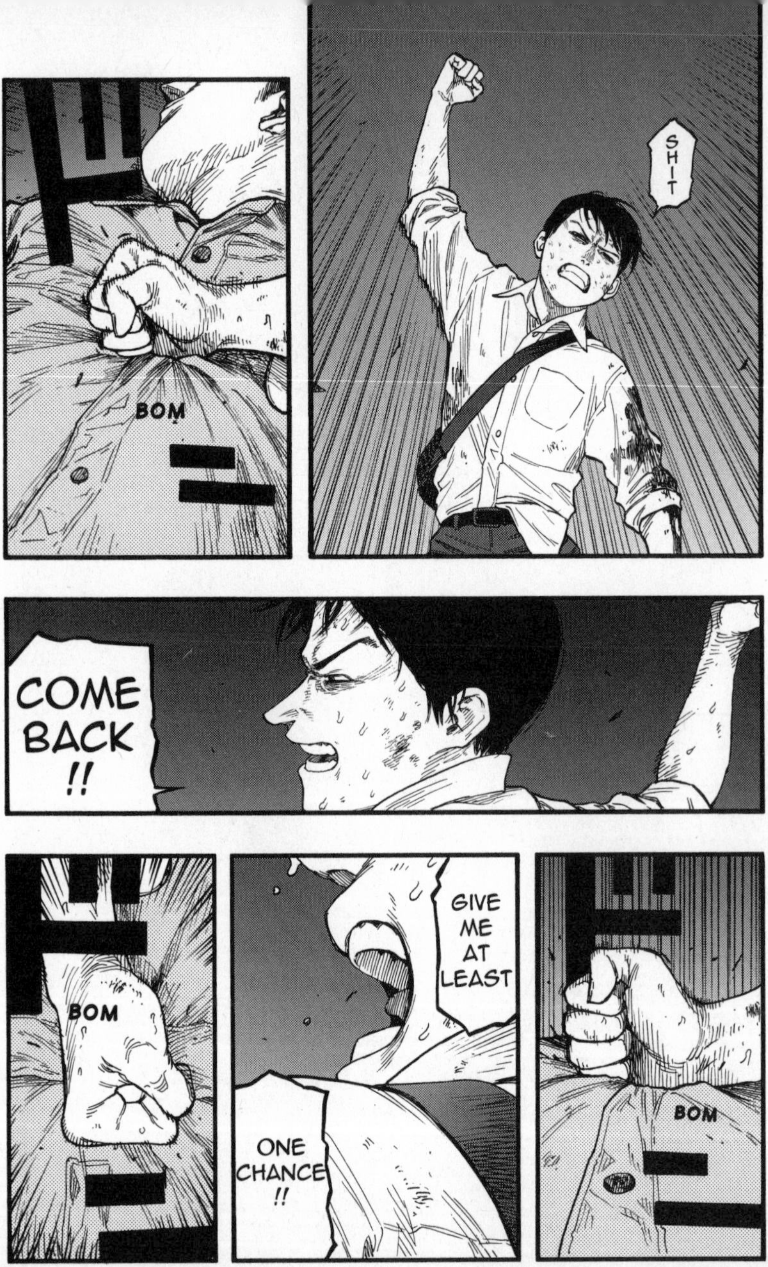
SHIT
BOM
COME BACK !!
BOM
GIVE ME AT LEAST
ONE CHANCE !!
BOM

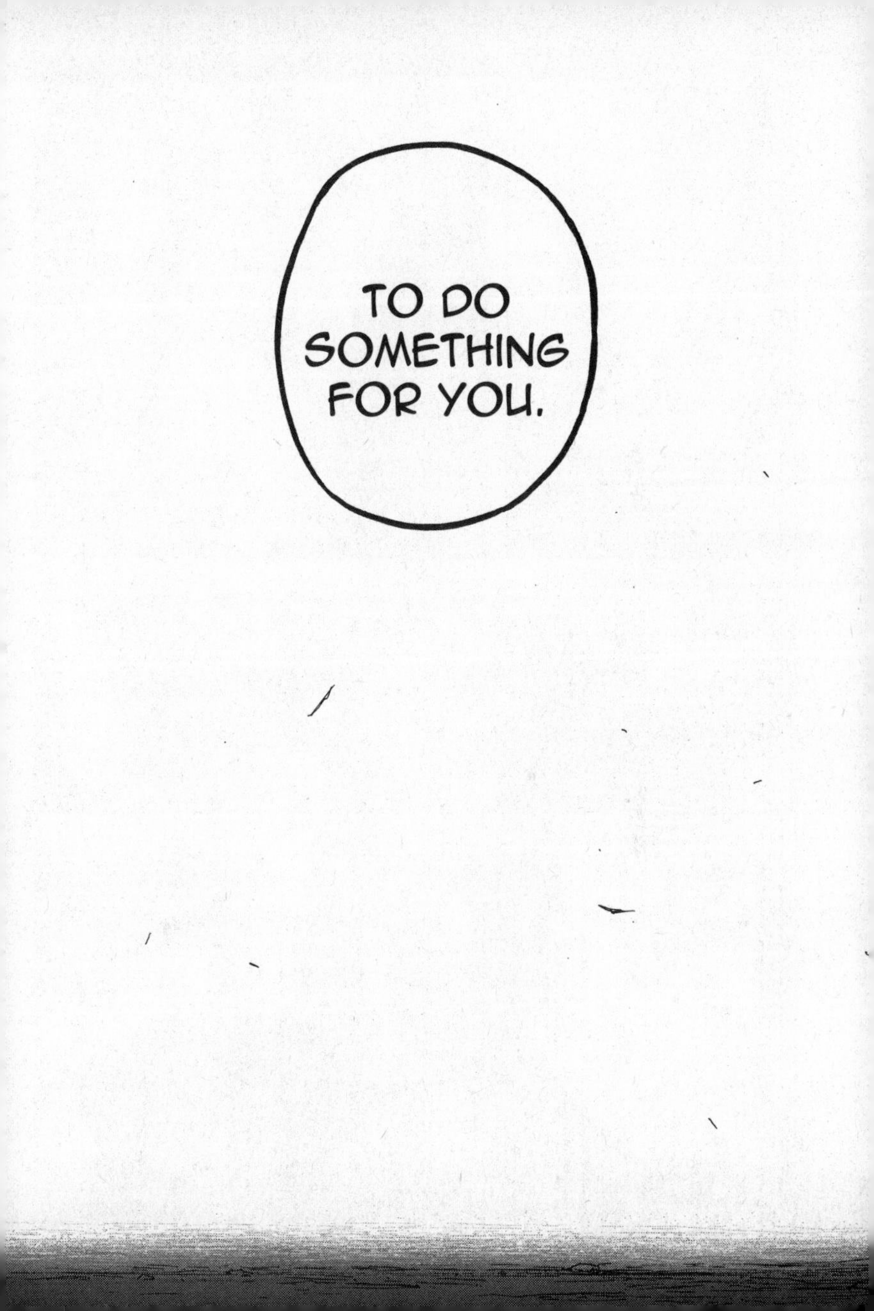
TO DO SOMETHING FOR YOU.

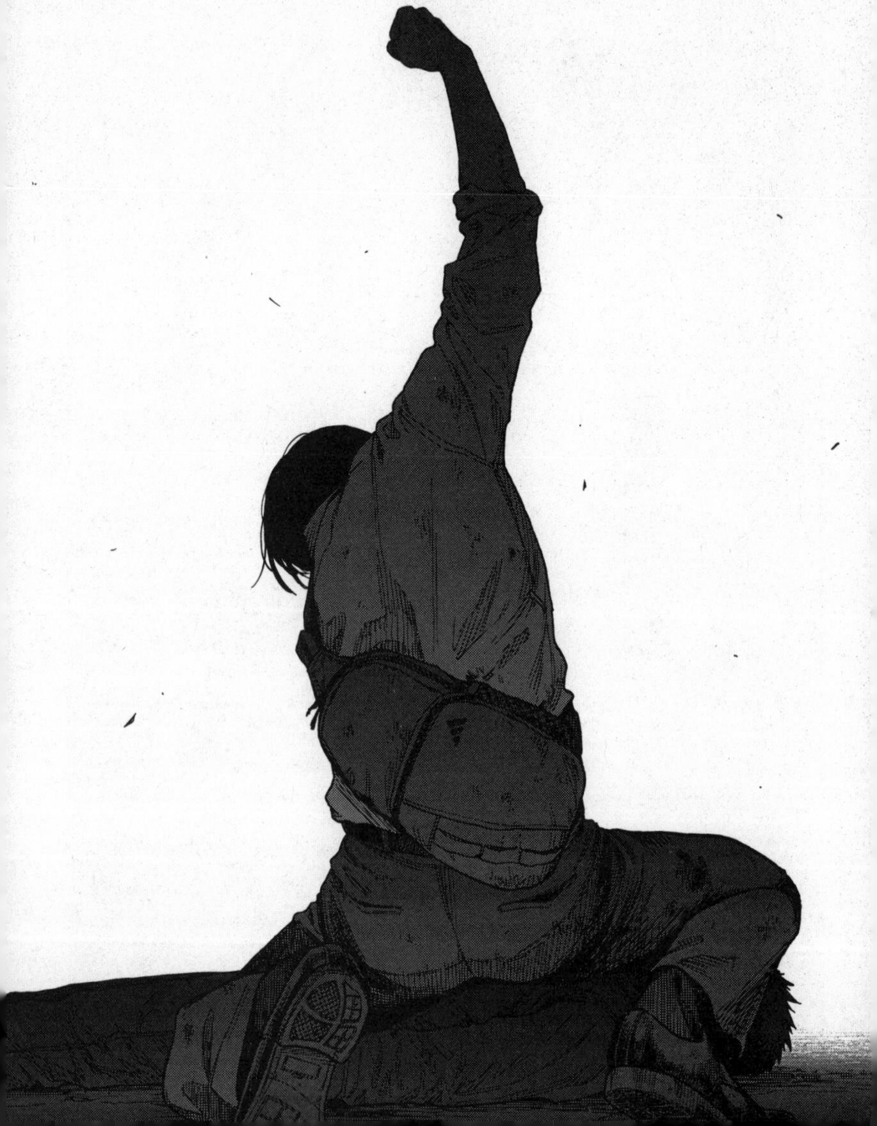

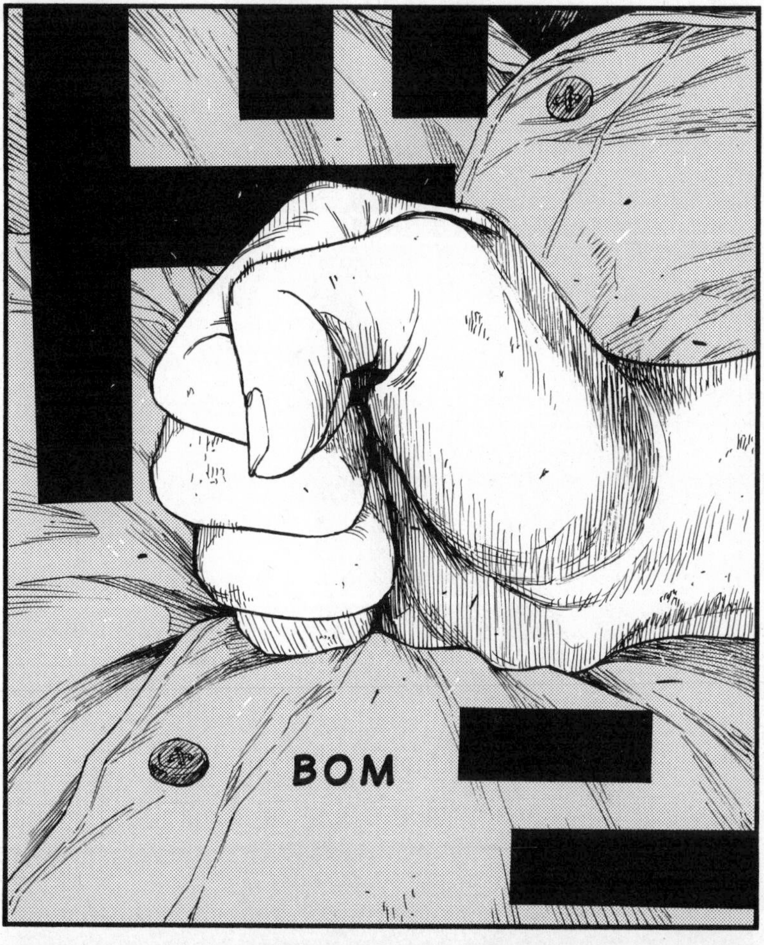
BOM

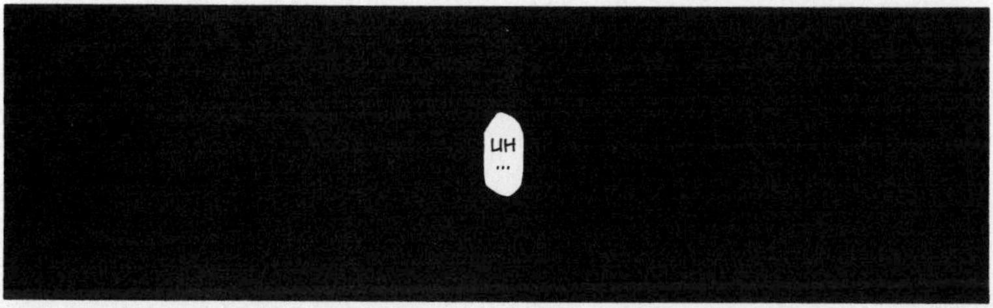
UH ...

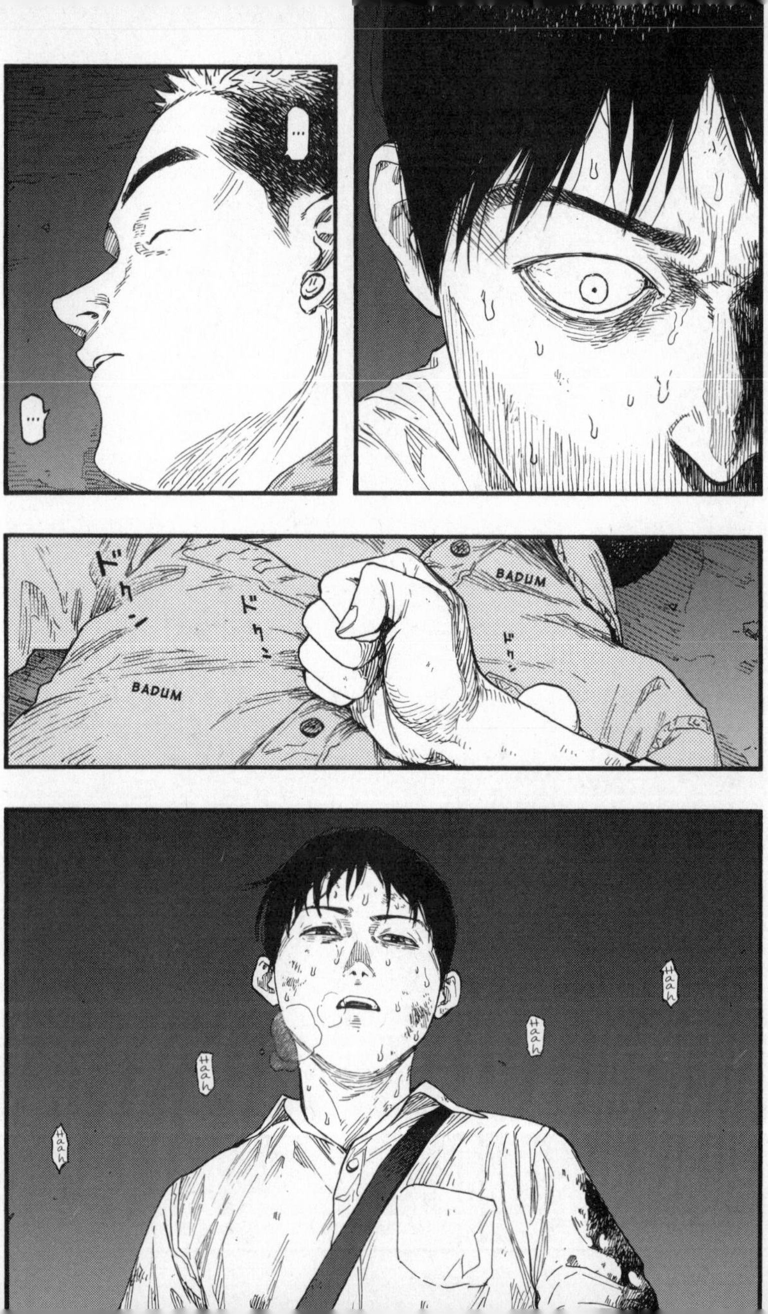
...
...
BADUM
BADUM
Haah
Haah
Haah
Haah

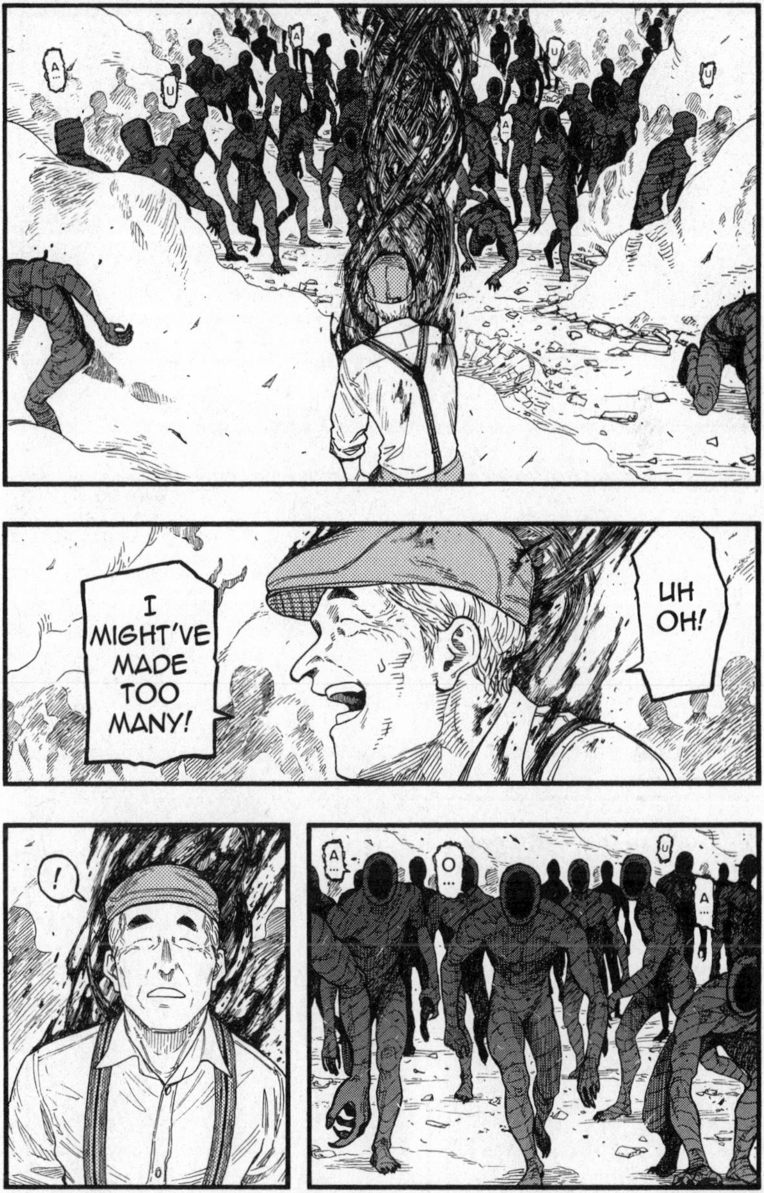
U
U
A...
A...
U
A...
UH OH!
I MIGHT'VE MADE TOO MANY!
U...
A...
O...
A...
!

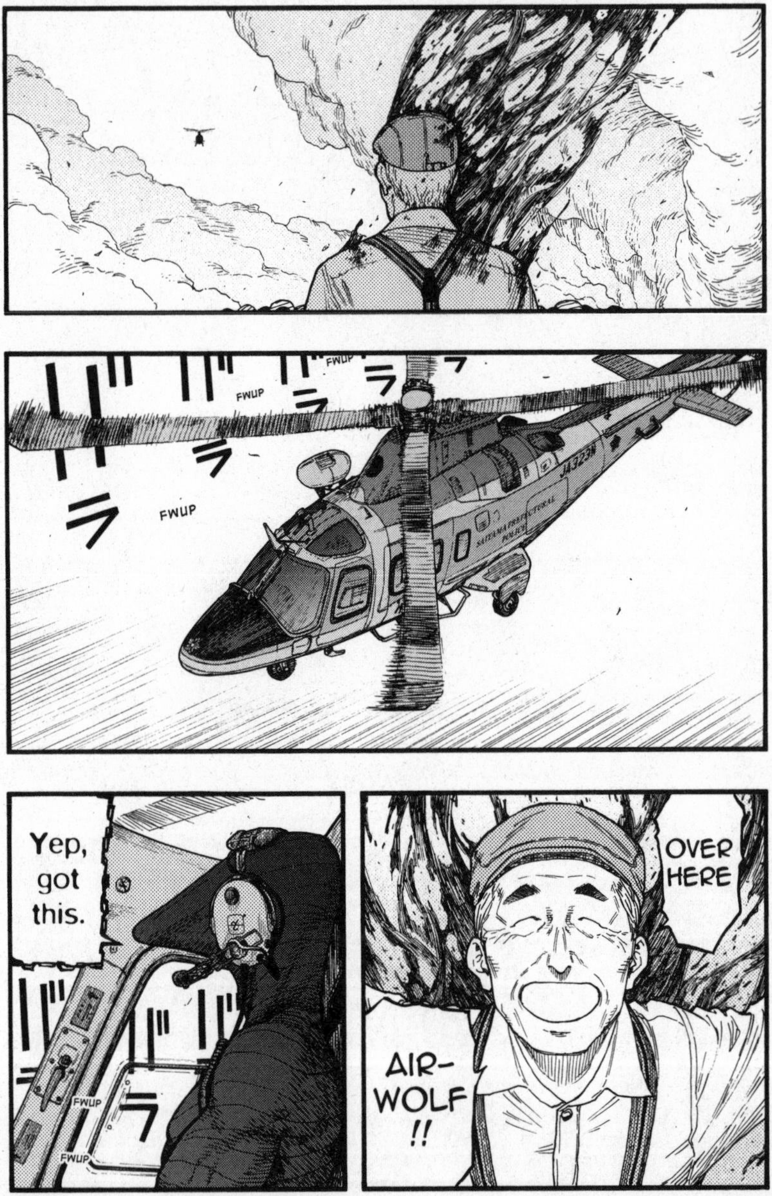
FWUP
FWUP
FWUP
OVER HERE
AIR-WOLF !!
Yep, got this.
FWUP
FWUP

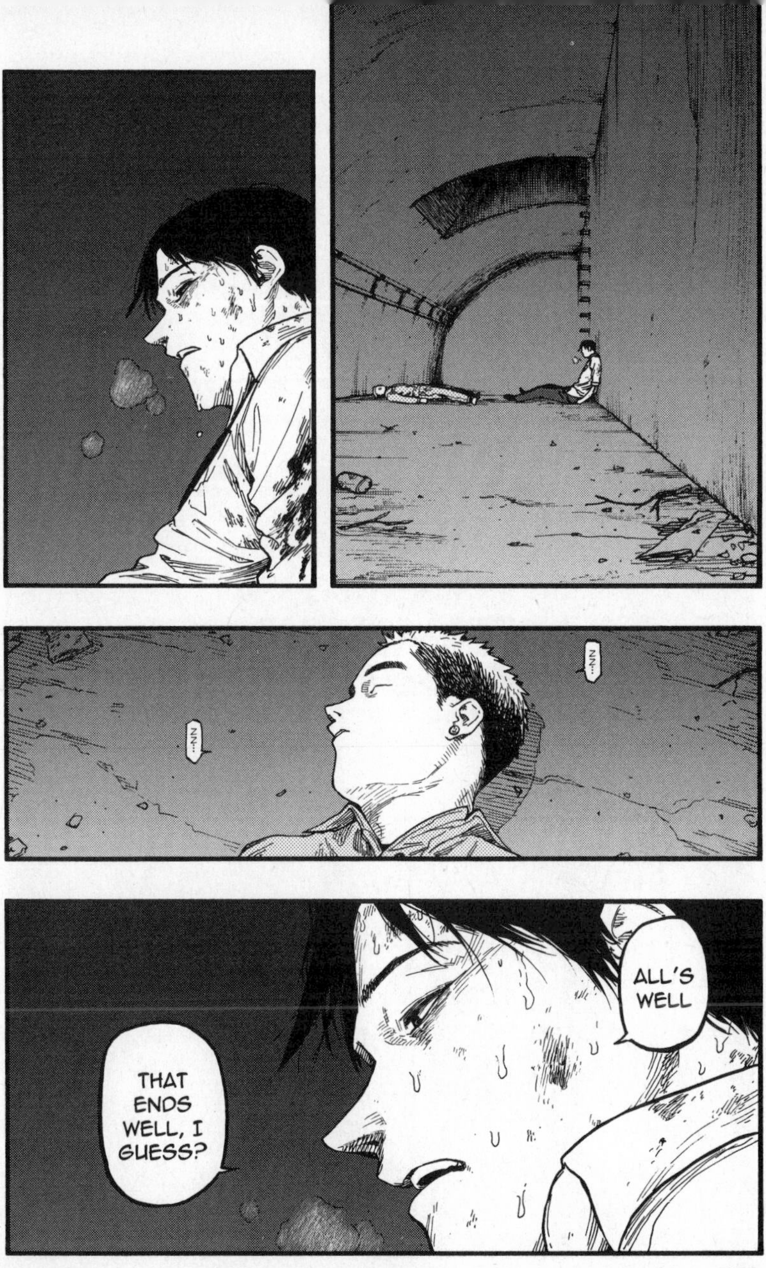
ZZ…
ZZ…
ALL'S WELL
THAT ENDS WELL, I GUESS?

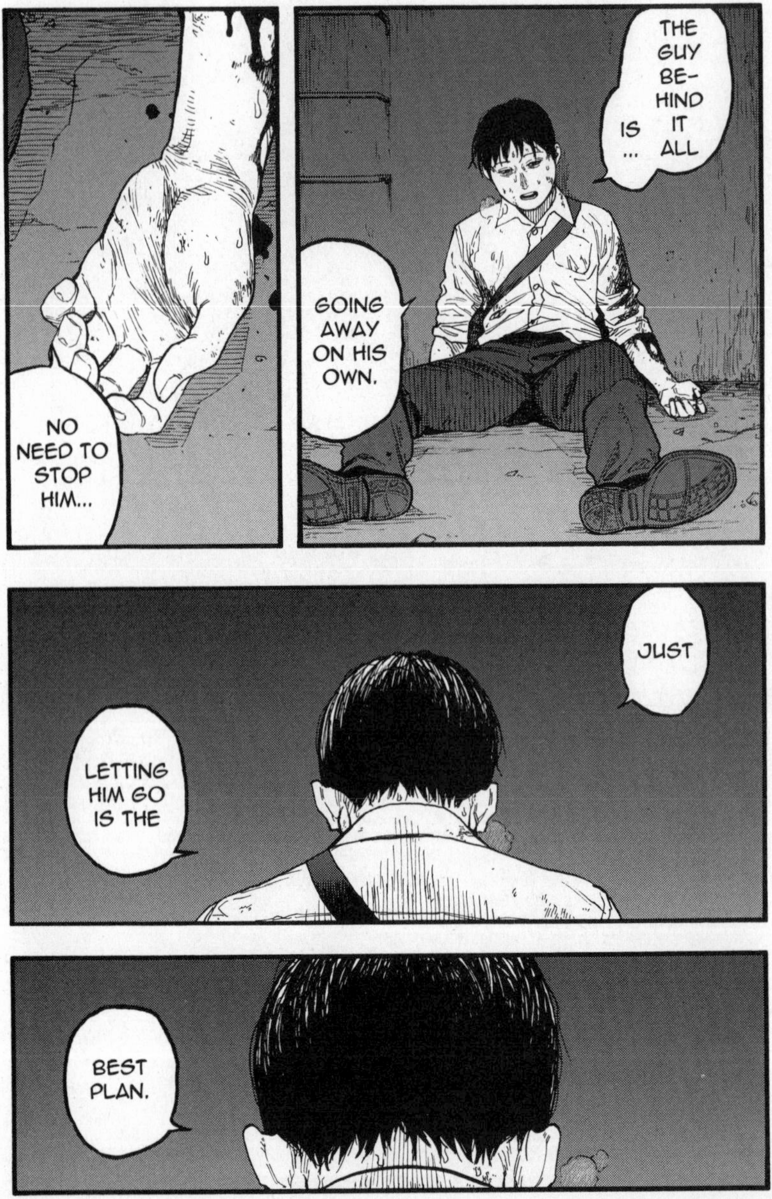
THE GUY BEHIND IT ALL IS...
GOING AWAY ON HIS OWN.
NO NEED TO STOP HIM...
JUST
LETTING HIM GO IS THE
BEST PLAN.

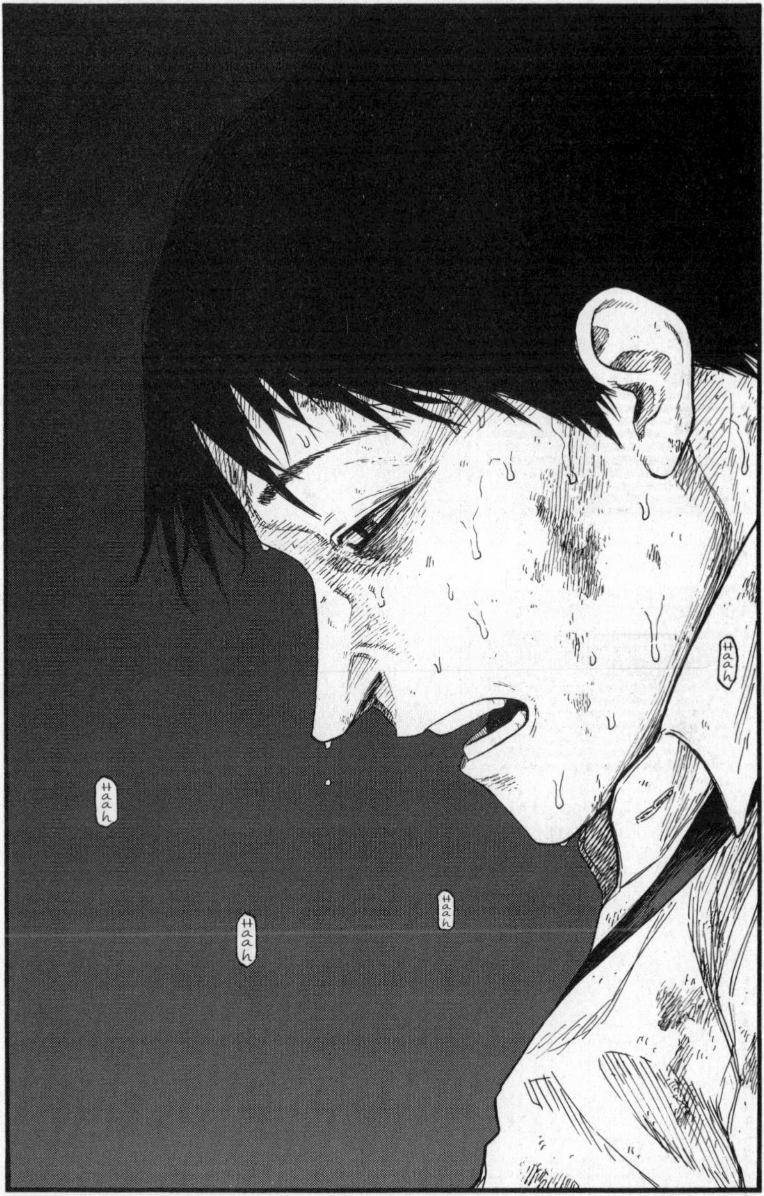
Haah
Haah
Haah
Haah

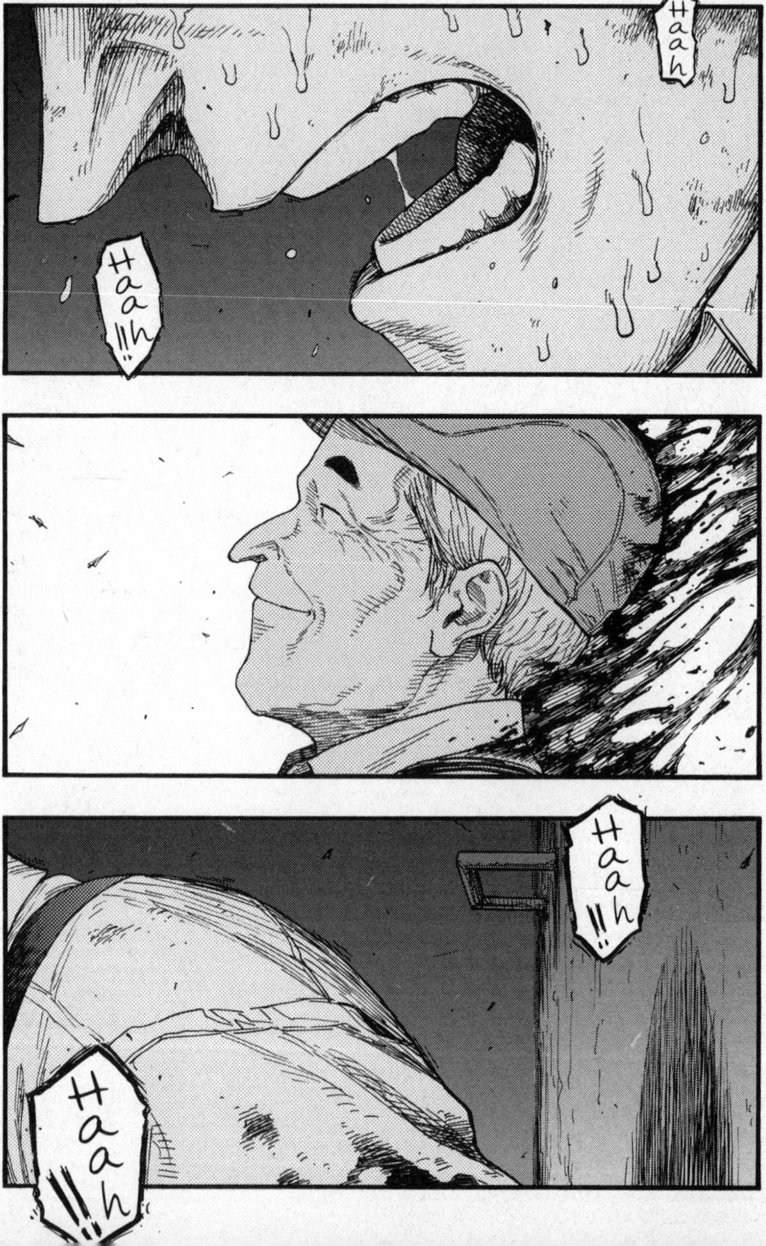
Haah
Haah!!
Haah!!
Haah!!!

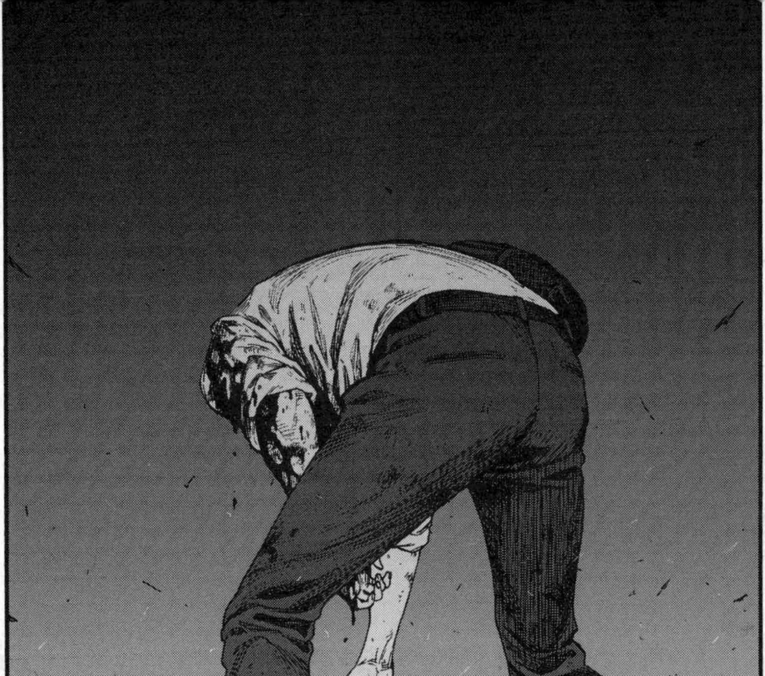

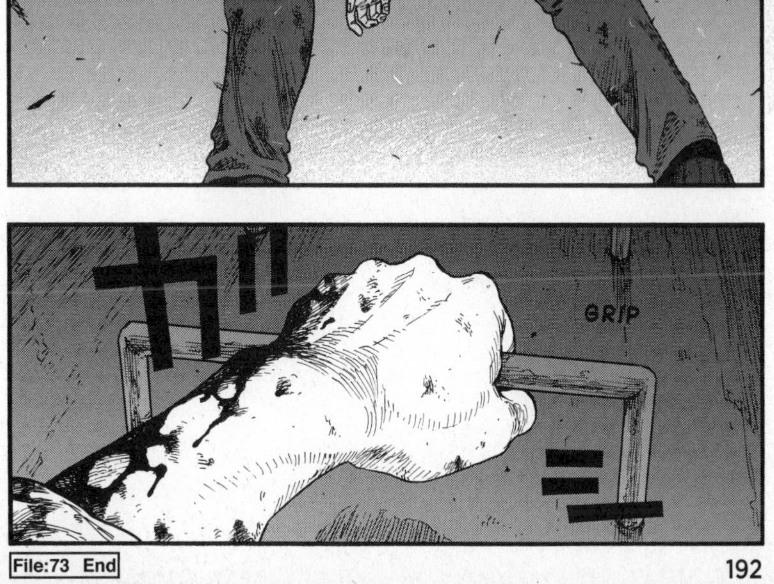
GRIP

COMIC: GAMON SAKURAI

ASSISTANTS: CROUTON SANCHI (almost all tone range masking)

SAWANOSHOW (Line drawings

[File 68: p. 5, panels 1, 4: inside panel: 95%] [File 68: p. 6, panel 1: car: 95%] [File 68: p. 8, panels 1, 4: car: 87%] [File 68: p. 9, panel 5: car: 99%]

[File 68: p. 10, panel 1: Izumi's hand, cell: 75%] [File 68: p. 11, panel 1: car: 93%] [File 68: p. 12, panels 2, 4, 5: car: 96%] [File 68: p. 13, panels 4: background: 96%]

[File 68: p. 15, panel 1: background: 99%] [File 68: p. 17, panel 1: background: 99%] [File 68: p. 20, panel 2: fighter jet: 99%] [File 68: p. 21, panel 4: fighter jet: 99%]

[File 68: p. 22, panel 4: hand, cell: 90%] [File 68: p. 23, panels 1, 4, 5: background: 92%] [File 68: p. 24, panel 1: background, fighter jet: 90%]

[File 69: Takagi's sweater logo: 90%] [File 69: bicycle: 95%] [File 69: scooter: 90%] [File 69: Kaito's cell logo: 99%] [File 69: p. 27, panel 4: hangers: 90%]

[File 69: p. 28, panel 3: book titles: 90%] [File 69: p. 30, panel 1: cicada: 99%] [File 69: p. 31, panel 4: background: 98%] [File 69: p. 32, panel 2: inside panel: 97%]

[File 69: p. 34, panel 2: right mob pair: 99%] [File 69: p. 34, panel 3: background: 90%] [File 69: p. 37, panels 1, 3: mob: 90%] [File 69: p. 38, panel 1: background: 98%]

[File 69: p. 40, panel 4: background: 95%] [File 69: p. 41, panels 2, 4, 5: sweater logo: 90%] [File 69: p. 41, panel 3: background: 99%] [File 69: p. 43, panel 2, 3, sweater logo: 95%]

[File 69: p. 44, panel 1: sweater logo: 99%] [File 69: p. 45, panel 4: background: 40%] [File 69: p. 47, panel 4: cell buttons: 99%] [File 69: p. 52, panel 2: multitool knife: 99%]

[File 70: p. 61, panels 1, 3, 8: fighter jet: 81%] [File 70: p. 61, panels 5, 6, 7: background: 93%] [File 70: pp. 62-63, panels 1, 3: fighter jet, Sienta: 77%]

[File 70: pp. 62-63, panels 1, 2: background: 50%] [File 70: p. 64, panel 1: background: 70%] [File 70: p. 66, panel 3: rear window defogger: 99%] [File 70: p. 67, panels 2, 3, 4, 5: car: 84%]

[File 70: p. 69, panel 1: background: 77%] [File 70: p. 73, panel 1: car: 91%] [File 70: p. 83, panel 4: shoes: 67%]

[File 71: p. 98, panel 1: car: 91%] [File 71: p. 102-3, panel 1: bike: 88%] [File 71: p. 105, panel 1: gun, hand: 69%] [File 71: p. 105, panel 2: bike: 90%] [File 71: p. 105, panel 3: gun: 82%]

[File 71: p. 106, panels 1, 2: bike: 81%] [File 71: p. 112, panels 1, 3: imagined background: 99%] [File 71: p. 113, panels 1, 3, 5: background: 90%] [File 71: p. 114, panel 2: cars: 80%]

[File 71: p. 116, panel 1: guns, small bag: 90%] [File 71: p. 116, panel 2: guns, bag logo: 90%]

[File 72: p. 135, panel 2: gun, hand: 70%]

[File 73: p. 164, panel 3: gun: 90%] [File 73: p. 165, panels 1, 3: gun: 99%] [File 73: p. 174, panel 4: person, car: 91%] [File 73: p. 175, panel 1: trio behind: 90%]

[File 73: p. 175, panel 3: inside panel: 89%] [File 73: p. 179, panels 2, 3: background: 90%] [File 73: p. 187, panels 1, 2: helicopter: 60%] [File 73: p. 187, panel 4: headset: 98%]

[File 73: p. 189, panel 1: soles: 99%])

KIMIYUKI MASAKI (Line drawings

[File 68: p. 5, panel 2: background: 90%] [File 68, p. 8, panel 5: background: 92%] [File 68: p. 9, panels 2, 4: background: 99%] [File 68: p. 10, panel 1: news vid: 99%]

[File 69: p. 31, panel 3: background: 99%] [File 69: p. 32, panel 1: background: 100%] [File 69: p. 48, panel 1: news vid: 89%] [File 69: p. 51, panel 2: background: 30%]

[File 69: p. 52, panels 1, 4, 5, 6: imagined scenes: 98%] [File 69: p. 54, panel 2: background: 99%] [File 69: p. 57, panel 4: background: 99%]

[File 70: p. 65, panels 1, 2, 3: background: 95%] [File 70: p. 66, panel 2: car except seats: 99%] [File 70: p. 70, panel 1: reporter: 95%] [File 70: p. 76, panel 1: gun: 95%]

[File 70: p. 82, panel 1: gun: 95%] [File 70: p. 84, panel 1: gun: 95%] [File 70: p. 86, panel 2: gun: 95%]

[File 71: p. 90, panel 1: gun: 95%] [File 71: p. 92, panel 4: gun: 95%] [File 71: p. 94, panel 6: tranq gun: 99%] [File 71: p. 95, panel 2: gun: 95%] [File 71: p. 96, panel 2: gun: 95%]

[File 71: p. 114, panel 2: background: 90%] [File 71: p. 118, panel 1: background: 99%] [File 71: p. 120, panels 1, 2, 4: background: 100%] [File 71: p. 122, panel 1: background: 85%]

[File 73: p. 167, panels 1, 3: grating: 99%] [File 73: p. 169, panel 3: grating: 99%] [File 73: p. 179, panel 1: background: 96%] [File 73: p. 188, panel 1: background: 91%])

CLIPSTUDIOOFFCIAL-3D MATERIAL [File 69: grade-school classroom interior: 85%]

CLIP STUDIO PAINT- LINE DRAWINGS VIA LT CONVERSION FUNCTION [File 69: p. 39, panel 4: background: 77%] [File 69: p. 45, panel 4: background: 50%]

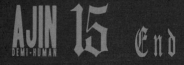

AJIN 15 End
DEMI-HUMAN

Ajin: Demi-Human, volume 15

Translation: Ko Ransom
Production: Risa Cho
         Hiroko Mizuno

© 2019 Gamon Sakurai. All rights reserved.
First published in Japan in 2019 by Kodansha, Ltd., Tokyo
Publication for this English edition arranged through Kodansha, Ltd., Tokyo

...blished by Vertical, an imprint of Kodansha USA Publishing, LLC.

...ginally published in Japanese as *Ajin 15* by Kodansha, Ltd.
...n first serialized in *good! Afternoon*, Kodansha, Ltd., 2012-

...his is a work of fiction.

ISBN: 978-1-949980-35-6

Manufactured in the United States of America

First Edition

Kodansha USA Publishing, LLC.
451 Park Avenue South
7th Floor
New York, NY 10016
www.readvertical.com